Northwick Banking Certificate Series

The Business of Banking

David Cox, FCIB, FCCA, CertEd
Michael Fardon, BA, MPhil, ACIB, CertEd

Northwick  **Publishers**

Published by

Northwick Publishers
14 Bevere Close
Worcester WR3 7QH
Telephone 0905 56876

Printed by Ebenezer Baylis & Son Limited
The Trinity Press, London Road, Worcester WR5 2JH

British Library Cataloguing in Publication Data
Cox, David, *1946 Apr. 15-*
    The business of banking.
    1. Great Britain. Banking
    I. Title II. Fardon, Michael, *1951-*
332.1'0941

ISBN 0-907135-50-1

Foreword

This book is specifically written for students of The Chartered Institute of Bankers, studying The Business of Banking in the Preliminary Section of the Banking Certificate.

The book, together with its accompanying *Study Guide,* provides a complete study package which gives a good introduction to the main aspects of banking and financial services. The topics covered include the use of cheques and 'plastic' money, the present-day structure of banking in the UK, the legal relationship between bank and customer, different types of bank customer, and the way in which the various clearing systems operate. Bank services for personal and business customers are looked at in detail as are the services provided by the major competitors of banks. An important chapter for all students is Chapter 1, which explains how to pass the examination.

Each chapter in the book concludes with a number of revision points, multiple-choice and short answer questions, and essay questions. Many of the questions are taken from past examination papers, other questions are of a similar standard to those set in the examination. Answers to all the multiple-choice and short answer questions are given in the *Study Guide.* Outline answers to selected essay questions from every chapter are also given in the *Study Guide.*

Readers will be aware that the financial services industry, of which banking is one part, is changing rapidly. New services are being introduced; the further use of computers and systems of electronic banking move ahead; the traditional roles of banks, and other financial services organisations, change as competition between them increases. It is essential for readers to keep up-to-date with the latest developments by reading articles in the financial press and in 'Banking World'. The last chapter in the book - Chapter 16 'Future Developments in Banking' - indicates some of the areas where there are likely to be major changes within the next few years.

David Cox
Michael Fardon
July 1989

Acknowledgements

The authors wish to thank the following for their assistance in the production of this book:

- Jean Cox, for keying-in the text to the computer
- Peter Gutmann, of National Westminster Bank PLC
- George Johnston, of Barclays de Zoete Wedd
- Banking Information Service
- the librarian and staff of The Chartered Institute of Bankers
- The Chartered Institute of Bankers, for giving permission to reproduce questions from past examination papers
- Bank of England
- Midland Bank plc
- National Westminster Bank PLC
- The Royal Bank of Scotland plc
- TSB Bank plc

The Authors

David Cox is Senior Lecturer in Banking at Worcester Technical College. He worked for Midland Bank plc for a number of years, and has fifteen years' full-time teaching experience, during which time he has taught students over a wide range of levels. He is also a qualified accountant and the author of a number of banking and accounting textbooks.

Michael Fardon, born and educated in Worcester, is a graduate of London University, where he was also awarded an M.Phil. degree. He formerly worked for Midland Bank plc, where he was involved in the areas of personal and small business finance as well as specialising in Corporate Finance for a number of years. He is a lecturer in banking at Worcester Technical College. His publications include a number of banking and accounting textbooks.

Contents

Chapter 1   How to Pass the Exam   1

2   The Theory of Money   6

3   Modern Forms of Money   16

4   Development of the UK Banking System   31

5   Banks and the Bank of England   49

6   Bank and Customer   60

7   Personal Customers   72

8   Business Customers   83

9   Funds Transfer: Paper Systems   96

10   Funds Transfer: Electronic Systems   115

11   Accounts and Services: Personal Customers   125

12   Investments for Personal Customers   144

13   Bank Lending to Personal Customers   156

14   Accounts and Services: Business Customers   171

15   Banks and Competition   180

16   Future Developments in Banking   209

Index   216

Chapter One
How to Pass the Exam

Preparation and practice are crucial ingredients for eventual success in any examination. There is a tendency to view *The Business of Banking* as an easy option. Students are often heard to say, "This subject is OK because it's what I do at work." These students concentrate on what they see as the harder subjects and they then fail *The Business of Banking*. They have neglected preparation and practice.

In this chapter we will set out a strategy for success in the exam; this strategy involves:

- efficient study
- effective revision
- examination technique

1.1 An Efficient Study Method: Resources and Preparation

As banking students you have a wealth of resources to help you in your study; the problem is how to use them efficiently. These are the resources:

Textbook
This book should be used both as preparation for lectures (if you attend College) and also as a reinforcement to what you have learned. Do not let it sit idly on your shelves, take it, read it, and compile a set of notes ready for revision purposes. If you own the textbook use a highlighting pen to pick out the important passages of text. At the end of each of all the other chapters there is a list of 'Revision Points' which should help you to form a structure for these notes.

Study Guide
A Study Guide has been written to accompany this textbook. It contains valuable notes, worksheets and answers to examination questions. See opposite page for details.

Syllabus and scheme of work
If you have not read the syllabus, ask your lecturer or tutor for a copy, or enquire of your Local Centre Education Officer, or telephone The Chartered Institute of Bankers (Tel: 0227 762600). Your lecturer or tutor will have worked out a scheme of work telling you which subjects you are studying at any particular time on the course. Make sure that you have a copy so that, if you are away on a course or on a holiday, you can make up the lost time by private study. It is important to know that you have covered all the areas of the syllabus; to omit sections on the basis that they will not come up in the exam is highly dangerous!

Background reading, listening and viewing

As a member of The Chartered Institute of Bankers (CIB) you will receive a copy of *Banking World* each month. Do not consign it to the bin in its plastic wrapper without opening it: following on from all the articles at the front there are sections specifically written for banking students. Read also the *Stage 1 News* produced by the CIB for students' study needs. In your branch you will find newspapers such as the *Financial Times* or *The Times*. These may look uninviting at first glance, but a quick scan of the pages will often reveal the latest developments in bank products and more general developments in the financial services industry. Cut these articles out for your file, but make sure the manager has finished with the paper first!

Do not neglect the radio and TV for your studies. There are a number of excellent specialist financial reporting programmes which will help you.

The workplace

Whether you work in a branch or in a specialised department you will be made aware of the latest developments in products and services by means of circulars, leaflets and training manuals. Use them. You will find that your studies will actually make you more efficient at work. If you surprise your supervisor by knowing about a product, the details of which may have slipped his or her mind, you will be well thought of. Collect copies of forms (with permission!) such as loan agreements and mandates, and study them together with this text. Take them to lectures and ask questions about them. Compare them with the forms from other banks which other students may have brought with them.

The High Street

Although to you the 'bank' means your branch or department, use your lunch hour to see what the other financial institutions are doing. Look critically at

- building societies
- finance companies
- retailers
- other banks

Are they promoting the same products as you? Are they better or worse than you?

1.2 An Efficient Study Method: Practice

As mentioned earlier, it is vitally important that you practise examination questions regularly, and preferably in a timed situation. The examination has three very distinct types of question, examples of which are given at the end of each chapter of this book.

- multiple-choice questions (i.e. choosing the correct answer out of four alternatives)
- short answer questions
- essay questions

We will discuss *how* these questions occur in the examination in Section 1.4.

Multiple-choice questions

The multiple choice questions in Section A of the examination are compulsory. There are two points to remember:

- always answer every question; even if you do not know the answer, there is a statistical chance that you will guess it correctly
- you only need to write down the letter indicating your choice; do not write down the whole sentence

Short answer questions

Short answer questions also form a part of the compulsory Part A of the examination. The main point to be made about your answers is that you do not need to write an essay, just a brief note. If the question says, 'List two characteristics of money' you should write, for instance,

(a) Acceptability
(b) Durability

You do not need to ramble on at length about the inefficiences of the barter system. (See Chapter 2, page 7.)

Essay questions

Essay questions, of which you have to write four, are the most difficult type of question to master, and should be practised frequently under timed conditions, i.e. in thirty minutes.

Let us take a typical question (covered by Chapter 15 in this book):

What are the main High Street competitors of the clearing banks and how do they compete?

The following points should be borne in mind:

plan	Plan your answer first in outline note form in your examination answerbook. List the competitors - building societies, finance houses, moneyshops, retailers, National Savings, insurance companies - and note down how they are competing with the banks. When you have finished writing your full answer, cross through your outline plan.
amount	You are not writing a novel: a well planned answer may not take more than two sides of paper. Write clearly and *concisely*.
introduction	Write a *brief* introductory paragraph to lead you into the answer. Here, for instance, you could write:
	'The clearing banks face fierce competition for their products. The main competitors in the high street are: building societies, finance houses, moneyshops, retailers, National Savings, insurance companies.'
	You would then start your section on building societies.
format	Do not write two sides of continuous prose without a break; it will be very difficult to read. Plan your answer in specific headed sections, and leave a blank line after each section. In the case of this question, you could use the heading 'Building Societies', underline it and then underneath list the ways in which they compete, using numbered points if you wish.

It is only by practising these answers that you will enter the examination room with a good chance of success.

1.3 Effective Revision

Revision should be based on two resources:

- a comprehensive set of notes compiled by you
- a 'bank' of past examination questions

Revision notes

Revision notes should be compiled *during the course of the year* based on:

- your lecture notes
- reading of the chapters of the textbook
- careful attention to the Revision Points at the end of each chapter
- use of the worksheets (designed for revision purposes) in the Study Guide which has been designed to accompany this textbook

It must be stressed that these notes should be compiled during your studies; do not leave them until a last minute panic! The format of the notes is up to the individual, but the use of headings, listed points, highlighting pens and different coloured ink for emphasis is recommended.

Past questions

This textbook has done the task of compiling questions for you. At the end of each chapter are sections containing all the relevant past CIB examination questions together with the type of questions that might be asked. Answers to selected questions may be found in the accompanying Study Guide, and also in The Chartered Institute of Bankers' Examiners' Reports, which are highly recommended reading.

Revision methods

Be systematic in revision. Draw up an action plan with dates and subjects. Try these methods:

- don't just read your notes - test yourself
- find a husband/wife/boyfriend/girlfriend to test you on the facts and the legal cases
- record facts on cassette tape and play them to yourself on your personal stereo when travelling by bus, train or tube, or in your car on the M25

Revision must be *active*. If you read passively, you are not making efficient use of your time.

1.4   Examination Technique

When you enter the examination hall the question of your success or failure will depend not only on your state of preparation but also on how you tackle the examination. Chief Examiners have frequently been heard to comment on the incoherent scripts they have to mark. Believe it or not, the Chief Examiner *wants* you to pass: it is up to you to use the three hours' examination time in the most efficient way.

Time management

The three hour examination requires you to answer five questions:

- a compulsory first question (Section A) - ten multiple-choice and ten short answer questions
- four out of eight essay questions (Section B).

It is recommended that you divide your three hours (180 minutes) as follows:

15 minutes	reading time and choice of questions
150 minutes	writing the answers - half an hour each
15 minutes	checking and correcting

It is *essential* that you spend the first quarter of an hour reading carefully and making your choice. There will doubtless be the student next to you who starts writing furiously in the first minute of the exam; it is distracting to you, but that student is writing without planning and is probably destined to fail.

Answering technique

All the following points are important 'mark earners':

- read the question carefully; do not write a prepared answer on a certain subject just because it is mentioned in the question

- take note of the instructions given: if it says 'list briefly', do not write an essay; if it says 'give the benefits to the customer', list the benefits; if it says 'discuss', do so.

- answer the compulsory question first; it is possible to obtain high marks here if you are well prepared

- answer your best essay question next, it will give you confidence; then move on to the other essay questions

- if you are running short of time towards the end of the exam, leave the question you are doing and start another question: most of the marks are gained in the first ten to fifteen minutes of writing the answer

- if you are desperately short of time, jot down in note form the points you would put in an answer; you should gain some marks

- re-read your answers carefully and correct any spelling or factual errors

One final point which cannot be stressed too strongly is that the examiner expects your script to be clearly set out and legible. The examiner is only human: if he or she is at the end of a long day of marking and your script is well set out in neat handwriting, with headings and listed points, the examiner's spirits will lift and you should score well. If, however, the *same* information goes down illegibly and in an apparently disorganised way, the examiner will have to work hard to find you the marks, and you will be less likely to gain them.

Lastly, enjoy *The Business of Banking* - it is the subject most closely related to the banking workplace - and good luck in the examination. With preparation and practice there is every good reason for a pass.

Chapter Two
The Theory of Money

In this chapter we will:

• establish a definition of money
• examine why barter - an economy without money - is inefficient
• explain the qualities and functions of money
• describe the origins and development of coins, banknotes and cheques
• discuss the problems caused by inflation

2.1 Money: a Definition

If you ask someone what money is, they will give you examples such as cash, credit cards, or money in bank and building society accounts. These are only examples; further thought will reveal that money has a number of important qualities and functions:

• money enables you to obtain what you want more or less anywhere you want, for example: personal possessions, a holiday, a night out

• money enables you to settle debts in the short term (the milk bill) and the long term (a mortgage)

In short, you could define money as follows:

Money is something which is exchangeable for goods and services, and is generally acceptable in the settlement of debt.

You could go further than this brief definition by examining in detail

• qualities of money (its necessary attributes)
• functions of money (what money enables you to do)

These qualities and functions are best seen when you examine an economy where there is no money, because the inefficiencies of this economy highlight how useful money is. Such economies are based on what is known as the *barter system*.

2.2 The Barter System

If you go into a primary school, you will see in operation a basic barter system: objects which are of value to the children - biros, badges, small toys - are exchanged on a 'swap' system which is based on a negotiated bargain. Larger boys tend to get better deals than smaller boys, but the principles remain precisely the same as the primitive 'barter' system which existed in the period in history when the human race started to trade but had not yet developed a money system. In Britain the barter economy developed from about 3000 BC and lasted until about 500 BC.

The basis of the barter system is that if a community produces sufficient goods they can be traded for goods produced by other communities. Take, for example, three commodities needed in pre-Roman Britain:

• pots - the universally-used storage container
• salt - valuable for preservation of meat and fish
• cattle - valuable for milk, haulage and food

What problems are involved in trading these three commodities? How do you buy a pot if you have got a cow? What happens if you suspect the cow you are buying is diseased? How much salt would you give for the cow? The drawbacks of the barter system are set out below.

Double coincidence of wants
If you want someone's cow you have to make sure that they want your pot or salt. The needs or 'wants' of buyer and seller must coincide.

Exchange rate
How do you determine how many pots or measures of salt will buy a cow? If the cowherd has a bigger stick than you, he may be able to negotiate a better exchange rate.

Giving change
If a cowherd wants to buy a pot, he has a problem: he cannot readily divide up his cow and give change. He will probably have to give something else instead.

Convenience factor
If you exchange cows, they are difficult to carry about and they can contract disease; pots are arguably more convenient, but they can be dropped; salt can be washed away.

In conclusion, the barter system is beset with problems and inefficiencies. The modern money system has developed to overcome these shortcomings. We will examine the history of coins and banknotes shortly, having first analysed money's qualities and functions.

2.3 Qualities of Money

As you will appreciate from the shortcomings of the barter system, money must have certain 'qualities' or characteristics to enable it to be efficient. These are best remembered by the word ADDPURSS:

A	cceptability
D	urability
D	ivisibility
P	ortability
U	niformity
R	ecognisability
S	carcity
S	tability

We will examine each of these in turn.

Acceptability

The necessity for a 'double coincidence of wants' means that money must be acceptable by everyone. There must be confidence in the money system. A modern example of money *not* being acceptable to everyone is in the South American Republic of Bolivia, where the inflation rate of the 'Peso' is so high that many Bolivians use United States Dollars instead of their own currency.

Durability

Money must be able to last (be durable) for a reasonable period of time; unlike the barter system where commodities are perishable or breakable. A 'reasonable period of time' for the UK currency is considered to be twenty years for coins and as little as six months for banknotes.

Divisibility

The barter system does not readily allow for the giving of change. An efficient money system should be *divisible* into units of different value to enable change to be given, and different amounts to be tendered. We will examine the definition of 'legal tender' in the next chapter (Chapter 3.1).

Portability

Although the cows used in the barter system have their own motive power, they do not slip easily into the pocket, wallet, or purse as modern money must. Money has to be *portable*. It is an interesting feature of modern money that it is becoming smaller. Coins have shrunk to such a size that critics of the system complain that they seem lightweight and 'cheap'.

Uniformity

One of the problems with barter was that commodity 'units' were rarely identical - one cow was never the same as another - and therefore bargaining power was affected. Units of modern money must be uniform or 'homogeneous' so that its purchasing power is not affected. Despite this, banks will always get the problem customers who insist on 'new notes please' or object to the notes paid in by the local fishmonger.

Recognisability

This may seem an obvious quality of money, but it must be recognisable as such, and hence become acceptable. There are problems occasionally when new coins are introduced, the new £2 coin being an example: people do not know whether they can be used as money or not.

Scarcity

Modern money, in order to maintain value, must be *scarce* or restricted in supply. In the UK, the Royal Mint and the Bank of England respectively, control the issue of coins and notes so that the money in circulation does not increase unduly. If the Bank of England, for instance, were allowed to print banknotes without restriction, the number in circulation would rise, their value (purchasing power) would fall, and the economy would soon be subject to high inflation.

Stability

Money must be stable in value or people will not want to use it. Modern money is by no means perfect in this respect: inflation (the fall in value of money) and exchange rate fluctuations (the variation in the value of money against other currencies) tend to destabilise the money system.

2.4 Functions of Money

As we have seen, 'qualities' of money describe its necessary characteristics or attributes. 'Functions' of money on the other hand, *describe what money enables us to do*. Money is traditionally said to have four main functions. They are easily remembered by the word SUMS:

S   tore of value
U   nit of account
M   edium of exchange
S   tandard for deferred payments

Store of value

Commodities in the barter system were often perishable. Modern money, as we have seen, is durable; it enables individuals to save and invest, so that at a future date the *value stored* can be realised and used to purchase goods and services, or to pass to other individuals.

Unit of account

Money as a *unit of account* enables individuals to set a price on goods and services, a function of money obviously lacking in the barter system. More than that, it enables *comparisons* to be made, e.g. a comparison of the profits of the major banks each year or the difference between your manager's salary and your own.

Medium of exchange

Money enables individuals to exchange *acquired value* for what they want. For example, as an employee you exchange your labour for money (not enough money you may claim!) which you then use to pay for what you need or want. Money is a very efficient *medium of exchange*. Consider the problems that would be caused if you worked for a greengrocer and were paid in sprouts and potatoes.

Standard for deferred payments

If in the barter system you wanted to buy a cow and pay for it in pots at a later date, a number of problems would be raised: how many pots, when and where? The modern money system enables the individual to use money as a *standard* (a unit of account) for *deferred payments* (payment made in the future). If you lend £5 to a colleague and ask her to pay you at next payday, or if you obtain a personal loan and pay back £50 a month over three years, money is being used as a standard for deferred payments.

2.5 The Development of Coins

The first coins

The origins of coins can be dated back to 2500 BC when the ancient Middle Eastern civilization of Mesopotamia used weighed measures of gold and silver for making payment. These precious metals obviously have the necessary qualities of money: acceptability, durability, divisibility, portability, uniformity, recognisability, security and stability, and also all the four functions of money. Although these weighed measures were 'money' they were not yet coins, and it was in the seventh century BC that the Ancient Greeks first struck recognisable 'coins' of gold and silver.

Significant developments in the British coinage

50BC Bronze coins	During the first century BC the first crude British coins copied from the neighbouring Roman Empire were circulated along with the iron bars that were the current 'medium of exchange'.
780AD The penny	In 780 Offa, King of Mercia, introduced the silver 'penny'. 240 pennies constituted a pound in weight of silver. The Latin word 'libra' meaning 'pound' was abbreviated to '£'. The abbreviation for penny was 'd' which stood for 'denarius', a European coin with Roman origins equivalent to the British penny. It is interesting to note that both abbreviations were used together until decimalisation in 1971. The '£' symbol is of course still used for our modern pound sterling.

1489 AD The 'Sovereign' coin	Henry VII in 1489 introduced the first pound coin (in gold) featuring himself enthroned in majesty (hence 'the Sovereign').
1662 Milled coins	Charles II, to prevent unscrupulous people 'clipping' the edge of coins for the gold or silver so obtained, introduced milled edges and the inscription 'Decus et Tutamen' around the edge of the larger coins. This means 'a decoration and a safeguard', and you can appreciate why! You will see this same legend inscribed on English modern £1 coins.
1816 The Gold Standard	Until 1816 the coinage had been solely based on the *sterling silver standard* which had linked the coinage to the value of silver, and ensured that each coin was 925 parts in 1000 pure silver. In 1816 the value of the coinage, based on a new gold sovereign also became linked to gold at £3 17s. 10½d. (£3.89) per ounce, eleven parts in twelve pure gold. This *gold standard* remained in force until 1914. While it was in force you could exchange a gold sovereign or a Bank of England banknote for an equivalent amount in gold at the Bank of England.
1971 Decimalisation	In order to harmonise with its European neighbours, the UK in 1971 adopted the unit of ten as a basis for the currency. The £, which used to comprise 240 pennies, now contains 100 'pence', or 'p' as they are generally known.

Intrinsic value and token value

One interesting feature about the development of the coinage is that whereas the earlier coins were actually worth what they were made of - that is how they came into being - the later coins were not, once the gold and silver standards had been abandoned. This is the difference between *intrinsic* and *token* value:

• **intrinsic value -** the value of a coin measured by the value of its metal content
• **token value -** the exchange value or 'face' value of a coin

If you take the modern pound sterling, a pound coin has an intrinsic value of a few pence but a token value of £1 (hence the profit made by the Royal Mint!), whereas a gold sovereign, legally a £1 coin, has a token value of £1 but an intrinsic value of a great deal more, which is why it is not used as loose change.

2.6   The Development of Banknotes and Cheques

The history of the modern banknote and cheque can be traced back in Britain to the late seventeenth century when London was developing as a commercial centre. Merchants, brokers and goldsmiths, who handled valuables and arranged payments for others, developed the first true 'banking' services, although they were not constituted as banks. The principal services were:

• loans on which interest was charged
• interest-bearing deposits
• foreign currency exchange
• notes and receipts

It is this last category of 'notes and receipts' which gave rise not only to the banknote but also to the cheque. The goldsmiths of London were prominent in the issue of notes and receipts, and we will use them as an example.

Goldsmiths' notes

Goldsmiths, as well as being craftsmen, used to hold gold in safekeeping for their clients. They issued receipts for these deposits promising to repay the amount deposited on demand. These receipts (or notes, as they were known) became acceptable among merchants in settlement of debt because, if one merchant wanted to pass on the receipt to a second merchant, all he had to do was to sign it on the back (endorse it), and hand it to the second merchant who could then claim the gold from the goldsmith.

Goldsmiths' notes were soon issued in fixed denominations and payable to 'bearer' (i.e. the person in possession of the note) rather than to a specified person. In this way, they became freely transferable between individuals, a much more convenient system. If you examine a modern banknote you will see that it also is in a fixed denomination and payable to bearer, the only difference being that it is not now exchangeable for gold. We will discuss the issue and backing of banknotes further in Chapter 4 when we examine the development of the banking system.

Early cheques

Although the word 'cheque' dates from the eighteenth century, early forms of cheque were common in the late seventeenth century, and known as 'notes'. If a depositor of gold at a goldsmith wanted to settle a debt with someone, he would write a formal 'note' instructing the holder of the gold to pay a certain sum in gold to that specified person. When banks were founded in the eighteenth century, cheques were written out by the account holders, instructing the bank to pay a third party. Printed cheques were introduced in the mid-eighteenth century, although hand-written cheques continued to be used well into the nineteenth century.

2.7   The Problems of Deflation and Inflation

We have discussed earlier in the chapter the qualities and functions of money. It is an obvious fact that if money varies in value over time, it becomes unreliable

- as a unit of account (year-to-year comparisons are difficult)
- as a store of value (savings will vary in value)

The stability of the money system is therefore an important policy objective for any government. Variation in value of money can take two forms: *deflation* and *inflation*.

Deflation

Deflation, which is comparatively rare at present, is a fall in the prices of goods and services caused by a falling demand for those goods and services. It is a sign of a sick economy and is typified by lack of confidence, falling output and a rise in unemployment.

Inflation

Most economies are inflation based, i.e. prices of goods and services rise and the purchasing power of money falls. Inflation is expressed in terms of a percentage rate. For instance, if inflation is running at 7½% at a specific date, your money will buy 7½% less goods and services than it would have done a year earlier. Inflation generally has two causes:

- **cost-push inflation** is caused by a rise in the cost of producing goods and services, for instance, a rise in the cost of raw materials (possibly imported) or a rise in labour costs (strong unions).

- **demand-pull inflation** is caused when demand for goods and services exceeds supply, for instance, when the Chancellor of the Exchequer reduces taxation or allows people to buy excessively on credit.

Hyper-inflation

Western economies generally keep inflation under control and can plan accordingly. Some other economies, notably those in South America, suffer from *hyper-inflation,* which is the situation where inflation runs out of control: shoppers queue in the early morning for goods to avoid the price rise later in the day; barter is reintroduced; civil unrest is common. Consider the effect of hyper-inflation on:

- your savings - they will reduce in value
- money you are owed - you will receive less in real terms
- money you owe - you will pay less in real terms

It is very clear that monetary stability is important to our economy.

Indications of inflation

Governments need to monitor the change in prices, and in Britain several *indices* have been introduced to indicate price changes in different sectors.

- **Retail Price Index (RPI)**   In January 1974 a 'basket' of household goods and services such as food, clothing, fuel bills, travel expenses for a typical household was valued and equated to the number 100. Subsequently, at regular intervals, this 'basket' has been revalued (inevitably it has risen in price) and the new value expressed as a number proportional to the original 100. For instance, if the revalued 'basket' cost twice as much, the new index number would be 2 x 100 = 200.

- **Tax and Price Index (TPI)**   Introduced in 1979 this index introduces the variations of the effect of direct taxation upon income.

- **Wholesale Price Index (WPI)**   This index measures the change of prices used in the manufacturing industry and highlights variations in cost-push inflation.

2.8 Revision Points

❑   Money is something which is exchangeable for goods and services, and is generally acceptable in the settlement of debt.

❑   The barter system which preceded money, had a number of inefficiencies:
- double coincidence of wants
- exchange rate
- giving of change
- convenience

❏ The qualities of money can be remembered by the word ADDPURSS:

- Acceptability
- Durability
- Divisibility
- Portability
- Uniformity
- Recognisability
- Scarcity
- Stability

❏ The functions of money can be remembered by the word SUMS:

- Store of value
- Unit of account
- Medium of exchange
- Standard for deferred payments

❏ Coins

- first appeared in Britain in the first century BC
- developed in gold and in silver
- gold standard introduced in 1816
- decimalisation in 1971
- intrinsic value - value of a coin's metal content
- token value - exchange value of a coin

❏ Banknotes and cheques

- developed from goldsmiths' notes in the seventeenth century
- banknotes became payable to 'bearer' and in set denominations, and were a claim on goldsmiths' gold
- cheques were written to a specific person giving them the right to claim gold from the goldsmith

❏ Deflation is the fall in price of goods and services, and is rare.

❏ Inflation is the rate of the rise in price of goods and services over a year. It can be:

- cost push - increase in the cost of production
- demand-pull - increase in the demand for goods and services
- hyper-inflation - inflation out of control (e.g. South America)

❏ Inflation is measured by:

- RPI - Retail Price Index
- TPI - Tax and Price Index
- WPI - Wholesale Price Index

2.9 Know your *The Theory of Money*

Each 'know your ....' test consists of multiple-choice and short answer questions: one mark is awarded in the examination for each correct answer. Many of the questions are taken from past examination papers; other questions are of a similar standard. Answers to the 'know your ....' tests are given in the Study Guide.

Multiple-choice questions
Choose the *one* answer you think is correct.

1.   Which of the following is a function of money?

   A Measure of scarcity
   B Valuation of savings
   C Standard of accounting
   D Store of value

2.   What function of money allows money to span time?

   A Standard of deferred payments
   B Unit of account
   C Medium of exchange
   D Store of value

3.   Which of the following is not a quality of money?

   A Durability
   B Recognisability
   C Unit of account
   D Divisibility

4.   Token value is:

   A The exchange value of a coin
   B The value of the metal out of which a coin is made
   C The value of a coin measured against inflation
   D The value of a coin as a collector's item

5.   Inflation is:

   A A rise in the purchasing power of money
   B A fall in the Retail Price Index
   C When the supply of goods and services exceeds demand
   D A fall in the purchasing power of money

Short answer questions

6.   Give *two* functions of money.

7.   List *two* characteristics of money.

8.   What *two* forms of money owe their origin to goldsmiths' notes?

9.   What is the RPI?

10. List *two* bad effects of inflation.

2.10 Essay Questions *The Theory of Money*

Where indicated, essay questions are taken from past examination papers; other essay questions are of a similar standard to the examination. Outline answers to selected essay questions are given in the Study Guide.

1. Whatever comes into use as money must possess certain qualities.
    Discuss these qualities as found in present day forms of money.
    [*The Chartered Institute of Bankers' specimen paper*]

2. You are taking part in a training exercise to develop an alternative to notes and coin as a method of buying and selling. You have the following options available to you:

    - 5,000 cigarettes
    - weekly stock of food for a family of four
    - game of Ludo, which contains: 2 dice, 4 sets of 4 coloured counters and a playing board
    - twenty-four bottles of assorted wines

    Which option would you choose? Justify your choice.

    [*question 2, Autumn 1987*]

3. What are the four functions of money? Discuss the extent to which present day forms of money fulfil these functions.

Chapter Three
Modern Forms of Money

In the last chapter we defined money by taking as our starting point what the term 'money' included. In this chapter we will examine in more detail modern forms of money:

* notes and coins
* bank deposits
* cheques
* 'plastic' money such as cheque cards, cash cards, credit cards, debit cards and charge cards
* near-money, i.e. items which can be readily turned into cash
* token money

3.1 Notes and Coins: Legal Tender

We have seen in the last chapter how notes and coins have developed into their modern forms. This development process is of course continuing: there are plans for new, lighter, coins, and discussions have been entered into about plastic notes, although opinion is divided about these.

The term *legal tender* is an important theoretical concept relating to notes and coins, although it is not often encountered in practice. The law states that a person being offered (tendered) money in settlement of debt *can* insist on

* the exact amount being given, i.e. they don't have to give change
* certain limits in denominations of coins

In practice, people give change and are not usually fussy about the denominations tendered because they are not in the habit of refusing payment! If, however, a bus driver states that "exact change must be tendered" he is in his legal rights to demand it. The maximum limits for denominations tendered are:

Bank of England notes	no limit
£1 coins (including gold sovereigns)	no limit
50p and 20p coins	up to £10
10p and 5p coins	up to £5
bronze coins	up to 20p

If you are involved in cashiering, you will notice that the legal tender amounts coincide with the amounts counted into bags at the till. You should also note that the following are *not* legal tender:

- cheques
- Scottish and Northern Irish banknotes

You may have encountered a shopkeeper who has refused a Scottish note: he or she is legally entitled to do so, although a bank will accept them.

Advantages of notes and coins as money
- acceptability — most cash is in fact legal tender
- durability — coins will last for 20 years
- divisibility — there are numerous denominations
- portability — cash is normally used for small transactions and so can easily be carried around
- uniformity — each unit is the same, except for small variations caused by wear and tear
- recognisability — they are readily recognisable and therefore acceptable
- scarcity — the issue of coins is controlled by the Royal Mint, the issue of notes by the Bank of England
- stability — they represent a stable currency

You will note that these advantages comprise 'ADDPURSS', the word for the qualities of money.

Disadvantages of notes and coins as money

There are certain practical disadvantages:

- security problem — cash can be stolen or lost
- durability — notes can be torn, burnt, or sent to the laundry
- portability — you cannot easily use coins for large items such as a house purchase (although £1 coins could not be refused, being legal tender for an unlimited amount!)

Common sense dictates that most of these disadvantages are not encountered in normal transactions.

3.2   Bank Deposits

A person may say "I have money in the bank." In a loose sense this is true, but if you examine the situation more closely, you will see that the person really means that they have a claim on the bank, and could withdraw that amount of money either in cash or by issuing a cheque.

Credit creation
Banks are arguably in a precarious situation because they have traditionally (from the time of the goldsmith) lent out *more* money, which is then redeposited with them, than they have notes and coins (or gold in the days of the goldsmiths). This process is known as *credit creation*. If all bank customers demanded notes and coins for their bank deposits on the same day, there would not be enough in the tills and the entire banking system could fail. The following statistics show the striking difference between actual money (notes and coins) and bank deposits (balances recorded on bank computers) as at the end of December 1988:

Total notes and coin held by UK banks	£3,405m
Total UK bank balances	£223,449m

We will see in the next chapter how *credit creation* works in practice and how public confidence in the banking system enables it to continue.

Sight and term deposits

Bank (and building society) deposits are either *sight* or *term:*

• **a sight deposit** is a deposit that can be drawn upon immediately, on demand.

• **a term deposit** (or time deposit) is a deposit that requires notice to be given before a withdrawal can be made

You will see that sight deposits rely on money's function as a medium of exchange. Term deposits are often savings accounts yielding a high rate of interest; they are used more as a store of value.

3.3   Cheques

The legal background to cheques

A cheque is a common form of money and is particularly useful as a medium of exchange when used with a cheque card issued by a bank or a building society. As we saw earlier, the cheque was first used in the seventeenth century and its use developed with the growth of trade and commerce until it was defined formally in law - the Bills of Exchange Act 1882 - as 'a bill of exchange, drawn on a bank, payable on demand'. This legal terminology needs some explanation.

Bills of exchange and cheques

A *bill of exchange* is a written order normally drawn up by a trader owed money, instructing someone else (usually the person to whom he has sold goods) to pay a specific sum, often in the future, to himself or to a third party. In simple terms it is a trader's formal way of stating to a buyer, for example: "You owe me a sum of money for the goods I have just sold to you; pay me (or someone else) in 30 days' time." The buyer signs his name on the bill of exchange to show that he accepts the obligation to pay.

A *cheque* on the other hand is a written order instructing a *bank* to pay someone *on demand,* i.e. pay them when the cheque is paid in or a request for cash is made.

Parties to bills of exchange and cheques

A cheque therefore is a specialised form of bill of exchange. They both have three parties: *drawer, drawee* and *payee.*

	cheque	*bill of exchange*
• drawer	the customer who writes out the cheque	the person who draws up the bill and is usually owed the money
• drawee	the bank that is instructed to pay the cheque on demand	the person who is expected to pay, usually in the future
• payee	the person who is to be paid by the bank, either by paying in the cheque or by cashing it	the person who is to receive the money from the drawee - often the same person as the drawer

Bills of exchange are rarely seen now, except in specialised areas of trade such as international settlement of debt.

Legal definition of a cheque

The Bills of Exchange Act 1882 does not define a cheque in *detailed* terms, but it does define a bill of exchange, and a number of terms in its definition of a bill of exchange apply equally to cheques. These terms (modified for cheques) are set out in the left-hand column below, and are explained on the right.

A cheque is . . .

an unconditional order	A cheque cannot be conditional, e.g. 'pay S. Robinson on his wedding day.' He may never get married.
in writing	A cheque must be in writing, whether in ink, pencil, typewriting, computer print or any other form of writing. The writing is usually on paper, but need not be so; valid cheques have been written on eggs, cows and whisky bottles! Banks *advise* customers to write cheques in ink on preprinted forms, largely to discourage fraud, but customers are under no *legal* compulsion to do so.
signed by the drawer	A cheque must be signed by the drawer (customer). Without an authorised signature a cheque is invalid.
requiring a bank to pay on demand	A cheque must be addressed to a bank and is payable on presentation either through the clearings or over the counter.
an exact sum	The amount of the cheque must be precisely stated.
to a specified person	The person to receive the money, the payee, should be stated,
or to their order	**or** the payee may pass the cheque to someone else by endorsing it (signing it on the back) so that they can be paid by the bank,
or to bearer	**or** the cheque may be made payable to 'bearer' (as a banknote is), in which case the person to whom it is handed (the bearer) can be paid by the bank.

This definition, which should be learnt, therefore reads as follows:

> *A cheque is an unconditional order in writing, signed by the drawer, requiring a bank to pay on demand an exact sum to a specified person, or to their order, or to bearer.*

We will discuss the way in which a cheque is cleared, and the obligations of the bank accepting and paying it, in Chapter 9, when we deal with funds transfer systems. In the meantime, it is important to look more closely at the details on a cheque and the different types of cheques encountered: order cheques and bearer cheques; crossed cheques and open cheques.

Key details on a cheque

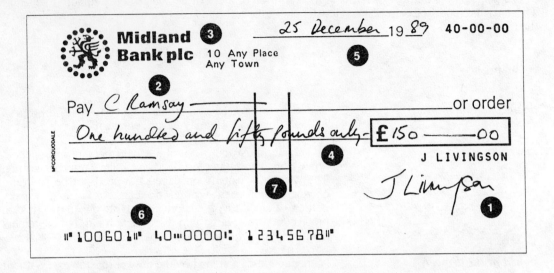

1. Signature   the drawer's authority to the bank to pay

2. Payee   the person who is intended to receive the money

3. Drawee bank   the name and address of the bank instructed to make payment

4. Amount   shows in words and figures the specific sum to be paid; they should agree!

5. Date   the drawer should write the date on the cheque indicating when it should be paid

6. Magnetic coding   the figures which will appear from left to right are:

                                • the cheque number

                                • the individual sort code of that branch (also printed at the top right of the cheque)

                                • the account number of the drawer

                                • the amount (not shown), which is encoded by the bank at which the cheque is paid in

7. Crossing   an instruction stating that the cheque must be paid into a bank account

It is often taken for granted that customers know how to write out cheques. This is not always the case, as a look through the morning's clearings will show, and banks should ensure that customers exercise care in writing cheques in order to avoid fraudulent alterations. Customers should:

• use ink and not pencil
• not leave space for fraudsters to add words or figures
• sign the cheque
• sign or initial any changes or corrected errors

Passing on the cheque: endorsements, order cheques and bearer cheques

Whereas notes and coins are an efficient medium of exchange, cheques as money may be restricted in the way that they can be passed from one person to another. If, for example, you are the payee of a cheque for £50 and you owe someone £50 you can pass it to them by *endorsement:* you sign it on the back. There are three types of endorsement: blank endorsement, specific endorsement and restrictive endorsement, and we will consider them by looking at a cheque which is payable to S. Robinson.

blank endorsement

> *S. Robinson*

Reverse of cheque

A blank endorsement is the signature of the person handing on the cheque, with no further instructions. In this case, the cheque can be passed to anyone without further endorsement. It could pass to C. Ramsay then to M. Ramsay and then to H. Ramsay. If H. Ramsay lost it and you found it in the street you could pay it into your bank account! (A blank endorsement makes a cheque into a bearer cheque - see next page.)

specific endorsement

> *Pay C. Ramsay*
> *S. Robinson*

Reverse of cheque

The person handing on the cheque indicates the person who is to receive the cheque and signs their own name. C. Ramsay in this case could either pay it into a bank account or endorse it over to someone else.

restrictive endorsement

> *Pay C. Ramsay only*
> *S. Robinson*

Reverse of cheque

In this case S. Robinson *restricts* the cheque to C. Ramsay; it cannot be passed to anyone else. C. Ramsay can pay it into her bank account.

These three types of endorsement illustrate the difference between a *bearer cheque* and an *order cheque*.

A **bearer cheque** can be passed ('delivered' in legal terminology) from one person to another *without endorsement*. A bearer cheque is either

• payable to 'bearer', (like a banknote), or
• payable to a person who has *blank endorsed* it (i.e. signed it and not indicated who is to receive it, as in the first illustration on the previous page).

Note that a bearer cheque cannot necessarily be *cashed* by the person who holds it, it must be an 'open' cheque (see below) for this to be possible.

An **order cheque** is made payable to a specific payee and can only be passed from the payee to another person by endorsement.

Cashing the cheque: crossed cheques and open cheques

A **crossed cheque** - a cheque which bears two parallel lines on its face - must be paid into a bank account; it cannot be cashed except by the account holder or an authorised representative of the account holder.

An **open cheque**, which has *no* crossing, may be cashed by the payee at the drawee bank; such cheques, for reasons of security, are rare - some employers issue open wages cheques to their employees.

It is important that the difference between an *open* cheque and a *bearer* cheque is fully understood. If you are not sure, read the last two pages again. You will no doubt realise that the majority of cheques issued are crossed order cheques. We will examine the different types of crossing, and phrases that appear on the crossing, in Chapter 9, when we discuss the clearing of cheques.

Advantages of cheques as money

• cheques can be issued for any amount, subject to availability of funds
• cheques are more secure than cash; they can normally be stopped if lost, and can easily be sent through the post
• cheques can easily be transferred between parties

Disadvantages of cheques as money

• shops will not normally accept cheques without a cheque card
• cheques are susceptible to theft and fraud
• a person accepting a cheque may find that it is dishonoured (bounced)
• it is less easy to use than cash and is noticeably slower (as you will see in a supermarket queue, although some larger stores have machines which will 'write' a customer's cheque)

3.4   Plastic Money

Plastic money is the term used to describe the plastic cards that are increasingly being used to make payment for goods and services. We will describe the mechanics of the appropriate payment systems in Chapter 10, and in this chapter concentrate on the way in which these plastic cards function as *money*.

Plastic money used today includes

- cheque cards
- debit cards
- credit cards (including store cards)
- charge cards

We will describe each of these in turn. You will note that cash cards or ATM (Automated Teller Machine) cards are not included here: they are not in fact *money* as such, but merely a convenient means for obtaining banknotes. It could be argued that they are obstructing the progress towards a 'cashless society' as they actively promote the use of banknotes as a medium of exchange.

3.5   Cheque Cards

A cheque card is a card issued by a bank or a building society guaranteeing payment of a cheque up to a certain limit.

Advantage of cheque cards as money
A cheque card, as a guarantee of payment, increases the acceptability of cheques as a medium of exchange; however, it has certain shortcomings.

Disadvantages of cheque cards as money

the limit

The limit, set at £50 in 1977, was extended in 1989 to £100 and £250 for certain customers, by the Association for Payment Clearing Services (APACS). In addition some customers can qualify for the Eurocheque card which guarantees special Eurocheques drawn abroad in foreign currency up to £100 equivalent. Many customers, still restricted to UK £50 cards, find this limit per transaction very frustrating; so too do the retailers.

the conditions

The guarantee of payment is only effective if certain conditions are fulfilled when the cheque is issued. The conditions are either written on the back of the card or available to customers at the bank. A typical set of conditions runs as follows:

[a] one cheque per transaction

[b] the cheque cannot be drawn on the account of a limited company

[c] the name and bank code on the cheque and card must agree

[d] the card is not out of date

[e] the cheque is signed, in the presence of the payee, by the person whose signature appears on the card

[f] the card number is written on the back of the card by the payee

[g] the card has not been defaced

The guarantee is therefore invalid if you wish to make a mail order purchase (conditions [e] and [f]), or if the card is stolen (condition [e]).

fraud
A cheque card and cheque book kept together are a temptation to criminals to such an extent that in 1988 the UK banks sustained losses of £22m from having to pay retailers who had accepted stolen cheque cards and forged cheques. It is interesting to note that condition [e] enables banks to avoid having to pay out in these circumstances, as the guarantee is invalid if a *thief* signs the cheque. Not many banks do in fact refuse to pay stolen cheques; if they did so, retailers might refuse to accept cheque cards!

In short, cheques backed by a cheque card are a useful medium of exchange, but have more shortcomings than the newer debit and credit cards which are gradually replacing cheque cards.

3.6   Debit Cards

A debit card is a plastic card with which the customer can make a purchase without writing out a cheque, but have the amount immediately passed as a debit to the account.

Examples of debit cards include Barclays Bank's *Connect*, Lloyds Bank's *Visa Payment Card* and the *Switch* card issued by a number of clearing banks.

The mechanics of how the debit is processed through to the customer's account using an imprinter or 'swipe' machine will be dealt with in Chapter 10, but it should be noted here that as money, a debit card is very versatile and a generally more effective medium of exchange than the cheque and cheque card.

Advantages of debit cards as money
- no limit on amount of payment
- speed and convenience of use - no cheque to write out
- many debit cards also function as cash (ATM) cards and cheque guarantee cards
- purchases can be made through the post or over the telephone by quoting the card number

Disadvantages of debit cards as money
- not all retailers accept them
- a debit card transaction is not necessarily a guarantee of payment (larger items can be returned)
- if a debit card is stolen there is no limit to the number of times it can be used by a thief (a cheque card is limited to the number of stolen cheques)
- customers are more likely to get into debt by overspending, as banks are finding to their cost!

3.7   Credit Cards

A credit card is a plastic card which enables the customer to purchase goods and services and to pay for them at a later date.

Credit cards are issued by the two main credit card organisations owned by the banks: Visa and Access. The mechanics of how the retailer claims the money and the customer pays will be dealt with in Chapters 9 and 10, when we examine funds transfer systems.

Advantages of credit cards as money

- no limit on amount of payment - the overall spending limit is set by the credit card company - it is often very generous
- speed and convenience of use - the retailer uses an imprinter or 'swipe' machine
- purchases can be made by post or over the telephone by quoting the card number
- some credit cards, e.g. Barclaycard, double as a cheque guarantee card
- most credit cards can be used to draw cash
- the attraction of 'buy now, pay later'
- credit cards are accepted abroad

Disadvantages of credit cards as money

- not all retailers accept credit cards because the retailer has to pay a percentage of the transaction value (often between 2% and 5%) to the credit card company
- customers can easily get into debt which they cannot repay
- high rates of interest are charged by the credit card companies

Store cards

A store card is a credit card issued by a specific store (or chain of stores). It can be used only at that store (or stores) and, while convenient to use, can be expensive in interest terms if you spread the cost of purchases over several months.

3.8   Charge Cards

A charge card is a plastic card which enables the holder to purchase goods and services worldwide.

Charge cards are often referred to as 'expense' cards or 'entertainment' cards, as they are cards used by high income earners and company representatives and definitely not by clerical bank employees! Examples include Diners Club and American Express. As the advertising media show, they are excellent as a medium of exchange: they enable you to purchase what you want in the most difficult circumstances. Their shortcomings include limited acceptability (not all outlets accept them) and expense: an annual subscription and payment in full on receipt of statement.

3.9   Liquidity, Near Money and Token Money

Liquidity is a term which means the readiness with which items can be turned into cash. Notes and coins are essentially very 'liquid' whereas a villa in Spain, although a valuable possession, cannot be readily turned into cash; it is said to be 'illiquid'.

Near money

There are certain items which are thought of as being a form of money, but are not as liquid as cash; they are known as *near money* or *quasi-money,* and are often held as a store of value.

Near money is a liquid item which has to be turned into cash before it can be used as a medium of exchange.

Consider how the following examples of near money function as a store of value rather than as a medium of exchange:

time deposits	bank or building society deposits which require a notice period before cash can be withdrawn
stocks and shares	they are a store of value which can be sold, but payment is not always immediate, it usually follows after a period of time
postal orders	these are often used as gifts or for postal payments, but have to be bought by the sender and cashed, or paid into a bank account, by the recipient

Token money

Certain forms of money such as luncheon vouchers or product tokens (i.e. '50p off your next purchase of Flasho washing powder') are 'token money'. They cannot be exchanged for cash but are a medium of exchange for a specific product, i.e. a meal or washing powder. Token money has limited acceptability and in the case of product tokens, limited durability ('offer expires 31 December 1989').

3.10 Revision Points

❏   Notes and coins, subject to certain limits constitute legal tender.

   • Bank of England notes - no limit
   • £1 coins and sovereigns - no limit
   • 50p and 20p coins - up to £10
   • 10p and 5p coins - up to £5
   • bronze coins - up to 20p

❏   Learn the advantages and disadvantages of notes and coins (see Section 3.1).

❏   Bank deposits are examples of money and can be:

   • sight deposits - money that can be drawn immediately
   • term (or time) deposits - money for which notice of withdrawal is necessary

❏   Cheques have three parties:

   • drawer - the customer
   • drawee - the bank
   • payee - the person receiving the cheque

❏   A cheque is:

   an unconditional order in writing, signed by the drawer, requiring a bank to pay on demand an exact sum to a specified person, or to their order, or to bearer.

❑ There are three types of endorsement:

- blank endorsement   - the signature only
- specific endorsement   - the signature and instructions to whom the cheque is to be paid ('Pay C. Ramsay')
- restrictive endorsement   - the signature and instructions to pay the cheque to one person only ('Pay C. Ramsay only').

❑ A bearer cheque can be transferred without endorsement.

❑ An order cheque needs an endorsement before it can be transferred.

❑ A crossed cheque has two parallel lines on its face and can only be paid through a bank account.

❑ An open cheque has no crossing and can be cashed by the payee at the drawee bank.

❑ Learn the advantages and disadvantages of cheques (Section 3.3).

❑ Plastic money includes:

- cheque cards
- debit cards
- credit cards (including store cards)
- charge cards

❑ Cheque cards:

- guarantee cheques up to the value of £50, £100 or £250
- the guarantee is only effective if the conditions of issue are fulfilled (learn them - see Section 3.5).

❑ Debit cards:

- include Barclays Bank's *Connect* and the *Switch* card offered by other banks
- avoid the use of cheques
- are used either with an imprinter or a 'swipe' machine

Learn the advantages and disadvantages (Section 3.6).

❑ Credit cards:

- include Visa and Access cards
- enable customers to purchase goods and services and pay for them later

Learn the advantages and disadvantages (Section 3.7).

❑ Charge cards are expense or entertainment cards:

- used by high income earners
- include American Express and Diners Club
- are expensive to use and require immediate settlement on receipt of the statement

❑   Near money is a liquid item which has to be turned into cash before it can be used as a medium of exchange, e.g.

- time deposits
- stocks and shares
- postal orders

❑   Token money cannot be exchanged for cash but is a medium of exchange for a specific product, e.g. luncheon vouchers.

3.11   Know your *Modern Forms of Money*

Multiple-choice Questions
Choose the *one* answer you think is correct.

1.   The fiduciary issue is backed by

   A gold
   B gold and silver
   C gold and government securities
   D government securities

2.   Which one of the following statements is correct?

   A Cheques are defined as money
   B Cheques are legal tender
   C Bank deposits are money but are not legal tender
   D Bank deposits are not money but are legal tender

3.   To obtain the guarantee provided by a cheque card

   A the card number must be written on the back of the cheque by the retailer
   B the card number must be written on the back of the cheque by the payee
   C two cheques must be issued if the item costs more than £50
   D two cheques with different dates must be issued if the item costs more than £50

4.   To obtain the guarantee provided by a cheque card

   A the customer must write the card number on the back of the cheque
   B the cheque should have the same code number as shown on the card
   C customers must write several cheques if the price is more than £50
   D alterations on the cheque card must be signed

5.   With a charge card

   A a customer can guarantee cheques
   B an annual fee is often payable
   C payments can always be spread over a period
   D customers can cash cheques at a bank

Short Answer Questions

6.   What is the normal limit of guarantee for a cheque card?

7.   What is the *fiduciary* issue?

8.   What is legal tender?

9.   Define *sight* and *term* deposits.

10. What is *credit creation*?

11. What are the three parties to a cheque?

12. Define a cheque.

13. What is a cheque crossing and what significance does it have?

14. Name three types of endorsement, and state briefly their effect.

15. What is the difference between a bearer cheque and an order cheque?

16. What is the difference between a bearer cheque and an open cheque?

17. State five of the conditions which must be fulfilled when a cheque is issued with a cheque guarantee card in order for the guarantee to be effective.

18. What is a debit card?

19. Distinguish between a credit card and a charge card.

20. What is *near money* (sometimes known as 'quasi-money')?

3.12 Essay Questions *Modern Forms of Money*

The numbers in brackets after subdivisions refer to the marks out of 20 for each question.

1.   What qualities must money possess? Discuss how these qualities are found in today's money.

[question 21, Spring 1987]

2.   Mike Gooch has just returned from holiday in Pakistan where he enjoyed bargaining in the markets for local goods. He became highly skilled in bartering items of clothing for a wide variety of produce and cannot understand why department stores will not allow him to 'buy' in the same way.

Explain why such a system would not work in the United Kingdom and list the assets that can be used to pay for goods and are acceptable as money.

[question 2, Autumn 1988]

3.   (a) Distinguish between legal tender and money.

[4 marks]

(b) Describe the various items that carry out some or all of the functions of money in a modern economy and state *two* major disadvantages of each.

[16 marks]
[question 2, Spring 1989]

4.   List the forms of money used in the UK at the present day, setting out in each case their advantages and disadvantages as money.

5.   (a) Define a cheque and explain what each part of the definition means.

[10 marks]

(b) What is the difference between a blank, a specific and a restrictive endorsement, and how can these endorsements affect the way a cheque is transferred?

[10 marks]

6.   'Cheque cards have many shortcomings'. With reference to this statement:

(a) state the disadvantages of cheque cards.

[15 marks[

(b) state how recent developments in banking are helping to overcome these problems.

[5 marks]

7.   In what ways is 'plastic money' superseding cash as a form of settlement? Illustrate your answer by reference to at least *five* types of plastic card.

Chapter Four
Development of the UK Banking System

In this chapter we will examine:

- the origins of banking and trace its history to the present day
- the contemporary banking system and the different types of banking institution which operate within its framework, including retail banks, merchant banks, and foreign banks
- the wide variety of financial markets operating in London

The watchdog of the banking system, the Bank of England, will be referred to throughout the chapter, but a detailed explanation of its complex present-day role will be given in Chapter 5.

4.1   The Origins of Banking

Moneylenders
There is no doubt that if banking did not exist it would become necessary to invent it. Early civilisations which had developed money (see Chapter 2) found it necessary to store it. As trading developed, merchants also found it necessary to borrow to finance their operations. The earliest bankers in the UK were moneylenders, some of whom came in the thirteenth century from Lombardy in Italy - hence 'Lombard Street', where the headquarters of The Chartered Institute of Bankers are situated. The money lenders traded from a bench (Italian 'banca') and greatly assisted the development of London as a trading and financial centre. Moneylenders charged high rates of interest and were unpopular: a well known example was Shylock the Jew in Shakespeare's *The Merchant of Venice* who lent money to a merchant on the security of 'a pound of flesh' from the merchant's body. Modern day borrowers are fortunately spared this unorthodox form of security, although the phrase persists in the English language.

Goldsmiths
As we saw in Chapter 2 the goldsmiths developed in seventeenth century England the basic functions of banking:

- taking deposits of gold
- loans
- issue of early banknotes ('receipts')
- paying of early cheques (called 'notes')
- foreign currency exchange

Raising of capital for trading ventures and also for political adventures became an attractive and profitable proposition for City of London merchants and led to the formation of the Bank of England in 1694.

The Bank of England

In 1694 William III needed to finance his war with the French. In that year, William Paterson, together with a group of wealthy merchants, raised £1.2m through a new privileged body, the Bank of England, which was granted a Royal Charter, and from then onwards became closely associated with the Government. Unlike the goldsmith bankers of the day who operated on their own or in partnerships, it was a 'joint stock company', the forerunner of modern day limited company banks. The £1.2m raised in 1694 was subscribed by 1,268 individuals, or 'shareholders' - to use current terminology.

We will examine the Bank of England's present supervisory role over the banking system in Chapter 5, and will now concentrate on how it developed as part of the UK banking system.

4.2   Goldsmiths and the Dangers of Credit Creation

An important function of the early goldsmiths was that of lending out the gold that was deposited with them on the assumption that not all the depositors would demand their gold back at the same time. Some of this gold would be redeposited with the goldsmiths, with the end result that the *recorded* deposits would exceed their holdings of gold, a potentially dangerous situation. This process of *credit creation* is illustrated in the following table which assumes that the goldsmith reckons he can safely lend out 50% of the gold deposited in his vaults:

	recorded deposits of gold	how the gold is used	
Step One			
Customer A deposits £100 in gold coins, and a receipt for £100 is issued	£100	Gold held	£100
Step Two			
Goldsmith lends out 50% of his deposit to Customer B		Gold held	£50
		Loan of gold	£50
	£100		£100
Step Three			
Customer B buys 50 barrels of ale from Customer C who deposits the £50 of gold coins paid to him with the goldsmith; a further receipt for £50 is issued	£100 £50 £150	Gold held (£50 + £50) Loan	£100 £50 £150

Clearly, this process can continue and the goldsmith could lend out 50% of the new £50 deposit of gold made in Step Three, and the £25 of gold coins lent out could be redeposited with him, creating yet another deposit. If the process continued to its logical (but unlikely!) conclusion, the goldsmith would hold £100 of gold coins, but have recorded deposits (evidenced by receipts or banknotes) of £200. The formula for calculating the figure by which the *original* deposit is multiplied is:

$$\frac{100}{\textit{Percentage of deposit retained (here 50\%)}} \quad = 2\ \textit{times}$$

Therefore, eventually, the goldsmith's total *recorded* deposits are £200 (original deposits of £100 x 2), but his actual holding of gold is £100. Deposits have been *created* by *credit* (lending). The customers' recorded deposits are liabilities (items owed by the goldsmith), and the gold held and loans made are assets (items owned by or owed to the goldsmith). We will examine these principles, in relation to the balance sheet of a bank, in detail in Chapter 6. At this point you should note that a present-day bank does not work to the 50% example considered above; instead it lends out rather more of its customers' deposits - see Chapter 6.

4.3   Country Banks and Joint Stock Banks

The history of banking has seen the development of two types of bank (see fig. 4.1):

- **the joint stock bank,** the forerunner of the present day limited company bank which raised capital from individual 'stockholders'

- **the country bank,** a small 'partnership' type of bank which rose to prominence in the eighteenth century and died out in the nineteenth century.

It is important to examine the principal Acts of Parliament which constituted and controlled both types of bank. Three consistent trends are evident in the development of the banking system:

- increasing control of the banks by the State through the Bank of England

- the development of the Bank of England's monopoly of the issue of banknotes

- an increase in size of banks over the years, caused by amalgamations and the tendency for smaller institutions to fail because of their vulnerability due to excessive credit creation and lack of public confidence

Principal Acts of Parliament relating to banking

Bank of England Act 1709

Under this Act, banks were limited to partnerships of a maximum of six partners. The exception was the privileged Bank of England, a joint stock bank. Consequently in the provinces, small *country banks* were formed by local merchants and landowners. They took deposits and, like the Bank of England, issued banknotes. An illustration of country banknotes is seen in fig. 4.2.

In 1810 there were 721 country banks, but in 1825 ninety of them failed. As we have seen, credit creation allows banks to issue more banknotes than they have gold in the vaults. The limited size and local nature of these country banks made them particularly susceptible to a loss of public confidence: they were unable to repay their depositors, they closed their doors and ceased trading.

Bank Act 1826

This necessary legislation followed the 1825 banking crisis. The restrictions of the 1709 Act were removed and the larger joint stock banks were allowed to set up 65 miles (105 km) from London. The 65 mile limit around the capital was designed to protect the monopoly of the Bank of England.

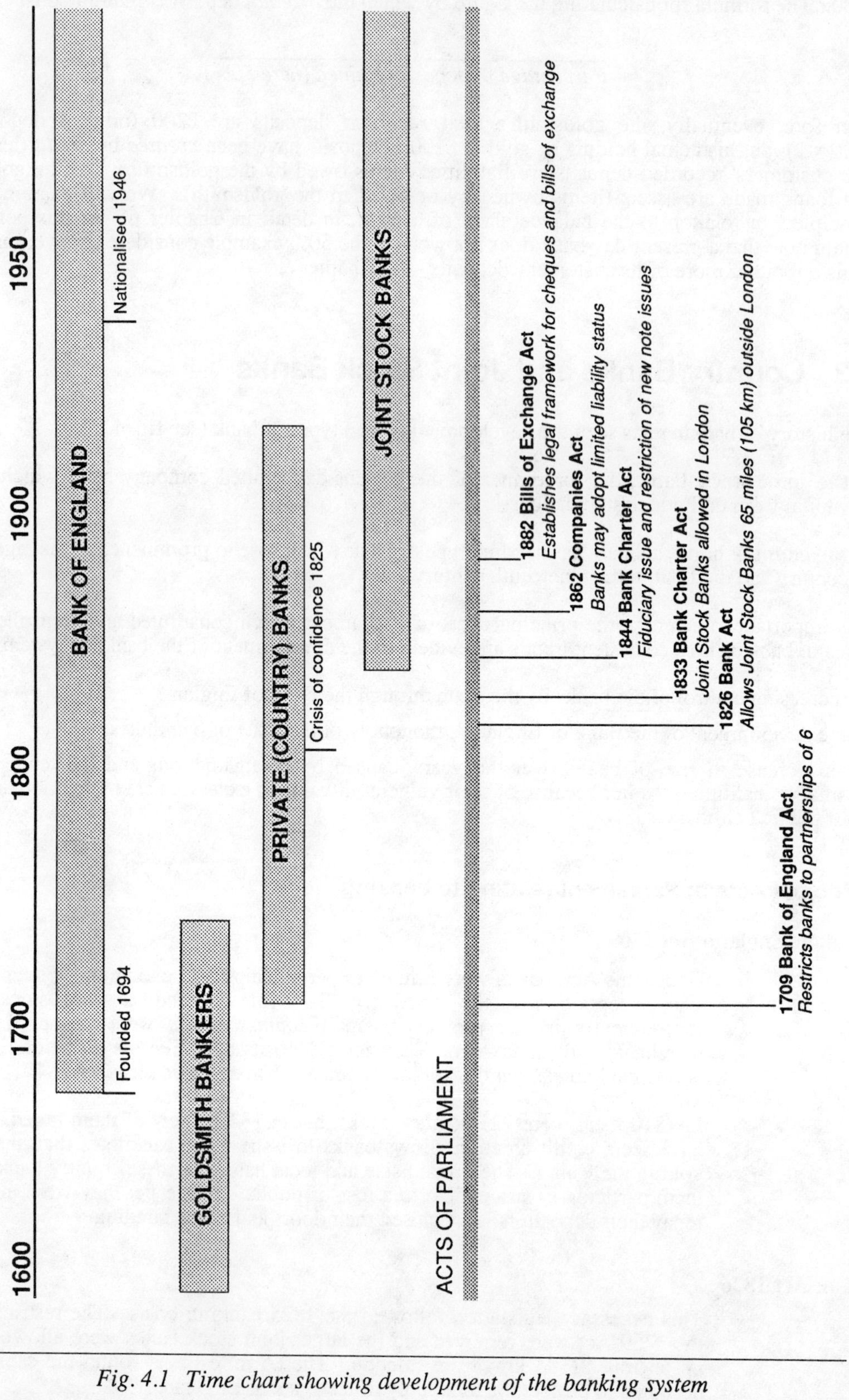

Fig. 4.1   Time chart showing development of the banking system

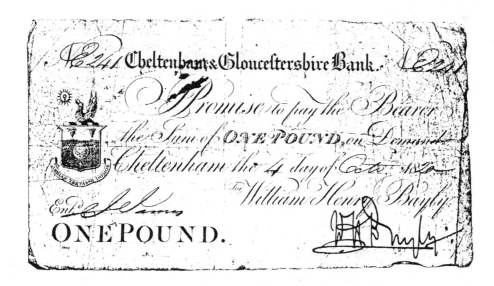

Fig. 4.2   Country banknotes

Bank Charter Act 1833

Joint stock banks were allowed to set up within the 65 mile (105 km) limit (i.e. in London), but they could not issue notes.

Bank Charter Act 1844

The Bank of England's power was strengthened in two ways:

• *bank note issue restriction*
If any of the 104 joint stock banks and 273 partnership banks merged they could no longer issue banknotes.

• *fiduciary issue*
£14m of banknotes were issued by the Bank of England, backed not by gold and silver, but by Government debt (i.e. the backing is the knowledge that the Government will repay its debt: fiduciary = trusting).   Today, all Bank of England banknotes are fiduciary.

Companies Act 1862

Prior to this Act, if a joint stock bank or partnership bank failed, the individuals who had contributed capital were *personally* liable to repay the depositors. The Companies Act 1862 ruled that individual stockholders could be protected and have *limited liability* (i.e. they were only liable for a limited amount) by forming a limited company. Many banks converted to limited companies, a factor which encouraged individuals to invest in them and which enabled them to grow in size.

4.4 Twentieth Century Amalgamations: Retail Banks

Reasons for amalgamation
At the beginning of the twentieth century the present day banking system was clearly emerging with 77 joint stock banks (nearly 4,000 branches) and only 19 private banks in existence in 1900. Further amalgamations took place as banks realised that larger banks meant

• a wider geographical coverage (many smaller banks were regional banks)
• a better competitive position
• savings in administrative costs
• the ability to offer a wider range of services

Present-day retail banks
In 1968 the last of the major amalgamations took place and produced most of the familiar 'High Street' bank names. National Provincial Bank and Westminster Bank, for example, merged to become National Westminster Bank. Interestingly, the proposal to merge Barclays and Lloyds was rejected by the Government's Monopolies Commission on the grounds that it would have produced unfair competition.

The main banks that emerged were:

• Barclays Bank
• Lloyds Bank
• Midland Bank
• National Westminster Bank (also incorporating Coutts Bank)
• Williams & Glyn's Bank (later merged with The Royal Bank of Scotland, and losing its name in the process)
• other names familiar in the regional High Streets are Yorkshire Bank and the Scottish and Northern Irish banks.

These banks are generally known as *retail banks* or *High Street banks* because they offer banking services to the general public in the same way that a High Street 'retailer' offers its goods.

You will notice that certain retail bank names are missing from the list set out above: TSB Bank, Co-op Bank, Girobank. These institutions have had a different history: they are not a result of joint stock bank amalgamations. Their development as retail banks is summarised in the next section.

4.5   The Development of TSB Bank, Co-op Bank and Girobank

TSB Bank
The Trustee Savings Bank (now known as TSB Bank), which was floated as a public limited company in 1986, owes its origins to thrifty Scots communities which, in the early nineteenth century, saved money under the supervision of local worthies or 'trustees' for investment in interest bearing accounts at other banks. In 1817, the Savings Bank Act provided a Government fund where the trustees' money could safely be invested. There then followed a period of development of small regional Trustee Savings Banks, which eventually merged into regional TSBs.

The TSB has developed into its present form in the latter part of the twentieth century:

1965	current accounts introduced
1975	TSB joins the clearing system
1977	personal loans and overdrafts introduced
1985	Government supervision ends
1986	TSB plc is floated on the Stock Exchange

Co-operative Bank
The Co-operative Bank is wholly owned by the Co-operative movement which runs the well-known Co-op stores. It was founded in the nineteenth century to provide banking services for the many co-operative societies which flourished at the time. The Co-operative Bank has a small number of High Street bank branches, but operates mainly from in-store 'Handybanks'. It provides a full range of banking services, and was the first bank to offer free banking to cheque account customers.

Girobank
Girobank was founded by the Government in 1968 as the National Giro. It formed a part of the Post Office whose counters it used as bank branches. Its aims were

- to provide a convenient money transmission service
- to attract members of lower income groups who, at that time (1968), did not often hold High Street bank accounts

In 1989 it was sold by the Post Office to the Alliance and Leicester Building Society.

Girobank has always been seen as a hybrid form of bank and sometimes regarded by the other retail banks as an outside competitor. It is dealt with in more detail in Chapter 15.3.

4.6   Specialised Banking Institutions

Anyone working outside central London will think of 'banks' as retail banks. If, however, you work in the City of London, you will see a bewildering variety of financial institutions, many of them foreign, which are either banks or owned by banks.

These include:

- merchant banks
- investment banks
- foreign banks
- consortium banks
- discount houses

Merchant banks

As we saw earlier in the chapter the first bankers were goldsmiths and merchants who engaged in banking as an extension of their trading activities. Merchant banks in the eighteenth and nineteenth centuries developed the following services:

- lending money for foreign trade

- foreign currency exchange

- guaranteeing payment to traders by 'accepting' bills of exchange - see Chapter 2.3; (accepting a bill of exchange meant a well-known and respected merchant bank signing its name on the bill so that it would be recognised in worldwide trading circles as a sure payment).

In the twentieth century, merchant banks have extended their activities to providing advice and finance to limited companies:

- raising company capital by the issue of stocks and shares (as issuing houses) for existing companies or privatisations (e.g. the Abbey National flotation)

- accepting bills of exchange

- direct lending in sterling and foreign currencies

- managing investments (portfolio management)

- giving general advice on company financial management

- dealing in securities (stocks and shares, and bonds)

- dealing in foreign currencies, and commodities (precious metals)

Merchant banking has always been thought of as a prestigious occupation, and a few of the old family firms, such as Hambros Bank, survive. Retail banks have recently invested in merchant banks as profitable and useful additions to their company (corporate) banking operations. For example, Midland Bank took over Samuel Montagu & Co. (now Midland Montagu) and TSB bought Hill Samuel & Co.

Investment Banks, the Stock Exchange and 'Big Bang'

In October 1986, the Stock Exchange (the London market where stocks and shares are traded) relaxed its rules in what was known as the 'Big Bang'. One of the results of this financial detonation was that UK and foreign banks could buy small independent UK firms which between them

- gave investment advice to the public
- bought and sold stocks and shares on the public's behalf
- held stocks and shares and quoted a price for them according to market supply and demand

As a result, trading in stocks and shares has now moved away from the Stock Exchange floor and takes place over the telephone between organisations such as Barclays de Zoete Wedd (BZW) which was formed by Barclays Bank buying the independent firms of De Zoete & Bevan, and Wedd Durlacher Mordaunt & Co., and merging them with Barclays Merchant Bank.

Investment banks or 'broker/dealers', such as BZW, carry out two specific functions:

- *market maker* - holding stocks and shares, and quoting a price
- *agency broker* - taking buying and selling instructions from the public, and giving specific investment advice

Clearly, these two functions need to be kept separate, otherwise the BZW givers of investment advice, for example, might be accused of being influenced by the BZW holders of stock, perhaps to dispose of less desirable shares! This separation is achieved by what is known as a 'Chinese Wall'; this is not a physical wall, but a wall of silence.

There are over 100 investment banks in the City of London, many of them foreign. Notable names include Nomura of Japan and Merrill Lynch of the USA. Their operations are overseen by what has become the International Stock Exchange, which regulates the way in which investment banks buy and sell both UK and foreign stocks, shares and bonds.

Foreign banks

As a major international financial centre, London has acted as a magnet to some 450 foreign banks which have set up representative offices, branches, or subsidiary companies in the capital. American, Japanese and European banks are particularly well represented. Their business in the UK consists mainly of

- foreign currency dealing
- international financing deals to foreign companies and governments
- selling banking services to UK customers, e.g. mortgages to personal customers, financing to business customers

Although the presence of foreign banks is most evident in the City of London, they can also be seen in the provincial High Street. Citibank of the USA has established Citibank Savings which has branches in many parts of the UK selling personal banking services.

The term 'overseas bank' is sometimes seen; it is used in two contexts:

- as a term used by the Bank of England to classify foreign banks (as described above)
- more traditionally as a British bank with branches established abroad

Consortium banks

A consortium bank is a bank which

- is owned by other banks
- is not controlled by any single bank (i.e. no bank has more than a 50% shareholding)
- has at least one overseas bank as shareholder

Consortium banks, like foreign banks, have been established to develop international financing deals to governments and companies worldwide. Scandinavian Bank Group plc, for example, established in London, has the following shareholders:

Bergen Bank, Norway	20%
Union Bank of Finland	20%
Skandinaviska Enskilda Banken, Sweden	14%
Privatbanken, Denmark	8%
Landsbanki Islands, Iceland	3%
General Public (it is listed on the Stock Exchange)	35%

Scandinavian Bank was established in London because the UK has fewer restrictions than the parent countries, and London is a major financing centre.

Discount houses

The eight discount houses of London are very specialised institutions and are unique to the UK. Together they form what is known as the *Discount Market*. They take deposits from the UK banks and invest them in short-term paper securities. This market and the other London *Money Markets* are dealt with in full in Section 4.9. Discount houses are important because some of their funds are on-lent short-term to the Bank of England; they then form an indispensable link between the UK banks and the Bank of England. Well-known names among the discount houses are The Union Discount Co. Ltd., Cater Allen Ltd., Gerrard & National Ltd., and King & Shaxson Ltd.

4.7   Financial Intermediaries

So far in this chapter we have described the development of the banking sector, but anyone who walks down a typical High Street, or opens the post in the morning, will realise that it is not just the banks that offer banking services. You can obtain a personal loan from a building society, a shop or the AA; you can invest your money with building societies, insurance companies and retail stores (Marks and Spencer). The 'financial supermarket' is not just a glib term coined by advertisers; it is a reality. We will examine the competition the banks face in terms of products in Chapter 15; in this chapter we will classify the competing institutions as types of *financial intermediary*.

A financial intermediary is a body which channels funds from those who have a surplus to those who need to borrow.

If you consider the operations of *financial* institutions, one of their most important functions is to accept money from the public and to on-lend it. They are *intermediaries* between those who have money they wish to deposit and those who do not and want to borrow.

Financial intermediation, as this process is known, has substantial advantages over lending to, or borrowing from, a friend:

- *risk*   your deposit is generally safe
- *amount*   a financial intermediary can combine a large number of small deposits to provide a large loan; this is known as 'aggregation'
- *period*   a financial intermediary can transform a series of short-term deposits (e.g. bank accounts) to provide a long-term loan (e.g. a mortgage); this is known as 'maturity transformation'
- *availability* you can deposit when you want, and borrow (if you are creditworthy!) when you want

4.8   Bank and Non-Bank Financial Intermediaries

As we noted in the previous section, banks are clearly not the only financial intermediaries; there is a distinction to be drawn between bank and non-bank financial intermediation.

Bank Financial Intermediaries (BFIs)

The bank financial intermediaries (BFIs) are characterised by the money transmission services which they offer. They include

- the retail banks - including TSB Bank and Co-op Bank
- Girobank

Non-Bank Financial Intermediaries (NBFIs)

Non-bank financial intermediaries (NBFIs) are savings institutions and other financial bodies which accept funds and provide financial benefits over a long term for individuals. Many NBFIs will be dealt with in Chapter 15, as they are competitors to the banks in the savings and financial securities fields. The chart below shows how they provide financial intermediation. If you are unfamiliar with the institutions or terminology, refer to Chapter 15.

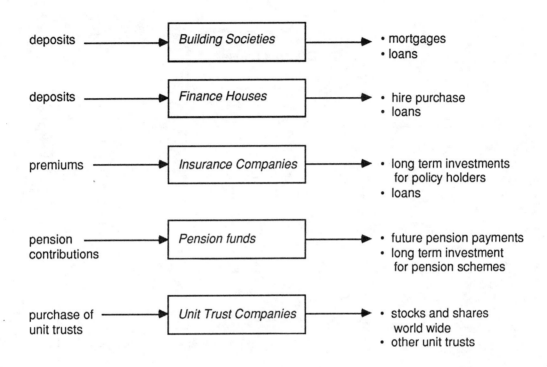

4.9 Other Financial Markets

There is clearly a wide range and a large number of bank and non-bank financial intermediaries in London. In order that they can function efficiently they need to

- borrow for short-term requirements
- lend short-term surpluses
- buy and sell foreign currencies
- 'hedge' - i.e. avoid fluctuations - in future interest rates and exchange rates

In order to meet these needs a number of markets, loosely described as 'money markets', have developed. These are illustrated in fig. 4.3 on the next page.

Parallel Money Markets

These markets involve deposits and loans of large amounts:

- on an unsecured basis - the name of the borrower (e.g. Lloyds Bank) being sufficient 'security'

- on a short-term basis - from overnight to periods of months

- between banks, building societies, insurance companies, industrial companies all dealing by telephone, often through brokers

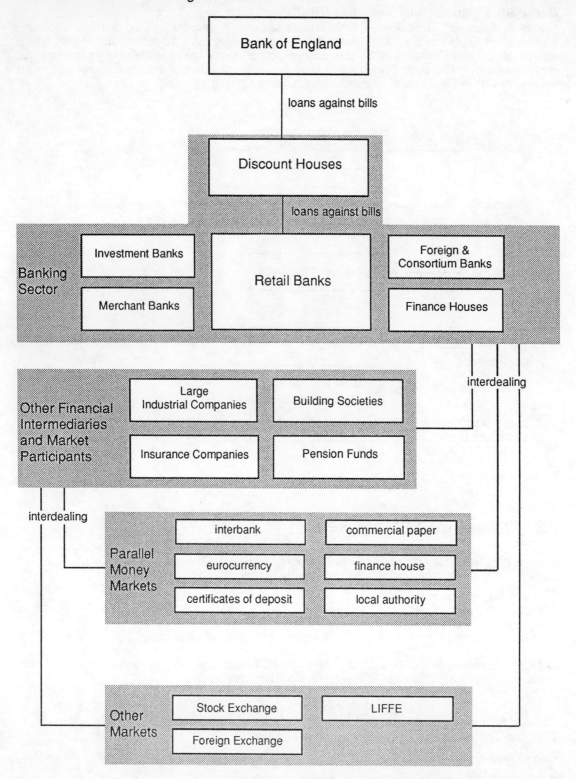

Fig. 4.3   Summary chart of financial institutions and markets

interbank market

> deposits and loans of large sterling amounts made between the institutions mentioned above, e.g. Lloyds Bank lending the Nationwide Anglia Building Society £5m overnight.

eurocurrency market

> deposits and loans of foreign currencies traded outside their country of origin (not just European currencies), e.g. US$2m lent by Midland Bank to British Petroleum in London for three months.

local authority market

> large deposits raised by local authorites to fund their expenditure, e.g. £2m lent by Barclays Bank to Hereford and Worcester County Council for seven days.

finance house market

> finance houses borrowing to finance hire purchase deals, e.g. National Westminster lending £5m to UDT (owned by TSB) for one month.

inter-company market

> large companies dealing between themselves, e.g. ICI lending British Gas £1m for one month (note: no banks are involved - hence it is not illustrated in fig. 4.3).

commercial paper market

> short-term certificates issued by companies and bought by investors (note: no banks are directly involved, except as brokers, bringing buyers and sellers together).

certificates of deposit market

> certificates issued by banks and building societies for fixed amount, fixed interest, fixed period deposits, bought as investments.

The London discount market

This market involves:

- the London discount houses
- raising funds from the UK banks against security
- investing the funds in a variety of investments

The investments include:

treasury bills

> 91 day fixed-interest certificates issued by the Bank of England and 'sold' at a discount.

commercial bills

> discounting of bills of exchange which have been accepted by banks (bank bills), or reputable companies (trade bills). Discounting means buying a bill of exchange at less than face value, holding it and receiving the face value on the due date from the accepting bank or company.

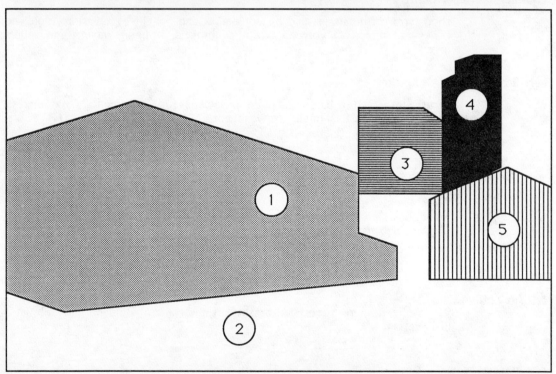

Fig. 4.4   View of part of the City of London, showing [1] the Bank of England, [2] Threadneedle Street (which gives the reference to the Bank of England as being 'The Old Lady of Threadneedle Street', [3] the Stock Exchange building, [4] National Westminster tower, [5] Royal Exchange (home of LIFFE)

Foreign Exchange market

Financial institutions buy and sell foreign currency:

* to enable customers to pay for imported goods

* to make a profit on the 'buy low, sell high' principle. The market is operated by dealers over the telephone in financial centres world wide. London is a favoured location because if operates at the same time as Tokyo (in the morning) and New York (in the afternoon).

London International Financial Futures Exchange (LIFFE)

LIFFE opened in 1982 to provide investors and borrowers with a 'hedge' (protection) against fluctuations in interest rates and exchange rates. Buyers and sellers can:

* trade interest-bearing investments in the future at a predetermined interest rate

* buy and sell foreign currencies at a predetermined exchange rate

A common LIFFE futures contract is the option to borrow or invest 3 month interbank deposits at a fixed interest rate. This helps financial institutions to 'hedge' against the possibility of interest rates fluctuating.

Fig. 4.4 shows some of the more important financial institutions in the City of London.

4.10 Revision Points

❑ Banking originated in the UK with:

* thirteenth century moneylenders
* seventeenth century goldsmiths (note issue)
* eighteenth century country banks (partnership banks)
* nineteenth century joint stock banks (forerunners of modern banks)

❑ The Bank of England was founded in 1694. Subsequent Acts of Parliament were:

* 1709 Bank of England Act - other banks limited to 6 partners
* 1826 Bank Act - joint stock banks allowed 65 miles (105 km) outside London
* 1833 Bank Charter Act - joint stock banks allowed in London (but not allowed note issue)
* 1844 Bank Charter Act - new note monopoly of Bank of England and £14m fiduciary issue
* 1862 Companies Act - banks may become limited liability companies

❑ Retail banks amalgamate in the twentieth century to form the 'big four'. Other retail banks have different origins:

* TSB - savings banks origin
* Co-op - owned by Co-operative movement
* Girobank - founded by Government, now owned by Alliance and Leicester Building Society

❑ Merchant Banks offer specialised services to companies:

* raising capital
* accepting bills of exchange
* lending
* investment management and dealing
* company financial management
* dealing in currencies and commodities

❑   Big Bang in 1986 allowed UK and foreign banks to buy firms dealing in stocks and shares.

❑   Investment Banks are:

- market makers - they hold stocks and shares for sale
- agency brokers - they buy and sell stocks and shares for the public and give investment advice.

'Chinese walls' divide these two functions.

❑   Other banking institutions include:

- foreign banks (450 in London)
- consortium banks (owned by other banks including a foreign bank)
- discount houses (8) which act as intermediaries between the banks and the Bank of England

❑   A financial intermediary channels funds from those who have a surplus to those who need to borrow. They are divided into:

- Bank Financial Intermediaries (BFIs) - i.e. retail banks
- Non-Bank Financial Intermediaries (NBFIs) - building societies, finance houses, insurance companies, pension funds, unit trust companies

❑   The parallel money markets (large deposits and loans between financial institutions) include:

- interbank market
- eurocurrency market
- local authority market
- finance house market
- inter-company market
- commercial paper market
- certificates of deposit market

❑   The London discount market involves the discount houses:

- raising funds from the banks
- investing in the parallel money markets
- investing in Treasury Bills and Commercial Bills

❑   Other markets include:

- Foreign Exchange market
- London International Financial Futures Exchange (LIFFE), which enables 'hedging' against fluctuations in exchange rates and interest rates

4.11 Know your *Development of the UK Banking System*

Multiple-choice Questions

Choose the *one* answer you think is correct.

1. The present day retail banks developed directly from

   A country banks
   B merchant banks
   C joint stock banks
   D goldsmith banks

2. Investment banks are

   A owned by the Stock Exchange
   B part of National Savings
   C foreign banks' UK representative offices
   D market makers in stocks and shares

3. Which one of the following is not a bank financial intermediary?

   A National Westminster Bank
   B National Savings Bank
   C Girobank
   D TSB Bank

4. The London discount market

   A enables banks to borrow money very cheaply
   B is a group of retail companies involved in financial services
   C invests in treasury bills and commercial bills
   D issues certificates of deposit to investors

5. LIFFE stands for

   A London International Financial Futures Exchange
   B London Interbank Facility for Foreign Exchange
   C London International Fraud and Forgery Evaluator
   D London Interbank Financial Futures Exchange

Short Answer Questions

6. How were banks restricted by the Bank of England Act 1709?

7. Name *two* measures introduced by the Bank Charter Act 1844.

8. Who owns Girobank?

9. Give *two* activities carried out by merchant banks.

10. What was 'Big Bang'?

11. What is a 'Chinese Wall'?

12.   What are the *three* requirements of a consortium bank?

13.   What is the main source and use of funds of a discount house?

14.   What is a financial intermediary? What are the two types?

15.   State *two* advantages of financial intermediation.

16.   Name two parallel money markets.

17.   Name *three* types of institution which trade on the interbank market.

18.   What is a certificate of deposit?

19.   Define 'eurocurrency'.

20.   Give examples of two contracts traded on LIFFE.

4.12 Essay Questions *Development of the UK Banking System*

1.   The activities of the banking sector impinge on all our lives. Briefly outline these activities and show how they affect us.

[question 22, Spring 1987]

2.   (a) Outline the historical development of the high street banks.

[12 marks]

  (b) Briefly state their main *functions* today.

[8 marks]
[question 3, Spring 1989]

3.   Many banks are *specialised* institutions. Describe the main functions of:
  (a) merchant banks   *[5 marks]*
  (b) investment banks   *[5 marks]*
  (c) foreign banks   *[5 marks]*
  (d) consortium banks   *[5 marks]*

4.   (a) Define *financial intermediary*.

[5 marks]

  (b) Give *two* examples each of BFIs and NBFIs and explain how the process of financial intermediation in each case is of benefit to both parties involved.

[15 marks]

5.   What are the principal London money markets? Give in your explanation the types of the institution that trade in the markets, and the types of investment involved.

Chapter Five
Banks and the Bank of England

In the last chapter banks were defined as *financial intermediaries* which transform customer deposits into loans. In this chapter we will take a closer look at a bank's source of funds and its use of those funds by examining a bank's *balance sheet*. A number of important points arise from this:

- banks lend out the majority of their deposits
- banks also invest their funds in a variety of different money markets
- they need to maintain these investments to provide *liquidity* (the ability to realise the money if depositors call in their deposits)
- banks lose out because quickly realisable investments are not as profitable (they earn less interest for the bank than loans)

We will then examine the role of the Bank of England which, as supervisor and regulator of the banking system, monitors the balance sheets and lending policies of banks, as well as carrying out the other functions of a central bank.

5.1   A Bank's Balance Sheet

A balance sheet is a financial statement of a business, showing the sources of funds and the way in which these funds are used at a particular moment in time. A balance sheet may be seen as an equation which always balances.

The two sides of this equation are:

- **sources**   *liabilities* (items owed by the business to others) plus *capital* (money introduced by the owners/shareholders)

- **uses**   *assets* (items owed to the business, and items owned by the business)

The equation appears as follows:

sources of funds liabilities + capital	**=**	**uses of funds** assets

If we relate this equation to a bank's balance sheet, the result is as follows:

sources of funds • customer deposits (liabilities) • capital (shareholders' investment)	**=**	**uses of funds (assets)** • investments made by bank • loans to customers • premises

In fig. 5.1 is set out the balance sheet of National Westminster Bank PLC (NatWest) as at 31 December 1988. This document is taken from NatWest's Annual Report and Accounts sent to shareholders. You may have seen your bank's Annual Report and Accounts being sent to influential customers. If you are able to beg or borrow a copy, you will find it useful for your studies, not only for the balance sheet, but also for the overall picture it gives of your bank's operations and marketing strategy.

Fig. 5.2 sets out pie charts showing the proportional make-up of both sides of the NatWest balance sheet equation. You may be surprised at the large proportion of deposits in the liabilities chart, and loans in the assets chart.

Before analysing these figures further, it is important to examine in more detail the items in the NatWest balance sheet.

5.2   Uses of Funds: Assets Employed

The NatWest balance sheet set out in fig. 5.1 presents the assets in the top half and the liabilities and capital ('financed by' section) in the bottom half. You will see that both halves of this vertical format are totalled: they balance. In a middle column there are references to detailed notes which appear elsewhere in the Annual Report and Accounts but are not reproduced here.

We have mentioned that liquidity of assets is important to banks (they want to be able to repay depositors). In order to reflect this importance, the assets are listed starting with the most liquid.

Highly liquid assets
NatWest's highly liquid assets include:

* coin and bank notes held in NatWest tills
* accounts held with the Bank of England and State banks abroad for settling clearing differences with other banks
* items in course of collection, i.e. cheques from other banks paid into NatWest and not yet cleared

These assets pay little or no interest; they are necessary but unprofitable.

Liquid assets: money market and Stock Exchange investments
NatWest, in common with other banks, invests in a wide range of safe, largely short-term, money market and Stock Exchange investments which, if there were a run on the bank, could readily be realised for cash. These appear in the balance sheet as follows:

money at call and short notice   this is principally money deposited with the
* London interbank market
* discount houses

♻ National Westminster Bank PLC

BALANCE SHEET OF
NATIONAL WESTMINSTER BANK PLC
AT 31 DECEMBER 1988

———◆———

	Notes	1988 £m	1987 £m
Assets employed			
Coin, bank notes and balances with the Bank of England and with State banks abroad		782	686
Items in course of collection on other banks		671	1,373
Money at call and short notice		2,763	3,049
Bills discounted		1,393	1,687
Dealing assets	10	46	68
Certificates of deposit		592	502
Investments	11	334	855
Advances and other accounts	12	33,194	27,561
Amounts due from subsidiary companies		10,645	10,003
Investments in associated companies and trade investments	14	155	122
Investments in subsidiary companies	15	2,205	1,565
Premises and equipment	16	2,184	1,501
		54,964	48,972
Financed by			
Ordinary shareholders' funds:			
Ordinary share capital	17	778	754
Reserves	18	3,664	2,699
		4,442	3,453
Preference share capital	17	14	14
Undated loan capital	19	1,302	1,068
Dated loan capital	20	1,581	775
Deferred taxation	21	8	28
Amounts due to subsidiary companies	22	1,624	1,702
Current, deposit and other accounts	23	45,293	41,378
Other liabilities	24	700	554
		54,964	48,972

Authorised by the Board to be signed at its meeting held on 21 February 1989

Boardman Chairman

T P Frost Group Chief Executive

J A Burns Group Chief Financial Officer

———◆———

Fig. 5.1   Balance sheet of National Westminster Bank PLC

National Westminster Bank PLC Assets Employed (Use of Funds)

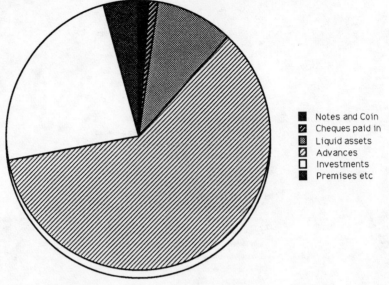

Notes and Coin
Cheques paid in
Liquid assets
Advances
Investments
Premises etc

National Westminster Bank PLC Sources of Funds

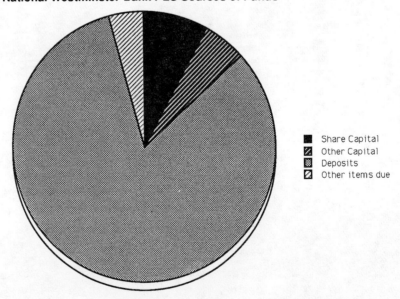

Share Capital
Other Capital
Deposits
Other items due

Fig. 5.2   Charts showing the make-up of NatWest's Balance Sheet at 31 December 1988

bills discounted	these are bills discounted and held by the bank until the due date when the bank will be paid
dealing assets	these are stock exchange investments held as part of NatWest's stock and share dealing services
certificates of deposit	certificates issued by *other* financial institutions for deposits made and invested in by NatWest
investments	safe stock and share investments held by NatWest

The assets listed so far are liquid and could be realised if the need arose. The remaining assets listed below are less liquid - 'illiquid' - but are more profitable for the bank.

Advances and other accounts

This is by far the largest figure among the assets on the balance sheet. 'Advances' means lending to NatWest customers. If you examine the interest rates at which banks lend to customers, you will appreciate the profitability of this asset.

Subsidiary and associated companies

Most of the remaining asset figures relate to financial companies in which NatWest has an ownership stake and which provide a source of profit. Among these are Access, BACS, Lombard North Central and NatWest Investment Bank.

Premises and equipment

NatWest's offices and computer equipment are valuable, but the least liquid assets on the balance sheet. They are, therefore, listed as the last of the assets.

Liquidity versus profitability

Now that you have seen the full range of a bank's assets you will realise that *liquidity* of assets (i.e. holding notes and coin and short-term investments) is less *profitable* than lending money when the return can be 20%. Banks, however, must maintain liquidity (the Bank of England demands it) to be able to repay depositors. Liquidity and profitability are therefore both important but conflicting objectives of any bank. It is the successful bank that achieves maximum profit and still retains an acceptable proportion of liquid assets.

5.3   Sources of Funds: Liabilities and Capital

The 'financed by' half of the balance sheet, which is set out in vertical columns underneath the 'assets employed' section, may be subdivided as follows:

ordinary shareholders' funds *(capital)*	'ordinary share capital' is money invested by shareholders in the bank, and 'reserves' represents money, including profits earned, belonging to them.
other capital *(capital)*	preference and loan capital is money invested in the bank by investors other than ordinary shareholders; it is money that is not likely to be withdrawn quickly (unlike deposits).

current, deposit and other accounts *(liabilities)*

sterling and foreign currency accounts including current (sight) accounts and deposit (time) accounts.

other liabilities

these include items owed to subsidiary companies, tax payable, and dividends due to shareholders.

5.4   The Bank of England and Bank Balance Sheets

The Bank of England was nationalised in 1946 by the Bank of England Act, and became a government-controlled central bank. One of its most important functions is the supervision of the banking system; this supervision involves the monitoring and control of individual banks' balance sheets.

Supervision by the Bank of England achieves two objectives:

*   **regulation of banks -** making sure that institutions which set up as banks in the UK are properly managed, have sufficient liquidity and sufficient capital

*   **regulation of bank lending -** as is evident from the credit creation principle (see pages 32-33) an increase in bank lending leads to an increase in the amount of money in the economy (an increase in bank deposits) and a subsequent increase in inflation; control of bank lending therefore helps to control inflation.

We will now deal with both of these objectives in detail.

Regulation of banks by the Bank of England
The Bank of England has had supervisory powers granted by two Acts of Parliament:

*   Banking Act 1979
*   Banking Act 1987 (which superseded the 1979 Act)

Banking Act 1979
*   required licensing of all banking institutions

*   established a Deposit Protection Fund, contributed by the other banks which, in the event of a bank failing, would repay depositors to the extent of 75% of their deposits, up to a maximum of £10,000 (i.e. a maximum payment of £7,500)

Banking Act 1987
*   requires all banking institutions (which must have minimum assets of £1m) to be licensed by the Bank of England

*   allows institutions to use the title 'bank' only when their capital exceeds £5m

*   requires banks to seek approval from the Bank of England if they are considering granting loans greater than 25% of their capital

*   requires banks to notify the Bank of England if they have granted loans of more than 10% of their capital

*   gives a right of veto to the Bank of England of proposed takeovers of UK banks, including foreign takeovers

*   requires banks' auditors (accountants who prepare their balance sheets) to disclose information to the Bank of England

*   increased the Deposit Protection Fund to 75% of deposits of up to £20,000 (i.e. a maximum payment of £15,000)

These measures therefore exercise control over bank balance sheets, determining minimum capital, monitoring large loans, and ensuring that the auditors advise the Bank of England of any irregularities at an early stage.

Regulation of bank lending by the Bank of England

The Bank of England, as noted above, needs to control the amount of bank lending in order to restrict the growth of inflation as part of the Government's *monetary policy*. As we have seen earlier, by the *credit creation principle,* the more a bank lends, the more that money is redeposited in the banking system, creating more bank deposits which in turn increase inflation. The Government's monetary policy is aimed at controlling the amount of money in the economy, and hence the rate of inflation (more money means less purchasing power and high prices).

The Bank of England can control bank lending in a number of ways:

* **interest rate policy**
  Economic theory states that if interest rates rise, people borrow less (and banks lend less). The Bank of England reserves the right to set a Minimum Lending Rate for banks. This, however, is rarely done; interest rates are normally indicated by the Bank of England on a more informal basis to the London money markets.

* **qualitative directives**
  The Bank of England reserves the right to restrict the type of lending banks can engage in; this is rarely resorted to.

* **liquidity requirements: cash ratio deposits and special deposits**
  The Bank of England restricts the banks' ability to lend by requiring them to keep a certain proportion of assets in liquid form, e.g. they have to keep 0.45% of their customers' deposits as *cash ratio deposits* in non-interest-bearing accounts at the Bank of England. They may also be required to make *special deposits,* which are interest-bearing accounts at the Bank of England.

* **open market operations (OMO)**
  OMO involves the Bank of England selling securities, such as Treasury Bills, in order to 'mop up' surplus money in the system and prevent banks from on-lending those funds.

The Bank of England also has other functions as a central bank; these are discussed below.

5.5 Functions of the Bank of England

Note Issue

The Bank of England is sole issuer of banknotes in England. The backing is entirely 'fiduciary', i.e. backed by government debt, not by gold or silver. Coins are issued by the Treasury at the Royal Mint, and not by the Bank of England.

Government's Bank

The Bank of England maintains accounts for government departments and also manages the National Debt, issuing *short-term* Treasury Bills to the discount houses and *long-term* Government Stock to the public through GEMMS (see next page).

Supervisor of GEMMS

Government stock is issued by authorised Gilt-Edged Market Makers (GEMMS) which, since 'Big Bang' in 1986, have been supervised by the Bank of England. Most GEMMS are Investment Banks (e.g. Barclays de Zoete Wedd).

Bankers' Bank

The Bank of England maintains accounts for the UK banks and discount houses. Banks need these accounts to settle their clearings and also to deposit cash ratio deposits and special deposits.

Lender of Last Resort

If there is a shortgage of money in the money markets the discount houses can borrow from the Bank of England to fund their investments rather than from the retail banks. Last resort lending is *not* money available for banks in difficulty.

Exchange Equalisation Account

The Bank of England maintains the UK gold and currency reserves which it uses to regulate the level of the pound sterling in the foreign exchange markets. If the pound is falling, it will buy pounds with the currencies that it holds, and if the pound is rising it will buy foreign currencies with sterling.

Banker to Foreign Banks

The Bank of England maintains accounts for foreign central banks and also for international financial institutions such as the World Bank and the IMF (International Monetary Fund).

Supervisor of Banking System

The Bank of England regulates the banks through the Banking Act 1987 (see Section 5.4).

Monetary Policy

The Bank of England, in consultation with the Treasury, helps regulate the economy through its control of bank lending (see Section 5.4).

5.6   Revision Points

❑   A bank balance sheet is made up of:

- liabilities (mainly customer deposits) and capital (shareholders' investments)
- assets (mainly lending to customers) and investments

These two elements balance (are numerically equal):

- liabilities and capital *equals* sources of funds
- assets *equals* use of funds

❑   Assets include:

- liquid assets - notes and coin, cheques paid in and not cleared, accounts with central banks, short-term easily realisable investments.
- loans (advances)
- investment in subsidiary and associated companies
- premises and equipment

❑   Assets are listed in order of liquidity (realisability). Banks are faced with the problem of achieving:

- maximum return on assets
- sufficient liquidity to repay depositors if necessary

This is known as *liquidity versus profitability*.

❑   Liabilities and capital comprise:

- customer deposits (the largest liability in money terms)
- shareholders' funds and other investments in the bank (capital)

❑   The Bank of England regulates banks by means of the Banking Act 1987:

- all banks must be licensed (minimum assets of £1m)
- all institutions wishing to be called 'banks' need a minimum capital of £5m
- the Bank of England supervises large lending (prior permission if loan is more than 25% of capital, notification if 10% to 25%)
- the Bank of England has a right of veto over proposed takeover of the banks
- liaison between the Bank of England and banks' auditors
- Deposit Protection Fund will refund 75% of deposits up to £20,000 (maximum payout £15,000)

❑   The Bank of England regulates bank lending as part of the Government's monetary policy by:

- interest rate policy
- qualitative directives
- liquidity requirements
- open market operations

❑   The functions of the Bank of England include:

- note issue
- banker to Government
- supervisor of GEMMS
- banker to banks (UK and foreign)
- lender of last resort (via discount houses)
- exchange equalisation (gold and currency reserves)
- supervisor of banking system
- instrument of monetary policy

5.7 Know your *Banks and the Bank of England*

Multiple-choice Questions

Choose the *one* answer you think is correct.

1. Which of the following is a liability in a bank's balance sheet?

    A Treasury bills
    B Advances to customers
    C Current and deposit accounts
    D Investments

2. Which of the following is an asset in a bank's balance sheet?

    A Customer accounts
    B Advances to customers
    C Loan capital
    D Money due to subsidiary companies

3. Which of the following is NOT a function of the Bank of England?

    A Lender of last resort
    B Banker's bank
    C Manager of gold and foreign currency reserves
    D Supervisor of company stocks and shares

4. The Bank of England is lender of last resort to

    A merchant banks
    B discount houses
    C commercial banks
    D National Savings Bank

5. The Bank of England carries out the function of

    A raising money for large companies through the Stock Exchange
    B giving sound financial advice on running large companies
    C supervising other banks under the Banking Act
    D attracting large deposits for the Government by paying a competitive base rate

Short Answer Questions

6. Give *two* of the liabilities on a retail bank's balance sheet.

7. List *two* assets in a retail bank's balance sheet.

8. Define *liquid assets* with reference to a bank's balance sheet.

9. Why is liquidity contrary to profitability?

10. List *four* measures of the Banking Act 1987.

11. Give *two* methods by which the Bank of England carries out the Government's monetary policy.

12.   What is the role of the Bank of England as *lender of last resort*?

13.   List *four* types of institution for which the Bank of England maintains accounts.

14.   What is the Bank of England's role in relation to GEMMS?

15.   What is the purpose of the Exchange Equalisation Account?

5.8   Essay Questions *Banks and the Bank of England*

1.   Banks deal with all sectors of UK activity - Government, Business and Personal. Explain how the financial system 'deals' with these sectors and illustrate your answer by reference to UK banking organisations.

[question 3, Autumn 1987]

2.   (a) What are the functions of the Bank of England?

[10 marks]

(b) Describe the role of *two* of the following financial organisations - retail banks; merchant banks; discount houses; Girobank.

[10 marks]
[question 3, Autumn 1988]

3.   (a) Many things act as money in our modern economy. How would you define money and briefly describe its main functions?

[9 marks]

(b) One of the functions of the Bank of England is to act as the note issuing authority for England and Wales. Explain briefly how it carries out this and its other functions.

[11 marks]
[question 2, Spring 1988]

Note: this question shows how the examination can 'mix' subjects together - here the theory of money and the function of the Bank of England.

4.   (a) Explain the main assets and liabilities on a retail bank's balance sheet.

[12 marks]

(b) State what liquidity is, and why it is important.

[6 marks]

(c) State how liquidity affects profitability.

[2 marks]

5.   State the main provisions of the 1987 Banking Act and explain why they are important for the banking system as a whole.

Chapter Six
Bank and Customer

In previous chapters we have examined the development of banks and their interaction with other financial institutions. In this chapter we turn to a relationship with which you will be more familiar: the bank and customer relationship. This involves:

- defining what is meant by 'bank' and 'customer'
- examining the legal relationships of debtor/creditor, agent/principal, bailor/bailee, mortgagor/mortgagee and the 'special relationship' between bank and customer
- comparing the rights and duties of bank and customer

6.1   Bank and Customer: a Legal Viewpoint

As this chapter is concerned with *legal* viewpoints, we will first explain how the law is quoted to support these viewpoints. The authority of English law is subdivided into *statute law* and *case law*.

Statute law
We have already seen how the development of the banking system has progressed through various Acts of Parliament - 'statutes' - such as the Bank Charter Act 1844 and the Banking Act 1987. Statute law is therefore a clearly defined set of regulations which must be adhered to.

Case law
Case law, which is quoted extensively in this chapter, is based on the decision of judges in court cases, and is a *guide* for judges in future cases, although if the facts of a future case are slightly different, the decision may go completely the opposite way! A typical banking case was *Woods v Martins Bank [1959]* in which the judge decided ('held') that if a person asks the bank for advice and *intends* to open an account, that person is a customer and can expect to be treated as such by the bank. There are two parties involved in any case:

- first name, the plaintiff - here, Woods, who brought the case
- second name, the defendant - here, Martins Bank (now merged with Barclays), which defended the case

It is important to remember the names of cases quoted in this chapter. The examiner will expect you to quote them, and they will be needed in your later studies. Note that you do not have to tell the whole story of the case in your answers, merely bring out the relevant points.

6.2 The Legal Definition of a Bank

The definition can be found in statute and case law:

Banking Act 1987

This Act, as noted in the previous chapter (see page 54) sets down the requirements of a body which may be granted a banking licence by the Bank of England:

- assets of not less than £1m for deposit-taking
- capital of not less than £5m before it can have the title of 'bank'
- good management

UDT v Kirkwood [1966]

Facts
This case concerned a loan made by a finance house (UDT) to a garage owner (Kirkwood). The loan went bad and UDT tried to recover the money. Kirkwood refused to pay on the grounds that the loan was void (i.e. not valid) because:

- UDT was not a bank
- UDT, not being a bank, should have been licensed as a moneylender under the Moneylenders Act 1900, and it wasn't

Decision
The courts finally decided that UDT *was* a bank because it provided the following services:

- crediting cheques and money to a customer's account
- debiting its customers' accounts with cheques and written orders
- maintaining accounts for its customers

Both these definitions, in statute and case law, are equally valid; they are merely different *authorities* for stating what a bank is if a dispute arises, as it did in this case of *UDT v Kirkwood.*

6.3 The Legal Definition of a Customer

There is no legal definition of a customer in statute law, but a number of cases provide the necessary authority.

legal point
a customer is a person who has an account or has applied to open an account

Ladbroke & Co. v Todd [1914]

Facts
Todd, a thief, opened an account with a stolen cheque, specially presented the cheque, withdrew the money and disappeared.

Decision
A person is a customer of a bank when an application to open an account has been accepted; the length of time the account is open is not important.

legal point
a customer is a person who has been provided with a specific service by a bank and who intends to open an account

Woods v Martins Bank [1959]

Facts   Woods was given investment advice by a Martins Bank manager but had no account at the time. The advice was bad and Woods sued. The bank tried to claim that Woods was not a customer and therefore was not owed a duty of care by the bank.

Decision   Woods was held to be a customer as he intended to open an account; the bank had to recompense him.

6.4   Legal Relationships between Bank and Customer

The basic bank and customer relationship (sometimes known as the banker/customer relationship), is one of *contract,* i.e. the bank agrees to open an account and the customer agrees to allow the bank to use his or her money as it wishes. There are also a number of other specific legal relationships between bank and customer; these are listed below.

Debtor and creditor
A debtor is a person who owes money and a creditor is a person who is owed money. The banking context of this is:

- Credit account: bank = debtor (it owes the customer money)
  customer = creditor (he/she is owed money by the bank)

- Overdrawn account: bank = creditor (it is owed money by the customer)
  customer = debtor (he/she owes money to the bank)

Principal and agent
In law a contract is a legally binding agreement between two parties, e.g. your contract of employment between you and the bank. In some circumstances you may need the services of a specialist to fix up a contract, e.g. an insurance broker to set up a contract (the policy) between you and an insurance company to insure your car. In this latter case, there are three parties involved: principal (you), agent (broker), third party (insurance company).

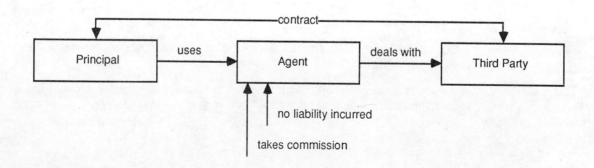

An agent is therefore a person used by a principal to arrange contracts with a third party. There are two basic rules applying to agents:

- they incur no liability on the contract (you cannot blame the insurance broker if the insurance company goes into liquidation)
- they can claim commission, as long as the principal is, or should be, aware of the fact

The bank can often act as agent for the customer, who is the principal. The following situations are examples:

- the bank arranges for the sale of stocks and shares for the customer
- the bank acts as estate agent for a customer buying a house

Bailor and Bailee

A bank offering safe custody facilities for a customer's valuables is providing a service known legally as *bailment*. There are two parties to the transaction:

- *bailor* - the customer, the depositor of the property
- *bailee* - the bank looking after the property

In law there are two types of bailee: *bailee for reward* (i.e. one that charges and is expected to employ the highest standard of care) and *gratuitous bailee* (i.e. one that does not charge and is only expected to act as a careful person would). This distinction does not really apply to banks because they apply the same high standard of care, whether they charge the customer or not.

A bank will normally advise a customer (bailor) to insure whatever is being deposited, as a bank will not be liable for loss or damage caused by theft, fire or flood, unless the bank were negligent and left the safe door open or the tap running in the staff kitchen!

Mortgagor and Mortgagee

A customer borrowing money from a bank and pledging property as security will normally sign a legal document known as a 'mortgage' giving power of sale to the bank if the customer defaults. There are two parties to this mortgage:

- *mortgagor* - the customer signing the mortgage
- *mortgagee* - the bank to whom the property is pledged

You will notice in this and the case of 'bailor/bailee', the bank in both cases has the suffix *'ee'* which denotes that it is at the receiving end of the transaction, just as an 'employee' is at the receiving end of employment.

The 'special relationship' between bank and customer

In certain cases of relationship such as parent and child, doctor and patient, there is said to be a 'fiduciary' relationship, a 'trusting' dependence of the weaker party on the advice of the stronger party.

If a bank gives advice to a customer, the relationship can sometimes be 'fiduciary'. The danger arises when the weaker party, e.g. a customer relying on a bank manager's advice, is persuaded to do something which is not in his/her interest. If this can be proved in a court of law it is known as *undue influence* and the customer's action - for instance, signing a mortgage over his or her home - can be held to be invalid. In a case like this, the bank's security might become void and the bank would not be able to recover money from a defaulting customer by selling the house.

In order for a customer to prove undue influence, two conditions must be fulfilled:

- the bank must have abused the fiduciary relationship, i.e. exerted pressure on a customer who was in a weaker/reliant position

- the customer must be put in a worse position as a result of the advice

There have been two important cases on this subject:

Lloyds Bank v Bundy [1975]

Facts   Farmer Bundy who often went to his Lloyds Bank manager for advice was persuaded to sign a mortgage over his farm to secure his son's borrowing. His son became bankrupt and Lloyds Bank wanted to sell Farmer Bundy's property and evict him.

Decision   Lloyds Bank had exerted undue influence and abused the fiduciary relationship between bank and customer. Farmer Bundy was put in a worse position as a result of the advice. The security was held to be invalid and Lloyds could not recover their money. The bank lost the case.

National Westminster Bank v Morgan [1985]

Facts   National Westminster Bank took over a mortgage given to Mr. and Mrs. Morgan by the Abbey National because the building society were going to repossess the house. The bank manager went to the Morgan's home to obtain Mrs. Morgan's signature to the mortgage. Shortly afterwards Mr. Morgan died, and NatWest wanted to sell the house to recover its loan. Mrs. Morgan claimed undue influence in that she had been pressurised to sign the mortgage by the NatWest manager.

Decision   Undue influence was *not* proved by the court:

- pressure had been brought to bear in a fiduciary relationship, *but*
- the Morgans were not worse off as a result (the Abbey National were about to repossess the property anyway).

The bank, therefore, won the case.

An important lesson for banks from these cases is that one way to avoid claims of undue influence in the 'special relationship' is to advise customers to obtain independent legal advice before signing security forms.

6.5   The Importance of Legal Definitions

When a customer opens a bank account, he or she enters into a contract with the bank, a legally binding agreement which implies certain rights which the bank can insist on from the customer, and certain duties which it is obliged to perform.

You may well ask why it is important to define bank and customer legal relationships and examine rights and duties, particularly when there is no written contract involved. The answer is that there normally *is* no need, because most dealings with customers run smoothly; the problems only arise when there is a dispute and certain questions need to be asked:

- Is the person actually a customer? If he or she is not, he or she cannot insist on certain duties of care by the bank.

- If the person is a customer, is the bank in breach of its duties?

- If the person is a customer is he or she in breach of contractual obligations to the bank?

A dispute can be resolved at a variety of levels: branch level, regional office level, or in the courts. Of these, court action is the least desirable for the banks, and it is case law decided in the courts which has established the rights and duties which are in question. A further person to whom personal customers can complain is the Banking Ombudsman, an independent arbiter, who can make awards of up to £100,000, but only when customers have taken complaints as far as they can with the banks.

6.6 Rights of the Bank

A bank has the right to:

- **use money** deposited with it as it wishes
  Case: Foley v Hill [1848]

- **exercise a lien** over items belonging to overdrawn customers passing through the bank's hands, e.g. cheques, but not items held for a specific purpose, e.g. safe custody - a *lien* is the right of the creditor to retain the property of the debtor until the debt is repaid, e.g. Sketchley Cleaners can retain your trousers if you do not pay the dry-cleaning bill

- **charge commission** appropriate to the service offered

- **be indemnified for loss** incurred when carrying out a service for a customer

- **be repaid on demand** for an overdraft, unless any written agreement specifies otherwise
  Case: Williams & Glyns Bank v Barnes [1980]

- **expect the customer to take due care when issuing cheques:** *London Joint Stock Bank v MacMillan & Arthur [1918]*

  Facts   In this case a fraudulent clerk altered a bearer cheque, made out carelessly by his employer, from £2 to £120, and disappeared with the proceeds.

  Decision   The court held that the bank was entitled to debit the employer with £120 as the amount in words had been omitted by the employer. Note: the same principle could apply to standing orders.

6.7 Duties of the Bank

Under the bank/customer contract the bank has a number of duties to the customer, most of them established by case law.

Joachimson v Swiss Bank Corporation [1921] established that banks have a duty to:

- **pay on demand** all cheques and written orders (such as standing orders)

- **collect cheques** that a customer has paid in, i.e. send off cheques in the appropriate clearing

- **give notice of closure of a credit account** so that a customer can make suitable alternative arrangements

Tournier v National Provincial Bank [1924] established that:

- **secrecy of customer accounts** must be strictly observed, with the exception of four instances where information can be revealed:

  compulsion by law: banks must reveal details of customers' accounts on receipt of court orders, on investigation under the Drug Trafficking Offences Act 1986, or by the Inland Revenue
  public duty: if the customer is an enemy national in time of war
  bank's interest: when enforcing repayment of a debt in the courts
  customer's consent: giving information to accountants when a signed authority from the customer is held

Other duties include:

- **advise customer of forgeries on account**
  Case: Brown v Westminster Bank Ltd. [1964]

- **exercise care and skill when dealing with customers** to avoid charges of negligence - if, for instance, a bank wrongly credits a customer with money, the customer can retain that money as long as the bank misled the customer, and the customer believed the bank and altered his or her position accordingly
  Case: United Overseas Bank v Jiwani [1976]

- **send regular statements of account** to customers who, incidentally, do not have to check the statement
  Case: Tai Hing Cotton Mill Ltd. v Liu Chong Hing Bank Ltd. [1968]

6.8   Bank and Customer: Written Contracts

We noted in Section 6.5 that a customer opening an account with a bank enters into a contract with the bank. It is interesting to note, however, that this contract is not in writing. Some customers may complain that the arrangement is too casual: they are not told about charges, nor about the rights and duties of the bank set out in the previous two Sections. Certain other bank/customer agreements *are* set out in writing, and as part of your studies you should examine some of these standard form contracts, including

- joint account mandates
- personal loan agreement forms
- cheque or debit card agreement forms

Fig. 6.1 sets out extracts from the terms and conditions applicable to both bank and customer relating to a debit card. The terms specifically cover:

- an automatic £100 overdraft
- the use of the card at retailers accepting SWITCH cards
- the use of the card to withdraw cash
- the use of the card to guarantee cheques
- the fact that the card belongs to the bank
- a disclaimer by the bank for failure of its computer equipment

You will note that the £100 overdraft should not be exceeded. Statute law protects the bank when a customer misuses a cheque card, running up an unauthorised overdraft. The Theft Act 1968, Section 16, has been used by the police in bringing a criminal prosecution against a bank customer who issued 25 cheques for £30 during the course of one session's gambling in a casino.
Case: Metropolitan Police Commissioner v Charles [1976].

Overdraft
● Provided that the terms of the agreement are complied with at all times, the card entitles the cardholder to use an overdraft facility on the account on such terms and up to such overdraft limit as shall be determined by the Bank from time to time. The overdraft limit will not be less than £100 or any higher existing overdraft limit on the account. Nothing in the agreement entitles the cardholder to use the card so as to overdraw the account beyond the overdraft limit, and all rights given to the cardholder under the agreement shall be treated as qualified accordingly.

Automated debits
● Subject to the terms of the agreement, the cardholder may use the card as a debit card (i.e. an alternative means of debiting payments to the account without issuing a cheque) to settle any purchase from retailers or suppliers who display the SWITCH logo.

Cheque guarantee
● Subject to the terms of the agreement, and to the Bank's Cheque Guarantee Conditions, the cardholder may use the card to guarantee payment of cheques which the cardholder is entitled to draw on any Current Account with the accountholder's branch. The Bank's Cheque Guarantee Conditions are available for inspection at any branch of the Bank.

● Any cheque drawn by the cardholder and bearing the card number may be debited by the Bank to the account on which it is drawn, even if the cheque is technically irregular, and the cardholder shall not be entitled to countermand any such cheque even if the agreement is terminated or any rights under it are cancelled or suspended.

Use of the card
● The card must be signed by the cardholder immediately on receipt and may only be used:
(a) by the cardholder
(b) subject to the terms of the agreement
(c) up to the expiry date embossed on the card
(d) in accordance with the operating instructions issued by the Bank or its agents from time to time.

● The card will remain the property of the Bank and the cardholder shall return it to the Bank on request.

● The Bank shall not be liable for any failure by any party to accept or honour the card.

● The Bank shall not be liable for any failure to perform its obligations under this agreement arising directly or indirectly from the failure or faulty working of any machine, data processing system or transmission link or any industrial dispute or anything beyond the Bank's control.

Fig. 6.1 Extracts from the terms and conditions applicable to The Royal Bank of Scotland's 'Highline' card

6.9 Developments in Customer Rights: the Jack Committee

In 1989 a committee headed by Professor Robert Jack and commissioned by the Government, proposed a major overhaul of banking law. Measures affecting bank/customer relations include:

- a full definition in statute law of secrecy - 'confidentiality' - of customer accounts
- closer control of disclosure of financial information about customers
- better explanation to customers of the secrecy rules

A fuller explanation of the Jack Committee proposals is set out in Chapter 16 'Future Developments in Banking' (page 211).

6.10 Revision Points

❏   A bank is defined in law

- by the Banking Act 1987
- in the case of *UDT v Kirkwood (1966)* as
  - crediting cheques and money
  - paying cheques and written orders
  - maintaining accounts

❏   A customer is defined in law as

- a person who has an account. *Case: Ladbroke v Todd (1914)*
- a person intending to open an account who is provided with a specific service. *Case: Woods v Martins Bank (1959)*

❏   Bank and customer can also enter into the following legal relationships:

- debtor and creditor (bank = debtor, if credit account)
- principal and agent (bank normally agent)
- bailor (customer) and bailee (bank) for safe custody
- mortgagor (customer) and mortgagee (bank)

❏   In the case of the 'special relationship' between bank and customer, undue influence can only be proved:

- where bank takes advantage when giving advice
- where customer is worse off as a result

Case: Lloyds Bank v Bundy (1975) - bank lost
Case: National Westminster Bank v Morgan (1985) - bank won

❏   Rights of the bank

- use money as it wishes. *Case: Foley v Hill (1848)*
- exercise a lien
- charge commission
- be indemnified for loss
- be repaid on demand. *Case: Williams & Glyn's Bank v Barnes (1980)*
- expect customer to take care when issuing cheques. *Case: London Joint Stock Bank v MacMillan & Arthur (1918)*

❑ Duties of the bank

- pay on demand all cheques and written orders
- collect cheques that a customer has paid in
- give notice of closure of a credit account

The case for the above three points is *Joachimson v Swiss Bank Corporation (1921)*

- secrecy of customer accounts - the four exceptions
  - compulsion by law (e.g. Drug Trafficking Offences Act 1986)
  - public duty (enemy account)
  - bank's interest (taking debt to court)
  - customer's consent (authority held to reveal details)

  Case: Tournier v National Provincial Bank (1924)

- advise customers of forgery on account. *Case: Brown v Westminster Bank Ltd. (1964)*
- exercise care and skill
- send regular statements, which do not have to be checked by customer. *Case: Tai Hing Cotton Mill Ltd. v Liu Chong Hing Bank Ltd. (1968)*

❑ Written contracts between bank and customer are normally subsidiary agreements:

- joint account mandates
- personal loan forms
- cheque card/debit card agreement forms

6.11 Know your *Bank and Customer*

Multiple-choice Questions

Choose the *one* answer you think is correct.

1. In which case must a banker refuse to disclose details of a customer's account?

   A When there is a court order not to do so
   B When the customer agrees to it
   C When instructing debt collectors
   D To a minor's parent

2. Which one of the following characteristics of a banker has not been identified by English case law?

   A Crediting money and cheques
   B Granting loans
   C Debiting accounts
   D Keeping accounts

3. The banker does *not* have the right to

   A be indemnified for losses
   B close accounts without notice
   C expect customer to use reasonable care when drawing cheques
   D repayment on demand of any overdrawn balance

4. Bank references should be taken to

    A obtain protection under the Cheques Act
    B check the address of the customer
    C find whether the customer is creditworthy
    D find whether the customer has bank accounts elsewhere

5. A bank has the right to

    A close a customer's account without notice whenever it wishes
    B disclose information to a customer's spouse
    C demand repayment of accounts overdrawn beyond an agreed limit
    D use a customer's money *only* as directed by the customer

6. In the fiduciary or special relationship the banker is expected to

    A use customers' money as specifically directed
    B act in complete good faith
    C take care of customers' property for which a special fee is received
    D give advice without making a special charge

Short Answer Questions

7. Give two reasons why banks take references on customers.

8. When a customer borrows money from a bank the customer is the .... and the bank is the ....

9. Name *two* banker/customer relationships.

10. Give *two* duties of a banker.

11. What case states that a person does not have to have a bank account to be a customer?

12. Name two circumstances where a bank may act as an agent for a customer.

13. Explain briefly the concept of bailment.

14. What is the 'special' relationship between bank and customer?

15. Give *two* rights of a bank.

16. What is the Banking Ombudsman?

17. Define a lien.

18. What is the significance of the case *London Joint Stock Bank v MacMillan & Arthur (1918)*?

19. List the *four* exceptions to the secrecy rule.

20. What is the legal position if a customer uses a cheque card when he/she knows there is no money in the account?

6.12 Essay Questions *Bank and Customer*

1.   Define a banker and a customer and explain the relationships between them.
[The Chartered Institute of Bankers' specimen paper]

2.   The nature of the relationship a banker has with his customer can vary according to the type of transaction involved. Give details of these relationships and the bankers' rights and duties involved.
[question 24, Spring 1987]

3.   (a)   The banker/customer relationship is a cornerstone of banking operations. Define a banker and a customer highlighting any key facts and characteristics.
[14 marks]
(b) Secrecy is a key element in the banker/customer relationship. Explain the circumstances under which a banker can disclose the affairs of the customer.
[6 marks]
[question 4, Autumn 1987]

4.   The banker/customer relationship is a key aspect in the business of banking.

(a) What is a banker and who is a customer?
[8 marks]
(b) Explain the contractual relationships and any other relationship that is important in a bank's business dealings.
[12 marks]
[question 3, Spring 1988]

5.   You receive the following letter from a slightly eccentric but important member of your local community. How would you reply?

Dear Sir,

We are concerned about the continued growth in the number of banking institutions in the UK.

It is virtually impossible to live in today's modern society without having a bank account of some sort or another and we worry that when individuals open an account they will not have any method of ensuring that you will deal with their account in a professional manner.

I believe that there are various legal rights and duties which underlie the way in which you do banking business. Could you tell me what these rights and duties are?

Yours faithfully,

Margaret Lawson

Margaret Lawson
Secretary to the Citizens Rights Association
[question 4, Autumn 1988]

6.   (a) A potential customer asks you 'Legally, what makes you a bank?' What would you say?
[5 marks]
(b) A customer wants to deposit some valuables with you but wants you first to explain the banker/customer relationship involved. Draft a brief explanation.
[5 marks]
(c) On opening an account a customer asks for a list of the bank's rights. Draw up a list which briefly sets out these rights.
[5 marks]
(d) A customer complains that you refused to give information on his account to his best friend. Tell him why you had to refuse.
[5 marks]
[question 4, Spring 1989]

Chapter Seven
Personal Customers

In the last chapter we discussed the legal relationship between bank and customer. In this chapter we will examine in more detail the precise nature of this relationship in the cases of various personal (i.e. non-business) customers:

- adults - aged 18 and over
- joint accounts
- minors - the under 18s
- married women
- personal customers operating in official capacities: executors, administrators and trustees

7.1 Personal Customers: Adults

An adult is defined in law as a person aged 18 and over. As far as the banks are concerned the accounts of adult customers have always formed the 'bread and butter' of banking, constituting the majority of their accounts. Competition for personal accounts is very much on the increase, and in Chapter 15 we will examine competition in the 'High Street', from building societies, and from other financial and retail organisations.

Opening the account

It is difficult to state *precisely* how banks open an account for an adult, because banks differ widely in their practice. These are some of the variations:

- obtain brief details and signature *or* ask the customer to complete a detailed application form
- obtain references and/or credit data search and/or identification

In this section we will examine the differences and the similarities and explain *why* the procedures are followed.

Customer details

The information normally required by the bank includes:

- full name
- home address and telephone number
- employer (if customer is in employment)
- signature (to enable bank to compare with signed cheques and other written instructions)
- age (to determine if customer is a minor, see Section 7.3)

TSB BANK Account Application

Application to operate accounts in sole/joint names

Account Stem └─┴─┴─┴─┴─┴─┘

Surname Customer 1   Surname Customer 2

Mr/Mrs/Miss   Mr/Mrs/Miss
Forename(s)   Forename(s)

Speedbank cards

Please issue a Speedbank card(s) for my/our account number └─┴─┴─┴─┴─┴─┴─┘

The card(s) to be issued to Customer 1 └─┘   Customer 2 └─┘   Customers 1 + 2 └─┘   *(please tick)*

I/We have read and accept the conditions of use overleaf and give the authority set out in Condition 1.
Both joint account holders must sign even if only one card is required.

* Please forward the card(s) to my/our address.   * I/We will collect the card(s) from my/our branch.

Signature   Signature

                                                      Date

Joint accounts only

In connection with this and any other accounts in our names we request you to honour cheques or orders for payment or comply with instructions relating thereto signed by either/both* of us (including cheques or orders for payment in favour of either or both of us); and in consideration of any overdraft or debt due to you which you may permit on this account or on any other account in our names, we agree to be jointly and severally liable. On the death of either of us the signature of the survivor may be accepted as a sufficient discharge for any credit balance on this or any other account or any part of such balances. The foregoing instructions shall remain in force until revoked in writing by either or both of us.

(* Delete whichever does not apply)

Registered Office: 60 Lombard Street, London EC3V 9EA. Registered in England and Wales: Number 1089268
TSB England & Wales plc is a Member of IMRO and AFBD

EW-1567-0588

Customer Number 1   Forename(s) - Customer 1   Surname

Customer Number 2   Forename(s) - Customer 2   Surname

New account number   Existing account number   Sub Type   Tariff

Present address - Customer 1   Postcode

Present address - Customer 2   Postcode

Correspondence address (if different from present address - Customer 1)   Postcode

(Sign below only if you have completed the correspondence address line above)

Signature   Signature

                                                      Date

Cheque book details - Bank use only

Sort Code   Account number
7 7 └─┴─┴─┴─┴─┴─┴─┴─┘

No. of books   Book type

Account name 1

Account name 2

Fig. 7.1a TSB Account Application form

Any party to cheque account number [_____] who does not require the Bank to send him/her a separate statement of account periodically should sign the statement below:-

I hereby authorise the Bank to dispense with giving to me in relation to the above account any statement required to be given pursuant to Section 78(4) of the Consumer Credit Act 1974.

Signature _____   Date _____

Note: At least one party to the account should not sign the statement.

Referee/Type of Identification [_____]

SPEEDBANK AUTHORITY AND CONDITIONS OF USE

To TSB England & Wales plc (the Bank)

In consideration of the Bank issuing to me/us from time to time TSB Speedbank Cards to enable me/us to use Speedbank terminals, I/we jointly and severally agree that:

1. The Bank is authorised to debit my/our account (the account number is stated in the application) with all amounts disbursed at the Speedbank terminals by use of any Cards which are issued to me/us (except disbursements made in respect of a Card after receipt by the Bank of notice of its loss or theft or that it is otherwise liable to misuse given in accordance with Condition 4) and I will be responsible/we will be jointly and severally responsible for any overdraft created by such debits but provided that the Card has not been used by a person who acquired possession of it with my/our consent, my/our liability will not exceed £50.

2. I/We will not overdraw the account if no overdraft arrangement has been made, nor overdraw the account in excess of any overdraft limit agreed by the Bank.

3. The Applicant(s) named in my/our application is/are the only person(s) who may use the Card(s).

4. I/We will exercise all possible care to prevent my/our Card(s) and any record of my/our Speedbank Personal Identification Number(s) (PIN) being lost or stolen or becoming liable to misuse. I/We will promptly notify **TSB England & Wales plc, PO Box 99, St Mary's Court, 100 Lower Thames Street, London EC3R 6AQ. Telephone 0273 204471,** of any such loss, theft or liability to misuse and will confirm such notification in writing.

5. I/We will not pass my/our Card(s) or disclose my/our Speedbank Personal Identification Number(s) to any other person and I/we undertake to destroy the PIN notification document on receipt and not to note the number(s) on the Card(s) or on anything carried or associated with the Card(s).

6. Speedbank Cards remain the property of the Bank, and must be surrendered to the Bank on demand.

7. The Card(s) must be surrendered to the Bank before the account is closed.

8. In the case of a joint account, the Bank is hereby authorised to issue to any one of the parties, any or all of the Speedbank Cards which are or may become available.

9. This authority for the issue of Speedbank Cards shall remain in force until receipt by the Bank of notice in writing to the contrary from me or any party to a joint account.

10. You may credit my/our account with all amounts deposited through Speedbank Auto-tellers. All deposit transactions are subject to verification.

11. You have the right at all times to vary these conditions and subject to any applicable statutory requirements any variation will become effective when you notify me/us by any means you consider appropriate.

SB notes

Date of birth [_____]   Sex [___]   Date moved to present address [_____]

Residential status *(please tick)*   Owned by you 1 | Rented Accomodation 3 | Owned/Rented by your parents 5 | Other 6

Marital Status *(Please tick)*   Single 1 | Married 2 | Widowed 3 | Separated/Divorced 4 | Other 5

Occupation [_____]

Employer's name [_____]   Date joined present employer [_____]

Will regular credits be paid direct into your cheque account by your employer? Yes | No   If no, will you undertake to pay £50 or more a month into your cheque account? Yes | No

Approximate value of your TSB savings £ [_____]   Approximate value of non bank savings £ [_____]

Home telephone number [_____]   Work telephone number [_____]

Bank use only

A	TWE	OO	TAPA	NBS	SB	CB	CC	TC	OD	EC

Notes [_____]

[_____]

Indicators [_____]   Means of recruitment [_____]

Marketing Indicators [_____]   End date for no marketing approach [_____]

Fig. 7.1b   TSB Account Application form

Some banks, as mentioned above, will ask further questions on the form, such as:

- number of dependants?
- houseowner or tenant?
- size of mortgage?
- length of time in employment?
- other borrowing commitments?

The purpose of this is twofold: firstly the customer's application can be credit-scored (see page 158) to establish creditworthiness, and, secondly, the information can be used by the bank's marketing department to sell certain products to the customer. For instance, the following information will be useful:

- **age** will determine which market segment (see Chapter 11.15) the customer belongs to: student, young professional, pensioner

- **type of employment** will enable the bank to decide whether to market goldcards or other products appropriate to the status of the customer.

Try and obtain an account opening form used by your branch and identify *why* each piece of information is required. A TSB Account Application form is illustrated on pages 73 and 74.

Establishing the identity and creditworthiness of a customer

If banks were lax in the way they opened accounts it would be easy for an individual to steal a cheque, open an account in the name of the payee, wait for the cheque to clear, withdraw the money in the form of cash and disappear. The person would be guilty of theft, the bank of conversion (depriving the true owner of their property), and the staff member who opened the account would be 'on the carpet'. The bank, in short, will have been *negligent*.

Banks, therefore, to avoid this form of fraud, take great care when opening accounts. As mentioned above, they vary in their practice, and as part of your studies you should find out the procedure adopted by your own bank. The procedure should include a combination of the following:

identification   inspection of suitable identification which should include a signature, e.g. driving licence, passport; this establishes *who* the customer is.

references   taking of one or two references, either from another customer or a 'reputable' person; if the bank does not know the referee, it may take a reference on the referee.

credit data search   the bank may make an enquiry by telephone or computer terminal from an independent computer database which contains the names and addresses of people who have had County Court actions brought against them for repayment of debt and, in some cases, records of other loan defaults.

References and credit data searches establish the *creditworthiness* and *identity* of the customer. It must be pointed out that if a bank considers a customer not to be creditworthy it can refuse to open an account.

Legal protection for a bank opening accounts

It would, clearly, be unfair if a bank took great care when opening an account and then discovered that the account holder was a thief, the account in a false name and the money originally paid in now withdrawn. The Cheques Act 1957, section 4, gives protection to the bank (the *collecting* bank) against claims from the true owner in such cases. It states that if a bank *collects* a cheque (i.e. the customer pays it in and the bank credits it to the account):

- in good faith (i.e. honestly)
- without negligence (i.e. the account had been opened with care - identification/references/credit searches, and there was nothing suspicious about the way the cheque was paid in)

then the bank, if the cheque were stolen, *is not liable to the true owner*.

Court cases in the past have decided what constitutes *negligence* when opening an account:

- not taking references *Case: Ladbroke & Co. v Todd [1914]*
- not checking on the referee *Case: Lumsden & Co. v London Trustee Savings Bank [1971]*

If, however, a fraud is committed and the bank opens an account in a false name, provided that the bank took the correct steps to obtain a reference it is protected against claims from the true owner as in the case of *Marfani & Co. v Midland Bank [1968]* when an account was opened in a false name but the referee only knew the account holder by that false name.

It should also be noted that obtaining the name of the customer's employer is an important safeguard. If the bank does not do so and the customer pays in cheques payable to the employer or forges their cheques, the bank will again be *negligent,* and be liable to the employer. Sometimes banks will even obtain the name of the husband or wife's employer to avoid negligence. This follows the famous case of *Lloyds Bank Ltd. v E.B. Savory & Co. [1932]* when a stockbroker's clerk stole cheques and paid them through the clearing into his *wife's* account. The bank, which had failed to obtain the name of the husband's employer had to repay the stockbroker.

7.2 Personal Customers: Joint Accounts

A joint account is an account operated by two or more personal customers. Normally joint accounts are operated by husband and wife, although boyfriend and girlfriend, or any combination is equally valid. Unlike a sole (single) account which merely requires a specimen signature and agreement to open the account, a joint account requires the completion by the customers of a *mandate,* which is a written agreement setting out very clearly the legal position of bank and customers.

Joint account mandate
The joint account mandate can either be a separate form or constitute part of the account opening form as in fig. 7.1. You should obtain one of your own bank's joint account mandates for your files and examine the clauses, which will normally include the following:

Signing instructions
The number of signatures required for cheques and other written instructions: 'both' or 'either', 'all' or 'any'.

Joint and several liability
This means that all parties to the account are liable for the whole amount of any debt. For example, if Mr. and Mrs. Robinson owed the bank £1,000 on joint account, the bank could bring a court action for £1,000 against *either* or *both* of them.

The following should be noted in the above case:

- if the bank receives more than £1,000 it should refund the difference in the proportion that contributions were made

- if Mr. Robinson pays £1,000 to the bank, he is entitled to demand £500 from Mrs. Robinson; whether or not he gets it is not the concern of the bank!

- if either party had a credit account in his/her name, the bank could use it to repay the overdrawn joint account, but *not* vice versa (i.e. a credit joint account could not be used to repay an overdrawn sole account)

Death of signatory
If one of the joint account holders dies, the signature of the surviving partner will release the money on the account.

Dispensing notice
The Consumer Credit Act 1974 requires that a separate bank statement should be sent to each joint account holder if that account is overdrawn. To avoid the ludicrous situation of, say, husband and wife receiving separate statements and the bank having to pay double postage, the mandate may include a *dispensing notice,* a clause stating that only one statement need be sent (see fig. 7.1).

Disputed joint accounts
Once a bank has *notice* of a dispute between joint account parties, e.g. a marital breakup, boyfriend leaving girlfriend, then any joint account mandate is effectively cancelled ('determined'). The practical effect of this is that the bank must insist on joint signatures to any payment out of the account. If the bank has no notice, the account will operate as normal. Thus, if a wife calls at the bank and says to the cashier, "He's leaving me, give me the balance of our account", the cashier cannot do so; if the wife says, "Give me the balance of our account", without stating why, the cashier can give her the money.

7.3 Personal Accounts: Minors

A minor is a person under the age of 18. In law there are certain restrictions on the liability of minors, and banks exercise great care in the operation of their accounts. The type of account offered will depend on the age of the minor. The table below sets out a typical range of accounts.

0 - 6 years	deposit account in the name of the parent
7 - 14 years	deposit account in the name of the minor
15 - 17 years	current account, with cash card, in the name of the minor

Minors and Borrowing
You will note that a minor is not normally given a cheque or debit card. The reason for this is that, under the Minors' Contracts Act 1987 a bank may not be able to recover an overdraft created by either of these cards. The Act states specifically that

- a contract for the borrowing of money by a minor is unenforceable, i.e. you cannot take a minor to court to recover a debt; only the goods bought with the borrowed money may be recovered

- an adult may guarantee a minor's debt, i.e. sign a formal bank security document stating in effect 'if the minor won't repay when requested to, I will.'

The effect of this Act is that a minor will not normally be granted, unless guaranteed by an adult (e.g. parent):

- a cheque card or debit card
- a credit card
- an overdraft or personal loan

The only exceptions to this rule are students under 18 who may receive a cheque/debit card as part of an overall package, and bank staff under 18. Banks often have problems with the former and occasionally with the latter!

7.4 Personal Accounts: Married Women

The law used to treat married women as being the property of their husband. Some husbands would like to think that this was still the case, but the Sex Discrimination Act 1975 treats as an offence any deliberate attempt, by a bank or any person, to discriminate between men and women.

The banks that still ask a woman for the name of her husband's employer when opening her account must therefore take care to ask a male customer the same question   (see the *Lloyds Bank Ltd. v E.B. Savory & Co.* case in Section 7.1).

We saw in Chapter 6, when discussing bank and customer legal relationships, that banks can run the danger of exerting *undue influence* over a customer when requesting him/her to sign a security form: such undue influence can render the security invalid.   Historically, banks have recognised that they can avoid this in the case of women customers - particularly when the husband's borrowing is being secured - by advising independent legal advice.   Nowadays, however, banks advise men and women alike to see a solicitor before they sign a security form.   In short, equality is now the overriding factor, and married women should be treated in the same way as their husbands.

7.5   Personal Customers acting in Official Capacities

Banks will often be asked to open accounts for personal customers acting in official capacities such as administrators, executors, and trustees.   All these roles involve looking after property:

- of dead people - administrators, executors, trustees
- of living people or organisations - trustees

Administrators

If a person dies and no will is in evidence, the person is said to have died 'intestate' (literally 'without a will').   The court will grant proof in the form of *Letters of Administration* to the personal representatives (usually the relatives) who become *administrators*.   Their job is to distribute the property of the deceased; this will often include a bank account (or accounts).   When administrators open a bank account for this purpose, they will be asked to produce the Letters of Administration and sign a bank mandate:

- making them jointly and severally liable
- specifying signing instructions, e.g. 'either' or 'both' to sign

If, of course, there is a single administrator appointed, a sole account will be opened and no mandate taken.

Executors

If a person has made a will, it will appoint *executors* to distribute the assets.   Power is given to the executors by the court in a document known as *Probate,* after which the will is said to have been 'proved'.   Executors (or a single executor) may open an account in the same way as an administrator, showing the court proof (probate) to the bank and signing a mandate, if there are joint executors involved.

Trustees

Normally after a period of twelve months, the property of the deceased person will have been distributed and the executor or administrator account may be closed.   If, however, there is property remaining and is being looked after for the benefit of, say, a twelve year-old grandson, the account holder will become a *trustee*.

A trustee is a person who is entrusted with the responsibility of looking after property for the benefit of a third party.   TSB students should note that the origins of the *Trustee* Savings Banks lie in the practice of a *trustee* looking after the savings of Scottish crofters.   The importance to the bank of trustee status is that:

- a new trustee account should be opened
- if there is more than one trustee, *all* must sign on the bank account (no delegation is possible)

Examples of trustee accounts include:

* trustees looking after a dead person's property (as above)
* a parent opening an account for a child, e.g. 'J. Robinson re L. Robinson'.
* a club official opening an account for an organisation, e.g. 'E. Clarke, Treasurer, Adelaide Bowls Club'

The important point for a bank in running a trustee account is that it should not allow the trustee to misapply the funds; if it does so, and should have realised that the trustee was acting wrongly, it will have to reimburse the third party (e.g. child, Bowls Club, etc.).

7.6 Revision Points

❏ When opening personal accounts a bank will have to bear in mind different legal considerations in the case of:

* adults
* joint accounts
* minors
* married women
* executors, administrators and trustees

❏ When opening an account for an adult a bank will normally:

* obtain personal details and specimen signature
* establish the identity and creditworthiness of a customer by asking for identification and obtaining references/credit data search

❏ If a bank observes the account opening formalities correctly (without negligence) and in good faith, it is protected by the Cheques Act 1957, section 4, against the true owner if a stolen cheque is paid in.

Negligence can be:

* not taking references - *Case: Ladbroke v Todd (1914)*
* not checking on the referee - *Case: Lumsden & Co. v London Trustee Savings Bank (1971)*

❏ Joint accounts:

* two or more personal customers
* joint account mandate taken including
  - signing instructions
  - joint and several liability clause (very important)
  - clause allowing one partner to claim the money if the other partner dies
  - dispensing notice
* in case of dispute, all signatures required

❏ Minors:

* a minor is a person under 18
* rights set out in Minors' Contracts Act 1987
* contracts of money lent to minors are unenforceable
* banks cannot recover money lent through the courts (only the goods purchased)
* an adult may guarantee a minor's borrowing
* banks therefore rarely issue cheque/debit/credit cards to minors or grant them loans

❑   Married women:

   • used to be treated as their husband's property
   • under the Sex Discrimination Act 1975 must be treated in the same way as men
   • if banks ask a wife for the name of her husband's employer (as they used to) they should ask a husband for his wife's employer

❑   Administrators:

   • act for a person who has died without a will under Letters of Administration (proof) issued by the court
   • a bank mandate should be signed (joint and several liability)

❑   Executors:

   • act for a person who has died and has made a will naming them
   • authority to act given by court in the form of probate (proof)
   • a bank mandate should be signed (joint and several liability)

❑   Trustees:

   • person(s) who look after property for the benefit of another person or organisation:
     - a dead person's property handed on for the benefit of someone still living
     - a minor's property looked after by an adult
     - a club official looking after the organisation's funds
   • trustees must *all* sign any authority (mandate, cheque, standing order)
   • trustees cannot delegate authority

7.7 Know your *Personal Customers*

Multiple-choice Questions

Choose the *one* answer you think is correct.

1.   Liability on a joint account is usually

   A joint
   B joint and several
   C first named
   D shared equally

2.   On an account with a Joint & Several liability mandate there is an overdraft of £1,000, and therefore

   A each party is liable for £500
   B each party is liable for £1,000
   C the drawer of the cheque causing the overdraft is liable
   D the first signatory on the mandate is liable

3.   For banking purposes a minor is anyone under the age of

   A 7
   B 16
   C 18
   D 21

4. If a minor borrows money the contract is

    A void
    B invalid
    C valid
    D unenforceable

5. If the bank holds a trustee account for two trustees of an estate

    A either can sign
    B both must sign
    C an executor must sign
    D the bank's trust company must sign

Short Answer Questions

6. List *four* details a bank needs to obtain when opening a personal account.

7. What is the danger to the bank of opening a personal account without taking references or obtaining a credit data search?

8. Define *joint and several liability*.

9. What is a *dispensing notice*?

10. What action should a bank take on notice of a disputed joint account?

11. Why is a bank reluctant to give a minor a debit card?

12. What effect has the Sex Discrimination Act 1975 on the running of personal accounts?

13. What is the authority to act of an administrator?

14. What is the authority to act of an executor?

15. Give *three* examples of a trustee account.

7.8 Essay Questions *Personal Customers*

1. You have been asked to open *three* accounts for a family: one for father and mother together, one for son aged 19, and one for daughter aged 13.

    In each case, outline the legal formalities required at the outset and explain the significance of this information when it comes to running the account.

    [question 6, Autumn 1988]

2. Describe the formalities for opening a personal bank account for an adult. Explain *why* each step is taken.

3. (a) Obtain a joint account mandate and explain the clauses that appear on it.

    [15 marks]

    (b) If you have notice of a dispute on a joint account, what action would you take, and why?

    [5 marks]

4. Anne Jones, a sixteen year-old girl in her last year at school wishes to open an account at your bank. She states that she needs a cheque card because otherwise she cannot buy goods at shops. How would you deal with this request? Give reasons for your actions.

5. What action would you take in the following circumstances?

(a) Mrs Anthony asks to open an account in her name. She objects to having to state the occupation of her husband on the account opening form. The form states 'Occupation of spouse ....'

[5 marks]

(b) Mr and Mrs Smith are acting for Mr Smith's father, who has recently died without leaving a will. They want to open a bank account to deal with the father's money.

[5 marks]

(c) The same situation exists as in (b) above, but a will has been found.

[5 marks]

(d) Louise Jones wants to open a deposit account for money which she is giving to her six month old niece, Elizabeth Wareing.

[5 marks]

Chapter Eight
Business Customers

In this chapter we will examine the bank accounts of business customers:

* sole traders
* partnerships
* limited companies

We will also look briefly at the bank accounts of non profit-making organisations, such as

* clubs and associations
* charities
* local authorities

8.1 Business Customers: the Marketplace

Banks compete fiercely for business customers because they contribute significantly to bank profits and also provide opportunities for selling the banks' products. You may find that your branch holds business accounts, or your business accounts may all be looked after by a specialised 'business branch'. The latter arrangement is becoming more common and gives the business managers the opportunity to specialise in business lending and to go out as salespeople to call on their own customers, and also those of other banks! At whatever type of branch you may work you should try, if possible, to look at some business customers' files and examine the documents we will be discussing in the course of this chapter.

There are three main types of business customer:

* sole trader
* partnership
* limited company

8.2 Sole Trader

A sole trader is an individual trading in his or her name, or under a trading name.

A sole trader is the most common form of business. A sole trader *is* the business: a person setting up as plumber, shopkeeper or financial consultant is entirely responsible for the profit or loss and success or failure of that enterprise. The table on the next page sets out the advantages and disadvantages of running a sole trader business.

advantages	disadvantages
• easy to set up	• long hours
• cheap to set up	• short holidays
• you are your own boss	• problems if you are ill
• control over the business	• total liability for debt
• you take all the profit	• risks to you and your family
• motivation: job satisfaction	• limited sources of money

Sole trader bank accounts

A bank opening an account for a sole trader must, if the trader is unknown, carry out all the procedures for opening a sole personal account, i.e. obtain identification/references/credit data search. The bank must take care over the name of the account:

• customer trading in own name:	*'Henry Ramsay, Business Account'*
• customer trading under a trading name:	*'Henry Ramsay trading as Superior Garden Services'*

If the customer is using a trading name, the bank should see some stationery (e.g. letterhead) which by law must show the name of the sole trader *and* the trading name.

The bank services available to business customers are covered in Chapter 14.

8.3   Partnerships

A partnership is a group of individuals working together in business, aiming to make a profit.

Examples of partnerships are doctors, dentists, solicitors, builders and decorators. All partnerships are regulated by the Partnership Act 1890 which sets out very specific terms:

Number of partners
There are normally between two and twenty partners (the exception being large professional firms of accountants and solicitors, which may have more than twenty partners).

Actions by partners
Any partner will bind the other partners (i.e. the partnership 'firm') by actions carried out in the normal course of business. For instance, a dentist ordering a new drill makes all the other partners liable on the order (i.e. the firm will have to pay for it), even if they don't like the drill.

Liability for debt
All partners are fully (jointly and severally) liable for all the debts of the firm. If a partnership is borrowing £100,000 from the bank, *every* partner is liable for £100,000 to the extent of their house and personal possessions.

The advantages and disadvantages of a partnership are set out below.

advantages	disadvantages
• more capital available	• each partner liable for whole debt of
• more varied expertise available	partnership
• holiday relief	• problems with disagreements
• sickness cover	(most common problem!)
• cross-fertilisation of ideas	• profit is shared
	• a partner has less independence in
	decision-making

Partnership bank accounts

A bank opening an account for a partnership must:

* obtain references/credit data search on unknown partners
* obtain the partners' signature to a bank mandate setting out signing powers and joint and several liability (confirming that each partner is fully liable for the whole debt of the partnership)
* see evidence of the genuineness of any trading name by examining stationery showing the trading name and the names of *all* the partners

Sometimes a partnership will be regulated by a *Partnership Agreement* setting out terms such as the share of profits, how to expel a partner, and so on. This 'rulebook' is not normally seen by the bank, as the bank relies solely on its mandate to regulate the running of the account.

8.4   Limited Companies

A limited company is a separate legal body, owned by shareholders and managed by directors.

A sole trader or partnership business is a risky enterprise because the success or failure of the business means the success or failure of the owner(s). The liability of the owner(s) for business debt is total. A limited liability company business, on the other hand, is quite different: the owners of the business are the shareholders and their liability for business debt is strictly limited (see fig. 8.1 on page 86):

* if the company fails they will only lose the money they have paid for their shares
* if the company fails and any instalments are due to be paid on the shares, these will have to be paid by the shareholders

A number of legal points should be noted:

* the Companies Act 1985 regulates the setting up and running of limited companies

* a company, as noted above, is a completely separate legal body from its shareholder owners: in the case of *Salomon v Salomon & Co. Ltd. (1897)*, Mr Salomon, a managing director and shareholder of a company, sued the company as a separate legal body for money owed to him personally

* limited companies unlike sole traders and partnerships, must send their annual financial accounts to Companies House in London, where they are available for public inspection

* limited companies are run by directors who are themselves shareholders; most shareholders are *not* directors

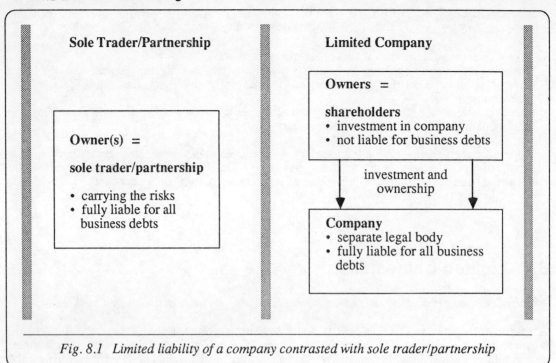

Fig. 8.1 Limited liability of a company contrasted with sole trader/partnership

Company documents

When a company is formed (incorporated) various documents are drawn up and registered at Companies House with the Registrar of Companies; the most important of these are the Memorandum of Association and the Articles of Association. As we will see shortly a bank opening an account for a company will need to inspect these carefully.

Memorandum of Association

This document establishes the constitution of the company, i.e. how it should be set up and what it can and cannot do. It is set out in a number of clauses:

- the name of the company followed by 'plc' or 'ltd' (see below for the difference between these)

- the location of the registered office of the company, i.e. whether in England and Wales, or Scotland (there are different legal systems in these two areas)

- a clause stating that the liability of the shareholders (members) is limited

- a clause stating how much share capital can be issued. e.g. 10,000 shares of £1 each - this is known as the *authorised* share capital, not all of which *need* be issued

- the *objects clause* setting out what the company can do in the way of business; it is normally wide-ranging (see page 90 - 'ultra vires' - for the importance of this clause to the bank)

You will note that the shares issued by a company are authorised in the Memorandum. There are a number of different types of share:

preference shares pay a fixed rate of dividend to the shareholder out of the company's profits and are paid before other shareholders receive their dividend (hence the term 'preference').

ordinary shares are the most common type of share and pay a variable dividend to shareholders out of profits *after* the preference shareholders have received their dividend; it would be very rare for an ordinary shareholder *not* to receive a dividend.

Articles of Association
This document could be termed the 'rulebook' of the company. It sets out details such as:

- when and how to call company meetings
- duties and powers of directors
- the issue and transfer of shares

A bank, as we will see, needs to take particular notice of the powers of directors, as the bank will be dealing with the directors on a day-to-day basis.

Certificate of Incorporation
When a company has been formed (incorporated) it is issued by the Registrar of Companies with a *Certificate of Incorporation*. This is a single sheet of paper with the company name, number and date of incorporation printed on it; it is often likened to the 'birth certificate' of a company.

Private and public limited companies
There is no significant variation between private and public companies apart from size and certain technical differences:

Public company
- the larger of the two types, with a minimum issued share capital of £50,000
- the name stated in the Memorandum must end with 'public limited company' (abbreviated to 'plc')
- a minimum of two directors
- the ability to raise money by an issue of shares to the public (i.e. shares quoted on the Stock Exchange) following the issue of a prospectus
- requires a Certificate to Commence Business in addition to the Certificate of Incorporation

Private company
- the smaller of the two types, with issued share capital of under £50,000
- defined in the Companies Act 1985 as a limited company which is not a public limited company
- the name stated in the Memorandum must end with 'limited' (abbreviated to 'ltd')
- a minimum of one director
- it is illegal to invite the public to buy shares

If you consider your own employer and your many company customers you will see that the public company (plc) is the larger organisation which may be quoted on the Stock Exchange, and the private limited company (ltd) is the smaller company, often owned by a family in business.

Mandate for companies registered under the Companies Acts

Guidance notes for the completion of this form of company mandate — please read carefully

1 Where a mandate is to be given for the first time to the Bank a resolution should be passed by the board of directors similar to that described in section C overleaf and entered in the company's minute book. Section C should be completed and after comparison with the entry in the minute book certified as a true copy by the chairman of the meeting and the secretary.

2 The secretary should also complete sections A and D and the persons authorised to sign should provide specimen signatures in section D.

3 a) It will often be convenient to complete section C by nominating as signatory the holders for the time being of certain offices, e.g. "any one director for the time being", "any two directors for the time being" or "any director and the secretary for the time being". If this practice is followed instructions may be varied later by following the short procedure outlined in paragraph 3b).

b) Where a company wishes to vary instructions previously given under paragraph 3a) simply because a new director, secretary or official (as the case may be) has been appointed, the secretary need only complete sections B and D.

4 If, however, named persons are nominated in section C the instructions can only be varied by the procedure outlined in paragraph 5.

5 Any other variation of an existing authority will require a fresh resolution of the board of directors and completion of sections B, C and D.

TO **Midland Bank plc**

Date _____

Insert name of company _____ ("the company")

Registered office _____

Address for statements _____

Complete section A or B and sections C and D as appropriate.

A **Authority**

You are requested to act as bankers to the company. Accompanying this authority or set out overleaf are:

1 Certificate of incorporation (for inspection and return).

2 Copy of the memorandum and articles of association.

3 Certified copy of a resolution of the board of directors *(see overleaf)*.

4 List of the directors* and officials authorised to sign with specimen signatures *(see overleaf)*.

_____
Secretary

Note: In the case of a public limited company the certificate of the Registrar of Companies that the company is entitled to do business should be forwarded for inspection and return.

B **Variation of authority**

You are requested to continue as bankers to the company but

*to act on new instructions/signatures as set out overleaf in sections **C** and/or **D**.

*to note the new address for statements

_____
Secretary

*Delete as appropriate

787-4

Fig. 8.2a   Company mandate form

C

We certify that the following resolution of the board of directors of the company was passed at a meeting of the board held on the _____ and has been duly recorded in the minute book of the company.

Resolved that

"1   The company authorises Midland Bank plc:

a) to honour all cheques and other orders or instructions authorising payment signed on behalf of the company by _____

_____("the signatory") whether any account of the company is in credit or debit;

b) to deliver up any item held by the Bank on behalf of the company in safe custody or for any other purpose against the written receipt or instructions of the signatory; and

c) to accept the signatory as fully empowered to act on behalf of the company in any other transactions with the Bank.

2   The company agrees that any indebtedness or liability incurred to the Bank under this authority shall in the absence of any express written agreement by the Bank to the contrary be due and payable on demand.

3   The secretary shall as and when necessary supply to the Bank list/s of current directors, and, if applicable, other, officials authorised to sign with specimen signatures and the Bank may rely upon such lists signed by the secretary."

_____   _____
Chairman   Secretary

D

Delete as appropriate   The following are the Directors* and officials currently authorised to sign.

Name—*in full*	Official Position	Specimen signature—*of any new signatory*

Date _____   _____
                                                              Secretary

Fig. 8.2b Company mandate form

8.5 Limited Company Bank Accounts

Opening the account
A bank opening an account for a limited company will need to examine the documents discussed above, specifically:

- the Certificate of Incorporation
- the Certificate to Commence Business in the case of a plc
- the Memorandum of Association and Articles of Association (normally contained in a single booklet)

These documents are normally stated in the bank company mandate, an example of which is illustrated in fig. 8.2. You will note that the following is requested on the mandate:

- the documents mentioned above (Section A)

- a signed directors' resolution to open a bank account and stating the number of people required to sign on the account (Section C)

- a list of people (normally directors) who are authorised to sign on the account, together with their specimen signatures (Section D)

Dealing with the directors
Banks deal from time-to-time with the directors of a company and need to take care when doing so.

lending money 'ultra vires' - if the loan is outside the amount a director can borrow (set out in the Articles) *or* is for a purpose outside the objects of the company (set out in the Memorandum), the loan will be 'ultra vires' (literally 'beyond the powers of') the directors or company, and may be void. In short, if the bank does not check the Memorandum and Articles carefully it may not get its money back if it lends.

paying cheques - if the cheques are not made out in the full and correct name of the company and the position of the person(s) signing is not made clear, that person(s) may be liable personally on the cheque, i.e. they may have to pay if the company is not able to.

8.6 Partnerships and Companies Compared

We will firstly examine the advantages and disadvantages of setting up a company and secondly look at these in the context of a partnership. Business customers contemplating expanding a sole trader business will often ask about these factors: is it better to set up a partnership or a limited company?

advantages of a limited company
- limited liability of owners
- you can sell shares in a company
- you can own shares without having to work in the business
- you can raise more money from outsiders by forming a company
- prestige

disadvantages of a limited company
- cost of setting up a company
- complex regulations which must be followed strictly (Memorandum and Articles)
- more paperwork - e.g. filing of annual accounts

Comparison of partnerships and limited companies

	Partnership	Company
Legal status	• the partners *are* the business	• separate from shareholders
Members	• normal maximum of 20	• no maximum
Liability	• partners each liable for entire partnership debt	• shareholders can only lose their investment
Legislation	• Partnership Act 1890	• Companies Act 1985
Regulation	• written or oral agreement	• Memorandum and Articles
Power to act	• a partner can do anything in the agreed ordinary course of partnership business	• activity limited by objects clause in Memorandum
Management	• all partners normally take an active part	• only directors and authorised officials
Transfer of ownership	• only possible by negotiation with the other partners	• sell the shares
Financial accounts	• private and not available to the public	• made available to the public at Companies House

8.7 Accounts for Non Profit-making Organisations

Banks will often open accounts for non profit-making organisations such as:

- social clubs and associations, e.g. the local Bowls Club
- charities, e.g. the local branch of Oxfam or Mencap
- local authorities

Clubs and associations

In legal terms clubs and associations do not exist separately, but only as a group of individuals who normally elect a committee. When opening the account, the bank should:

- open the account in the name of the club/association
- ensure the committee has passed a resolution to open the account
- obtain a signed mandate giving signing instructions
- obtain the rulebook (if there is one)

Occasionally a club will be constituted as a limited company, e.g. a football club, in which case it will be treated as such by the bank.

Charities

Charities are often companies 'limited by guarantee', i.e. the members have not bought shares but instead guarantee to pay a certain amount if the company is 'wound up' (ceases to operate). Banks must therefore treat such charity companies in the same way as any limited company. Companies limited by guarantee often omit the word 'limited' from their name.

Local authorities

If a bank opens an account for a local authority (e.g. a County Council) it will ensure:

• the account is in the name of the authority
• the council has passed a resolution authorising the account
• a mandate is taken specifying signing powers of council officials

The bank normally deals principally with the council Treasurer or Chief Financial Officer.

8.8 Revision Points

❑ There are three main types of business customer:
   • sole trader
   • partnership
   • limited company

❑ A sole trader
   • is an individual trading in his or her own name, or using a trading name
   • is wholly liable for business debts

   You should learn the advantages and disadvantages of sole traders.

❑ When opening a sole trader bank account, a bank must:
   • check the genuineness of a trading name by examining stationery
   • otherwise treat it as a sole personal account (references, etc.)

❑ A partnership is a group of individuals working together in business, aiming to make a profit
   • 2 to 20 partners (except solicitors, accountants)
   • the partnership is liable for the action of partners in the ordinary course of business
   • partners are all wholly liable for partnership debts (joint and several liability)

   You should learn the advantages and disadvantages of partnerships.

❑ When opening a partnership bank account, a bank must
   • obtain references on unknown partners
   • obtain completion of mandate (joint and several liability)
   • check genuineness of trading name (examine stationery)

❑   A limited company is a separate legal body, owned by shareholders and run by directors
- regulated by the Companies Act 1985
- shareholders have limited liability
- financial accounts sent to Companies House
- documents include Memorandum of Association (learn the clauses), Articles of Association, and Certificate of Incorporation
- public limited company (plc) has issued capital of over £50,000, needs Certificate to Commence Business, a minimum of two directors and may be quoted on the Stock Exchange
- private company (ltd) has no minimum capital, minimum of one director, not quoted on Stock Exchange
- shares may be ordinary (dividend out of profit) or preference (fixed rate of dividend, paid before that of ordinary shareholders)

❑   When opening a company bank account, a bank must
- examine the Memorandum and Articles of Association, Certificate of Incorporation (and Certificate to Commence Business, if plc)
- obtain signatures to mandate
- take care not to lend or deal 'ultra vires', i.e. outside the objects of the company (Memorandum) or powers of the directors (Articles), otherwise the lending or dealing may be void

❑   You should learn the advantages and disadvantages of a company (Section 8.6)

❑   You should learn the differences between partnerships and companies (Section 8.6)

❑   Non profit-making organisations often open bank accounts:
- clubs and associations
- charities
- local authorities

In each case a bank must ensure:
- there is authority to open an account
- a mandate is taken
- if it is a club or charity, that the legal status of the organisation is known: is it an association, limited company, company limited by guarantee?

8.9 Know your *Business Customers*

Multiple-choice Questions

Choose the *one* answer you think is correct.

1.   A sole trader

    A must trade under a separate trading name
    B is wholly liable for his/her business debt
    C is limited in liability to the amount of money invested
    D cannot trade until he/she has received a Certificate to Commence Business

2.   In a partnership

   A any partner can bind the firm by actions carried out in the normal course of business
   B the main partners only are liable in law for the debts of the firm
   C all partners have liability for the debts of the firm in relation to their capital investment
   D the partners are required to register the partnership agreement in writing

3.   In a partnership

   A each partner is fully liable for all debts
   B the partner authorised to sign is mainly liable
   C partners are liable in proportion to their seniority and income
   D liability is shared equally between full partners

4.   The minimum share capital of a Public Limited Company is

   A £25,000
   B £50,000
   C £100,000
   D £250,000

5.   The objects clause of a limited company is

   A a clause setting out the remedies for an objecting director
   B a clause setting out the number of shares that can be issued
   C contained in the Articles of Association
   D contained in the Memorandum of Association

Short Answer Questions

6.   What will a bank need to see when opening a sole trader account in a trading name?

7.   What is the liability of a sole trader for business debt?

8.   Define a partnership.

9.   How many partners can there be in a partnership?

10. What is the liability of partners for actions carried out by other partners in the ordinary course of partnership business?

11. What is the liability of a partner for business debt?

12. Name *two* documents the bank would want to see when opening an account for a public limited company.

13. Complete the following sentence using no more than 12 words:
    '*Ultra vires* lending is ....'

14. Name *two* types of company share.

15. State *three* differences between a private limited company and a public limited company.

16. List *five* clauses you would expect to see in the Memorandum of Association of a limited company.

17. Name the *two* Acts of Parliament which regulate partnerships and companies.

18. What is a company limited by guarantee, and what type of organisation is often constituted as a company limited by guarantee?

19. List *three* of the procedures a bank undertakes when opening an account for a club or association.

20. List *two* procedures a bank will undertake when opening an account for a local authority.

8.10 Essay Questions *Business Customers*

1. Banks apply different considerations to different types of customer. Give examples of these special considerations for each main type of customer. Briefly explain the importance of the considerations to a banker.

[question 23, Spring 1987]

(Note: when this question was asked it also applied to personal customers, which of course made it very wide ranging. For the purposes of examination preparation, apply it here to business customers only.)

2. In respect of partnerships and public limited companies, contrast:

   (a) the requirements for opening a bank account

[10 marks]

   and

   (b) the factors the bank needs to consider when granting a loan.

[10 marks]
[question 6, Autumn 1987]

3. From a legal point of view, a business can be organised in a number of different ways.

   (a) Outline the main advantages and disadvantages of each type of organisation.

[15 marks]

   (b) List the factors a banker will be concerned about when dealing with each type of organisation.

[5 marks]
[question 4, Spring 1988]

4. List the main considerations a bank would have in mind when opening an account for

   (a) a sole trader

[5 marks]

   (b) a partnership

[5 marks]

   (c) an angling club

[5 marks]

   (d) a local authority

[5 marks]

Chapter Nine
Funds Transfer: Paper Systems

In this chapter we shall:

- examine the organisation of the clearing system
- explain how a cheque is cleared
- describe the difference between the paying bank and the collecting bank
- explain the reason for returning cheques
- examine alternative methods for clearing cheques - Town clearing and special presentations
- explain the paper credit clearing system
- explain the paper system for clearing credit and debit card transactions

Electronic systems of funds transfer are considered in the next chapter.

9.1 The Banks' Clearing System

The clearing system is the means by which transfers are made between banks of paper transactions, e.g. cheques and bank giro credit slips, or of electronic transactions in the form of computerised debits and credits. Transactions can be

- inter-branch, i.e. between branches of the same bank
- inter-bank, i.e. between different banks

All inter-bank clearings are under the overall control of the Association for Payment Clearing Services (APACS); the members of APACS are banks and building societies which take part in the clearings. Separate clearing companies deal with particular clearings, as illustrated below.

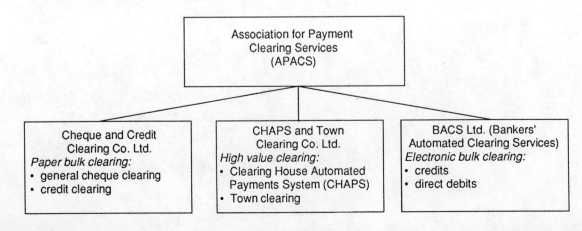

APACS also supervises the development of Electronic Funds Transfer at Point of Sales (EFTPOS) through a fourth company called Eft Pos UK Ltd.

Membership of each operating company is open to financial organizations which make use of a particular clearing, and the main participants are the London and Scottish Clearing Banks. A number of building societies have become members of Cheque and Credit Clearing Co. Ltd., and BACS Ltd.

Paper-based clearing systems are:

• general cheque clearing
• credit clearing
• Town clearing

These are discussed in this chapter, together with special presentations of cheques.

Electronic-based clearing systems are:

• CHAPS (Clearing House Automated Payments System)
• BACS (Bankers' Automated Clearing Services)

These are discussed in the next chapter, together with EFTPOS (Electronic Funds Transfer at Point of Sale).

Girobank clearing

Girobank - which operates mainly through post offices - runs a clearing system which is outside the scope of the banks' clearing. When a Girobank account holder wishes to pay another account holder, he or she fills in a transfer form and posts it to Girobank's computer centre at Bootle in Merseyside, where the accounting transfers are effected. As all accounts are maintained in one place, the transaction is carried out immediately on receipt of the transfer form. Non-account holders wishing to pay money to a Girobank account can pay in cash at a post office, together with a completed credit form.

9.2 General Cheque Clearing

Every day each branch bank receives cheques paid in by customers. These cheques fall into three groups:

• those that are issued by customers of the branch
• those that are issued by customers of the other branches of the bank
• those that are issued by customers of other banks

The first group can be debited to the customers' accounts straightaway (unless the cheque is to be returned). The second group will pass through the bank's own internal clearing system (known as the inter-branch clearing); however, some of these cheques may be 'cleared' by means of truncation (see Chapter 10.5). The third group of cheques will pass through the general cheque clearing operated by Cheque and Credit Clearing Co. Ltd. Both the inter-branch and the general cheque clearing operate in a similar way, the main difference being that, in the general clearing, settlement for cheques exchanged is made between the banks.

The general cheque clearing normally takes three working days, and the procedures are shown in fig. 9.1. Note that, in the example shown, Midland Bank owes Barclays the amount of the cheque but settlement will be made on a 'net' basis through accounts held at the Bank of England, e.g.

Barclays Bank	£50 million	of cheques drawn on Midland
Midland Bank	£40 million	of cheques drawn on Barclays
settlement	£10 million	paid by Midland to Barclays

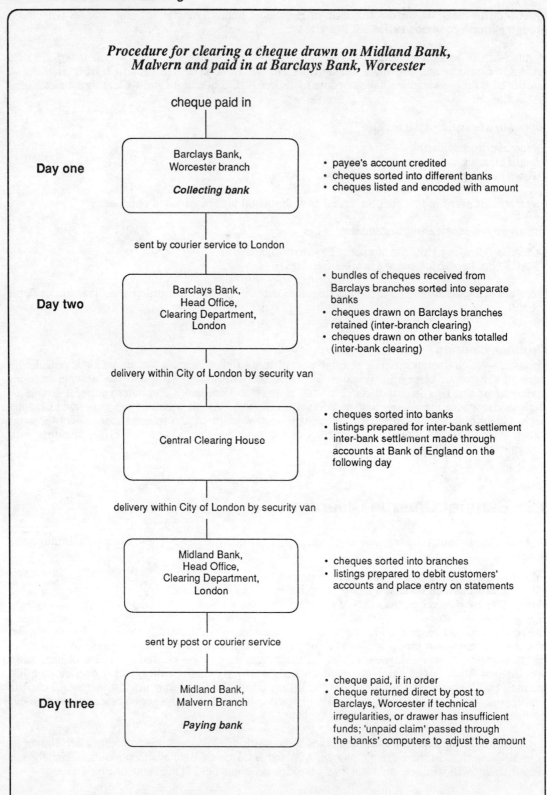

**Procedure for clearing a cheque drawn on Midland Bank,
Malvern and paid in at Barclays Bank, Worcester**

cheque paid in

Day one

Barclays Bank,
Worcester branch

Collecting bank

- payee's account credited
- cheques sorted into different banks
- cheques listed and encoded with amount

sent by courier service to London

Day two

Barclays Bank,
Head Office,
Clearing Department,
London

- bundles of cheques received from Barclays branches sorted into separate banks
- cheques drawn on Barclays branches retained (inter-branch clearing)
- cheques drawn on other banks totalled (inter-bank clearing)

delivery within City of London by security van

Central Clearing House

- cheques sorted into banks
- listings prepared for inter-bank settlement
- inter-bank settlement made through accounts at Bank of England on the following day

delivery within City of London by security van

Midland Bank,
Head Office,
Clearing Department,
London

- cheques sorted into branches
- listings prepared to debit customers' accounts and place entry on statements

sent by post or courier service

Day three

Midland Bank,
Malvern Branch

Paying bank

- cheque paid, if in order
- cheque returned direct by post to Barclays, Worcester if technical irregularities, or drawer has insufficient funds; 'unpaid claim' passed through the banks' computers to adjust the amount

Fig. 9.1   General cheque clearing

Note from fig. 9.1:

- the cheque takes three working days to clear

- the cheque is cleared via the Central Clearing House (owned jointly by banks and building societies) in London

- it is assumed in this example that the cheque is paid; if it had to be returned (see Section 9.3) it would normally be posted by Midland Bank, Malvern, first class to reach Barclays Bank, Worcester on Day 4.

- the bank which takes the cheque in over its counter and credits its customer's account is known as the *collecting bank*

- the bank on which the cheque is drawn (which debits its customer's account) is known as the *paying bank*

As the clearing handles a huge quantity of cheques each day, it is highly automated with cheque sorting and listing equipment. The magnetic encoding across the bottom of each cheque enables much of the processing to be done automatically.

We will now examine the role of the paying bank and the collecting bank in more detail. It is important that you appreciate these points because when you are either a cashier accepting a cheque over the counter (as collecting bank) or examining the morning's clearing (as paying bank), it will enable you to understand the various checks and procedures involved. Before reading further, if you are at all unsure about the definition of a cheque, you are recommended to re-read Chapter 3.3 (pages 18 - 20) as revision.

9.3 Obligations of the Paying Bank

When a cheque is presented for payment to the paying bank, either through the clearings (the normal procedure for crossed cheques), or over the counter (if it is an open cheque being cashed by the payee or a crossed cheque by the account holder), the bank must honour the cheque provided that:

- the customer has sufficient funds or overdraft limit
- the cheque is technically in order
- there is no legal bar to payment

If any of these conditions is not fulfilled, the bank should return the cheque to the collecting bank by first-class post, with the reason for return written in red across the top left-hand side of the cheque. The collecting bank will then normally debit its customer's account and forward the cheque to the customer. In the sections below are set out the reasons for non-payment and the appropriate answer written on the cheque by the paying bank.

Does the customer have sufficient funds or an overdraft limit?

Situation	Answer on cheque
No funds or hope of funds	*Refer to Drawer* or *RD*. The cheque will be returned to the payee, who will contact the drawer.
No funds at present, but a chance of funds, e.g. salary due shortly	*Refer to Drawer Please Represent* or *RDPR*. The cheque will be returned to the collecting bank and sent through the clearing again.

Note that a paying bank could be taken to court for libel if it returned a cheque for lack of funds in error, e.g. if it failed to pay a salary into a customer's account.

Is the cheque technically in order?

A bank can return a cheque if it is not correctly drawn (except if it is issued in conjunction with a cheque card). The following list explains what is meant by 'technical irregularities' and, as above, gives the answer written on the cheque when it is returned.

Situation	Answer on cheque
Not signed by drawer	*Drawer's signature required.* The signature must be present, even if a cheque card has been used to guarantee the cheque.
Date	*Postdated cheque.* A cheque dated in the future must be returned.
	Out of date. A cheque more than 6 months old is said to be 'stale' and must be returned.
	Note: if the cheque is undated, the paying bank can insert the date.
Payee's name missing	*Payee's name required.* If the payee's name is missing, the cheque must be returned; otherwise the bank will not know if it has paid the right person.
Crossing	A bank must pay a cheque to the bank named in the crossing or crossing stamp. If, for instance, a cheque has gone through the clearing twice and has the crossing stamps of two different banks on it, the cheque should be returned *Cheque crossed to two banks.* Of course, if a cheque is not crossed it can be paid to the payee over the counter. For further details of crossings, see the next section (pages 103 to 106).
Alterations	Alterations must be signed (or initialled) by the drawer, otherwise the cheque should be returned *Alteration requires drawer's confirmation.*
Mutilation	A mutilated cheque is one that is badly damaged or torn, even if it has subsequently been repaired. It should be returned *Mutilated cheque.* Occasionally, if the payee has damaged the cheque (e.g. slit it in half when opening the post), the collecting bank will stamp and sign the reverse of the cheque accepting responsibility; in this case the cheque can be paid.
Words and figures differ	If the amount in words and figures differs, the cheque should be returned *Words and figures differ,* as otherwise the bank will not know if it is paying the correct amount.

Is there a legal bar to payment?
In certain circumstances a bank *cannot* for legal reasons pay its customers' cheques.

Situation
Stopped cheque

Answer on cheque
Payment countermanded by order of drawer, when written instructions are received. If the customer telephones instructions, the words *awaiting confirmation* should also be added.

It is essential that the customer:
* quotes the correct cheque number
* effectively communicates the instructions to the paying bank

Death of the customer

The bank should return the cheque *Drawer deceased* once it has notice of the death.

Bankruptcy of customer

The bank should return any cheques *Drawer involved in bankruptcy proceedings* once it has notice of a bankruptcy petition.

As you will appreciate, it is the *notice* to the bank which is crucial in all these cases.

The paying bank: forgeries and protections
The paying bank sometimes faces the danger of debiting its customer's account when either:

* the customer's signature is forged (if the chequebook has been stolen) *or*
* the cheque has been correctly issued but then stolen and paid in by the thief, so that the paying bank is paying the wrong person.

The principal danger is that of *conversion:* depriving the rightful owner of their property. The law has certain protections for the paying bank.

Forged drawer's signature
In these circumstances, the paying bank has no right to debit its customer's account. Banks lose a great deal of money each year because of stolen cheque books and cheque cards. The only protection for the paying bank is if the customer *knew* about the forgeries, but did not inform the bank. *Case: Greenwood v Martins Bank [1932].*

Cheque stolen from payee
If a cheque were stolen from the payee and the thief obtained payment from the paying bank, the paying bank would be protected from the claims of the true owner (payee) in the case of:

A forged endorsement

If the thief forged the payee's endorsement, the bank is protected by section 60 of the Bills of Exchange Act 1882 (all cheques) and section 80 of the Bills of Exchange Act 1882 (crossed cheques), as long as it acted

* in good faith (s.60 and s.80)
* in the ordinary course of business (s.60 only)
* without negligence and according to the crossing (s.80 only).

In short, it will not have to repay the payee if these conditions are met.

A missing endorsement

If the thief managed to pay the cheque in without an endorsement, the paying bank is protected by section 1 of the Cheques Act 1957, as long as it acted

• in good faith
• in the ordinary course of business

Again, it will not have to repay the payee if these conditions are met.

The term 'in good faith' means 'honestly' (it is presumed that banks are honest!) and 'in the ordinary course of business' means precisely what it says - in the normal clearings for crossed cheques, and in normal opening hours for open cheques paid over the counter.

These protections are very useful for a paying bank which pays thousands of cheques daily and cannot in fairness be required to check the authenticity of every endorsement or realise when one is missing. If a bank on the other hand, pays a cheque with technical irregularities, it has no protection in law. It should be noted though that, with the high volume of cheques presented for payment each day, most banks physically inspect only those cheques above a certain amount. Nevertheless, the legal responsibility remains with the bank and, if a cheque is paid in error, it will be liable.

9.4   The Role of the Collecting Bank

Obligations of the collecting bank: avoiding conversion

The collecting bank is the bank accepting a cheque for the credit of its customer's account. The collecting bank should ensure that a cheque being paid in for the credit of an account rightfully belongs to that account holder. If the bank fails in this obligation, for instance by accepting a stolen cheque for its customer's account, it is guilty of *conversion,* i.e. depriving the true owner of their property. There are certain protections given to the bank by the Cheques Act 1957 which we will discuss below, but first we will look at the details on a cheque that a cashier should examine when accepting it over the counter. These comprise:

• endorsements
• crossings
• technical details

Endorsements

An endorsement is used to transfer a cheque to another person. The *payee* or person transferring the cheque signs the cheque on the back, so endorsing it. We have seen already in Chapter 3.3 that there are three types of endorsement:

• *blank endorsement* - the signature of the *payee* (this makes it a bearer cheque, and it can be paid into any account)

• *specific endorsement* - 'pay X', followed by the signature of the *payee* (this means it can be paid into X's account)

• *restrictive endorsement* - 'pay X only', followed by the signature of the *payee* (this means it can only be paid into X's account)

The most common form of endorsement is the normal signature of the endorser, followed, if required, by courtesy titles, such as Mr., Mrs., Ms., Dr., etc. For example, if the payee is endorsing the cheque:

Payee	*Endorsement*
Mrs. A. Green	Normal signature, e.g. 'A. Green', 'A.B. Green', or 'Alice Green', followed by a courtesy title, if wished, e.g. 'A. Green (Mrs.)'
Dr. J. Jones	Normal signature, e.g. 'J. Jones', or 'Julian Jones' followed by the courtesy title, if wished, e.g. 'J. Jones (Dr.)'

If a cheque is payable to a wife, but is made out using her husband's initials or Christian name, she should endorse the cheque with her usual signature, adding the words 'wife of . . .' For example:

Mrs. John Smith	Normal signature, e.g. 'Jane Smith', followed by 'wife of John Smith'

If a cheque is payable to a husband *and* wife, and the wife wishes to pay it into her sole account, she must obtain her husband's endorsement before paying it in (and vice versa). For example:

Mr. & Mrs. P. Robinson	'P. Robinson (Mr.)'

In short, endorsements should be checked carefully by the collecting bank to ensure that the correct person is receiving the money. If, in the last case quoted above, the wife had paid joint money into her account *without* her husband's endorsement, the husband could bring a claim of *conversion* against the bank because it would have deprived him of his money.

You should note that some cheques have an 'R' printed on their face. These require the payee's signature (**R**eceipt) on the reverse before they can be paid. This is not strictly speaking an endorsement; it is a receipt for the amount of the cheque.

Crossings

A crossed cheque is a cheque with two parallel lines on its face. A crossed cheque must be paid into a bank account, the only exception being when it is cashed by the account holder or authorised representative.

A collecting bank must check the crossing of any cheque paid in, because certain crossings contain wording which restricts the way in which they can be paid in.

Types of crossings

There are two main types of crossings on cheques:

• general crossing
• special crossing

General crossing

Two parallel lines drawn across the face of the cheque, with or without the words 'and company', 'and co.', 'not negotiable', 'account payee'.

Examples of general crossings:

The effect of all these general crossings is that the cheque must be paid into a bank account. The words 'and company' have no legal significance, dating back to the times when the names of banks ended with the words 'and co.' 'Not negotiable' and 'account payee' have a special significance, and are described below.

Special crossing

The name of a bank (with or without branch details) written or stamped between parallel lines *or* written or stamped without parallel lines. A branch crossing stamp is an example of a special crossing. Other phrases can also be included in a special crossing:

The effect of a special crossing is that the cheque must be paid into an account with the bank (but not necessarily the branch) named on the special crossing. It is also an instruction to the *paying bank* (see Section 9.3) to make payment for the cheque only to the bank named in the crossing.

Note that the branch crossing stamp, besides crossing the cheque specially, helps to identify the bank from which the cheque was received if the cheque is to be returned unpaid by the drawee bank.

'Not negotiable' and 'account payee' crossings

A general or special crossing can include the words 'not negotiable' and/or 'account payee'.

Not negotiable

These words mean that no-one can get a better title (right to the cheque) than the person they got it from. Therefore, no-one can obtain a perfect title after a cheque has been stolen (see fig. 9.2). Contrast this with a cheque which does not have the words 'not negotiable' in the crossing: here the cheque is fully negotiable, i.e. if a person accepts the cheque in good faith and gives value (e.g. money) for it, he or she has a legal right to the cheque and can sue all parties to the cheque for payment, even if it has been stolen, and the cheque stopped by the drawer.

Important note: a 'not negotiable' crossing does *not* mean that a cheque cannot be transferred to a person other than the payee; it can be transferred by endorsement, in the usual way, and can therefore be paid into a bank account other than that of the payee.

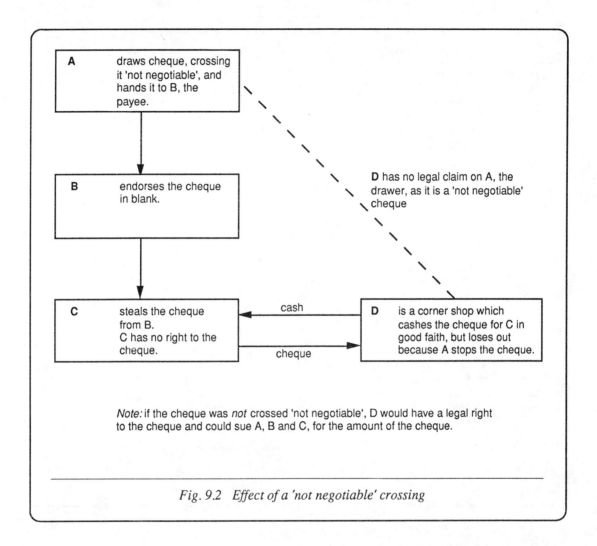

Fig. 9.2 *Effect of a 'not negotiable' crossing*

Account payee

These words written in the crossing are an instruction to the collecting bank that the cheque should be paid only into the account of the payee. If it is accepted for the credit of another account, the bank can be liable for loss if the account holder is not the true owner of the cheque: the bank will be guilty of *conversion*. In practice, a bank might accept such a cheque if it is for a small amount after making enquiries from the account holder, or the drawer, as to why it is not being paid into the account of the payee. *Note:* the wording 'account payee only' has the same significance as 'account payee'.

Fig. 9.3, on the next page, summarises the decisions taken by a collecting bank cashier when presented with cheques including an 'account payee' crossed cheque.

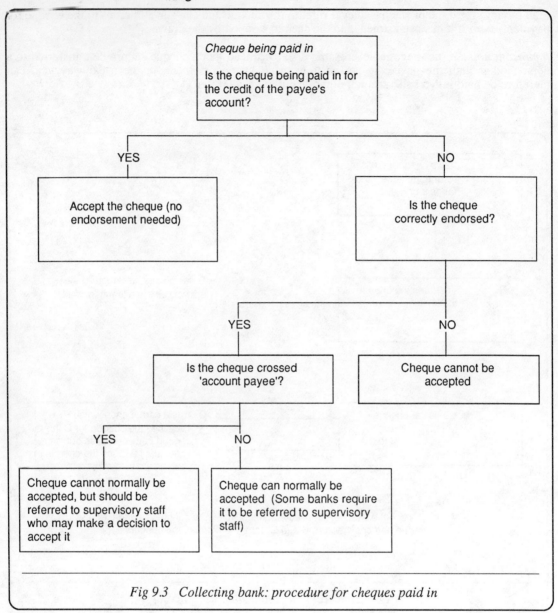

Fig 9.3   Collecting bank: procedure for cheques paid in

Future developments with crossings

It seems only a matter of time before the complex issue of crossings on cheques is simplified. The Jack Committee Report (1989) on Banking Services, Law and Practice (see Chapter 16.5) has recommended that the crossing 'rules' should be simplified and that only one crossing will be recognised, with the meaning 'not negotiable'.

Technical details to be checked by the collecting bank

A collecting bank will normally check the same details as a paying bank *must* check, i.e.

- signature of drawer must be present
- the date must be in order, i.e. not postdated or out of date; if it is not present the payee or bank can insert it

- the payee's name must be present
- alterations must be signed or initialled by the drawer
- if a cheque is mutilated and the bank is willing to accept it, the bank must stamp and sign it on the reverse and give the reason for mutilation
- if words and figures differ, the collecting bank *may* accept it, but only if the amount in words is the lower amount, in which case the collecting bank will write 'we claim £x' (the lower amount) on the cheque.

The collecting bank: protection against conversion

A collecting bank may be faced with a situation whereby a fraudster, who holds an account at that bank, has stolen a cheque made payable to another person, forged that person's endorsement and paid it in at the collecting bank. What if the payee discovers the theft and claims the money from the collecting bank, claiming *conversion*? The law is quite clear on this point: the Cheques Act 1957, section 4, states that a bank which:

- credits its customer with the value of a cheque
- acts in good faith (i.e. honestly)
- acts without negligence

cannot be liable to the owner and will not have to recompense that person. Obviously, the meaning of the word 'negligence' is crucial. Negligence includes:

- not opening the account correctly (e.g. not obtaining references) - see Chapter 7.1.
- not taking care when accepting the cheque (e.g. taking an 'account payee' crossed cheque for an account other than the payee's without enquiry).

This is why cashiers and staff who open accounts must exercise care when carrying out their duties. If they do not, they could lose the bank money.

9.5 Alternative Methods for Clearing Cheques

So far in this chapter, we have concentrated on the general cheque clearing, through which the majority of cheques pass. Two alternative methods for clearing cheques are:

- Town clearing
- special presentations

Town clearing

This is a fast system for clearing high value cheques paid in and drawn on banks in the City of London. The Town clearing is restricted to

- bank branches in the City of London which have a letter 'T' after the sort code number
- cheques paid in at, and drawn on, a Town clearing bank which are for £10,000 or more

Cheques which are to pass through the Town clearing are taken by messenger to the Central Clearing House before 3.45 p.m. Then they are taken to the branches on which they are drawn. If a cheque is unpaid, it must be returned to the presenting bank by 4.30 p.m.

The Town clearing serves the banks, insurance companies and other financial institutions which operate in the City of London and provides them with a speedy clearing system for high value items.

Special presentations

An alternative speedy clearing system is available for all cheques: a bank customer paying in a cheque at the collecting bank can request a *special presentation*. This involves the collecting bank in one of two actions

- the cheque is sent direct to the drawee bank by first class post, and a telephone call is made next morning by the collecting bank to discover if the cheque is paid

- if the cheque is drawn on another bank in the same locality, it is taken by a member of staff and, if paid, is exchanged for a bankers' payment.

A charge is made for special presentation of cheques. Once the drawee bank confirms that the cheque is paid, it cannot be stopped by the drawer.

9.6   Bank Giro Credits and the Credit Clearing

Bank giro credits (BGCs) - or *credit transfers,* as they are often called - enable a person to pay money into someone else's bank account. The bank giro credit system is particularly useful for:

- paying bills such as gas, electricity, telephone, community charge, subscriptions, etc., and often the bill will have a credit form preprinted on it (see fig. 9.4)
- employers making wage and salary payments
- banks making manual standing order payments on behalf of customers

The first example of these - paying bills - is a paper-based system and is passed through the credit clearing (see below). The other examples - wages and salaries, and standing order payments - can also be paid electronically by putting the details on a computer disc or tape and passing them through Bankers' Automated Clearing Services (BACS), which is the electronic bulk clearing (see Chapter 10.1).

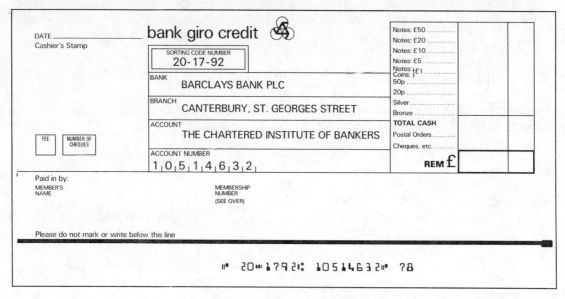

Fig. 9.4   A pre-printed giro credit form

Credit clearing

The credit clearing handles paper-based bank giro credits that are paid in at bank branches in much the same way as the cheque clearing. Like cheques, credits may be inter-branch or inter-bank: both are sent by the receiving branch to the bank's clearing department at head office. They are then sorted, with inter-branch items being dispatched to the branch of the payee; inter-bank items are

placed in bundles for each bank and taken to the Central Clearing over to the different banks and settlement is made, e.g.

Lloyds Bank £25 million of credits for Nation
National Westminster Bank £20 million of credits for Lloyds
settlement £5 million paid by Lloyds to Na

The credit clearing takes three working days and, with the use of standar encoded, the sorting and listing procedures are highly automated.

9.7 Clearing Credit Card and Debit Card Transac....s

Transactions involving credit cards and debit cards are processed by retailers and other merchants, either by means of an imprinter machine (paper-based transactions), or by means of a 'swipe' machine attached to a computer-linked till (electronic transactions). The latter is an EFTPOS (Electronic Funds Transfer at Point of Sale) transaction - see Chapter 10.3 - and the debit to the buyer's credit card account or bank account is made automatically.

Paper-based transactions are handled as follows:

- the retailer pays in to the bank, using a separate credit, copies of the vouchers signed by cardholders, and a summary listing those copies
- the bank credits the retailer's bank account with the total of the credit
- the vouchers are passed through a central clearing and are received by the credit card company, or the bank in the case of debit cards
- each voucher is debited to the cardholder's credit card account, or debited by BACS to the bank account (debit cards)
- a direct debit is passed via BACS to the retailer's bank account by the card company in respect of commission charged on the transactions (generally between 2 per cent and 5 per cent of the sales value)

9.8 Revision Points

❑ The banks' clearing system is under the control of the Association for Payment Clearing Services (APACS). The separate clearing companies are:
  - *Cheque and Credit Clearing Co. Ltd.,* which deals with the paper bulk clearing of cheques and credits
  - *CHAPS and Town Clearing Co. Ltd.,* which deals with the high value clearing
  - *BACS Ltd.,* which deals with the electronic bulk clearing of credits and direct debits
  - *Eft-Pos UK Ltd.,* which supervises the development of EFTPOS

❑ Girobank operates its own clearing system for transfers between accounts effected mainly through post offices.

❑ The general cheque clearing features a three working days' clearance period, via the Central Clearing House in London.

❑ The *collecting bank* is the bank which takes a cheque over its counter for the credit of its customer's account, or the credit of an account at another branch. The *paying bank* is the bank on which a cheque is drawn.

A bank must honour its customer's cheque provided that:

- customer has sufficient funds or overdraft limit
- cheque is technically in order
- there is no legal bar to payment

The paying bank will check the following technical points:

- drawer's signature
- date
- payee's name
- crossing
- alterations
- mutilations
- words and figures

❑ Legal bars to payment are:

- stopped cheque
- death of the customer
- bankruptcy of customer

❑ If a cheque is to be returned to the collecting bank, the appropriate reason should be written on the cheque, which is then posted by first class mail direct to the collecting bank.

❑ The principal danger for the paying bank is that of *conversion,* i.e. depriving the rightful owner of property. Protections for the paying bank are:

- in the case of a *forged drawer's signature,* that the customer knew about the forgeries but did not inform the bank, otherwise there is no protection

- in the case of a *cheque stolen from the payee* with a forged endorsement

  - if the cheque is open *or* crossed, that the bank acted in good faith and in the ordinary course of business (section 60 of the Bills of Exchange Act 1882)

  - if the cheque is crossed (not open), that the bank paid the cheque in good faith, without negligence and in accordance with the crossing (section 80 of the Bills of Exchange Act 1882)

- in the case of a *cheque stolen from the payee,* with a missing endorsement, that the bank acted in good faith, and in the ordinary course of business (section 1 of the Cheques Act 1957)

❑ The collecting bank should examine:

- endorsements
- crossings
- technical details

❑ Endorsements are checked by the collecting bank to ensure that the correct person is receiving the money.

❑ The two main types of crossing are:

- general crossing
- special crossing

Each of these crossings can include the words 'not negotiable' and/or 'account payee'

❑ 'Not negotiable' means that no-one can get a better title (right to the cheque) than the person they got it from; it can be paid into an account other than the payee's.

❑ 'Account payee' is an instruction to the collecting bank that the cheque should be paid only into the account of the payee.

❏ The collecting bank will check the following technical points:

- cheque signed
- date
- payee's name
- alterations
- mulilations
- words and figures

❏ The collecting bank is protected from claims of conversion by section 4 of the Cheques Act 1957 when it credits its customer with the value of the cheque, provided that it:

- acts in good faith (i.e. honestly)
- acts without negligence (when opening or running the account)

❏ The Town clearing provides same day settlement for:

- bank branches in the City of London
- cheques of £10,000 or more

❏ Special presentation is where a cheque is:

- sent direct to the paying bank by the collecting bank
- taken to the paying bank by a member of staff of the collecting bank (both banks being in the same locality)

❏ Credit clearing deals with paper-based bank giro credits

❏ Credit card and debit card paper-based transactions are paid in by retailers to their bank, are cleared centrally, and the retailer's bank account is credited with the amount.

9.9 Know your *Funds Transfer: Paper Systems*

Multiple-choice Questions

Choose the *one* answer you think is correct.

1. A cheque dated seven months ago is

   A a post-dated cheque
   B an out-of-date cheque
   C legal tender
   D not negotiable

2. Which one of the following words does *not* describe a type of endorsement?

   A Blank
   B Specific
   C General
   D Restrictive

3. Which one of the following is an incorrect endorsement of a cheque under English law?

   A Payee Dr J Brown endorsed James Brown Dr
   B Payee Dr J Brown endorsed Dr James Brown
   C Payee Mrs Alice Jones endorsed A Jones
   D Payee Mrs Alice Jones endorsed Alice Jones

4.   A cheque payable to H. Sanderson is endorsed by her 'pay S. Green only'. What type of endorsement is this?

   A Blank
   B General
   C Restrictive
   D Specific

5.   A special crossing consists of

   A two parallel lines
   B two parallel lines with 'Account J Smith'
   C the name of a bank across the cheque
   D the words 'not negotiable'

6.   'Not negotiable' means

   A the cheque cannot be transferred
   B the cheque cannot be endorsed
   C the cheque must be paid into the account of the payee
   D the holder cannot receive better rights than the person from whom it was received

7.   Town clearing deals with cheques of more than what amount?

   A £1,000
   B £10,000
   C £50,000
   D £100,000

Short Answer Questions

8.   What does APACS stand for?

9.   In a day's general cheque clearing National Westminster Bank has £75m of cheques drawn on Lloyds; at the same time, Lloyds has £65m of cheques drawn on National Westminster. Which bank will make a settlement payment.

10.   What are the *three* circumstances under which a paying bank must honour a cheque?

11.   State *three* points to be considered concerning the date of a cheque.

12.   You want to return a cheque because there are insufficient funds. What would you write on the cheque?

13.   What reply would be given by the drawee bank when returning a stopped cheque?

14.   What are the main Acts of Parliament that protect the paying bank?

15.   Define conversion (no more than 18 words).

16.   State *three* of the types of endorsement.

17.   What does an 'R' mean on the face of a cheque?

18.   Complete the following sentence:
       'Account Payee' is an instruction to the .... banker.

9.10 Essay questions *Funds Transfer: Paper Systems*

1. (a) Give the definition of a cheque.

    [6 marks]

    (b) The role of the paying bank is to debit cheques to a customer's account.

    When must the paying bank honour and when should it not pay customers' cheques?

    [10 marks]

    List the factors that should be scrutinised to ensure that cheques are paid correctly.

    [4 marks]

    [question 7, Autumn 1988]

2. What advice would you give to a cashier in the following situation?

    An open cheque for £250, drawn by your customer J Bloggs and payable to C Farnsbarnes, has been presented for payment in cash. The cashier tells you that the cheque was endorsed C Farnsbarnes in her presence, but she feels nervous about cashing it as the presenter is unknown to her.

    [The Chartered Institute of Bankers' specimen paper]

3. (a) What is the practical effect of crossing a cheque?

    (b) Explain the types of crossing that appear on cheques.

    (c) What is the effect of adding the words 'account payee' to a crossed cheque?

    [question 25, Spring 1987]

4. Define what is meant by the *crossing* and *endorsement* of cheques and explain why they are so important.

    Give examples of particular types of crossings and endorsements, stating in each case whether they apply to the paying or to the collecting banker.

    [question 5, Spring 1989]

5. (a) Define a collecting banker and state his main duty.

    [6 marks]

    (b) What features on this cheque should be considered by the collecting banker?

    [14 marks]

    [question 5, Spring 1988]

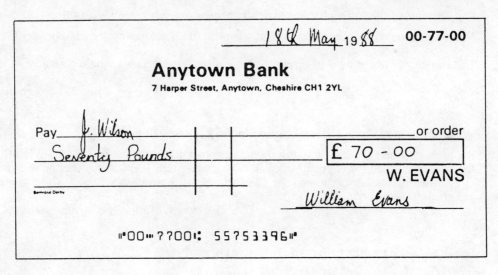

18th May 19 88   00-77-00

Anytown Bank

7 Harper Street, Anytown, Cheshire CH1 2YL

Pay___J. Wilson_____ or order

Seventy Pounds   £ 70 - 00

Bemrose Derby   W. EVANS

                                                    William Evans

⑈00⑈7700⑈: 55753396⑈⑈

J. Wilson

Chapter Ten
Funds Transfer: Electronic Systems

In the previous chapter we looked at paper-based methods of funds transfer. Banks, in order to cut costs, are trying to reduce the daily movement of paper in and out of the Central Clearing House in the City of London. The past few years have seen the development of electronic systems, using computers, to make payments. In this chapter we will consider:

- BACS Ltd. and the electronic bulk clearing
- the CHAPS system for dealing with the high value clearing
- EFTPOS (Electronic Funds Transfer at Point of Sale)
- ATMs (Automated Teller Machines)
- the use of truncation for cheques and bank giro credits
- home banking

10.1 Bankers' Automated Clearing Services (BACS)

BACS Ltd. is the company which operates Bankers' Automated Clearing Services under the supervision of APACS (Association for Payment Clearing Services). Besides the London and Scottish Clearing Banks, a number of building societies are members of BACS Ltd.

The clearing handles electronic funds transfers, for:

- standing orders
- direct debits
- salary credits
- other credits, such as traders settling amounts due

Standing orders are used where a customer has regular payments to make for fixed amounts, e.g. mortgage payment, hire purchase payments. The bank is given written instructions to debit the amount from the customer's account and to send the money amount to the beneficiary.

Direct debits are also used for regular payments such as insurance premiums, mortgage payments, rates, gas, electricity and water bills, etc. They differ from standing orders in two ways:

- they can be used for either fixed or variable amounts and/or where the time intervals between payments vary
- it is the business that is to receive the payment that prepares the debit to the payer's account and this is passed through the banking system to be taken out of his or her account

Certain safeguards protect the payer against irregular use of the direct debit system (see next page).

Operating the BACS system

The BACS system is used by banks themselves and by customers (who have to be sponsored by a bank in order to be able to obtain authorisation to use the system). The user prepares details of the transactions, i.e. sort code number, account number, account name, amount, reference number. The details are sent to BACS at the computer centre in Edgware, Middlesex in the form of a computer disc or tape, or transmitted by telephone link using the BACSTEL service. At BACS the information is read by computer and validated. The entries are then sorted electronically into the various banks for which they are intended. The entries are then placed on magnetic tapes, one for each bank, which are then passed to the bank. The tapes are run into each bank's own computer system and the funds transfers involved are made. The three-day processing cycle of BACS is described in more detail in fig. 10.1.

Advantages of using BACS for credits

The main advantages to a business customer using BACS for credits (standing orders, salary payments, other credits) are:

Reduced clerical costs
Paperwork is less - there are no cheques or paper vouchers to prepare.

Lower bank charges
Most banks make a lower charge for electronic transfers than paper-based entries.

Cash flow benefits
The debit and credit transactions take place on the same day with the payer having control over the date of payment.

Interest saved
Where payments are being made, e.g. for wages and salaries, the debit to the payer's account is not made until the same day as the credit is applied to the payee's account. Compared with the paper-based bank giro credit system, where there is a period of three working days between funds being debited to the payer's account and being credited to the payee's account, there will be a saving in overdraft interest because the payer pays later and has to borrow for a shorter period of time.

Increased security
BACS offers a much more secure method of payment for wages than payment in cash.

The banks use the BACS system for their own payments, such as standing orders, because it reduces the volume of paper in the clearing system. Payments are cheaper to prepare and reduce the workload on the staff.

Advantages of using BACS for direct debits

A business customer, using direct debits for collecting payments, makes savings in administration - it prepares the debits to payer's accounts, instead of having to wait for standing order payments to be received through the clearing system. Any direct debits which cannot be paid are returned quickly, and steps can then be taken to chase up the debt. Variable amount direct debits (VADD) are particularly useful to organisations which are likely to be collecting differing payment amounts, such as insurance premiums, annual subscriptions, mortgage payments.

With direct debits, there are safeguards to protect the payer against irregular use of the system:

- only organizations approved by banks are allowed to operate it

- direct debits must be made strictly in line with the payer's instructions

- any changes in the amount or date of payment for variable amount direct debits must be advised to the payer beforehand

- if an incorrect direct debit is made, the organisation must reimburse both bank and payer

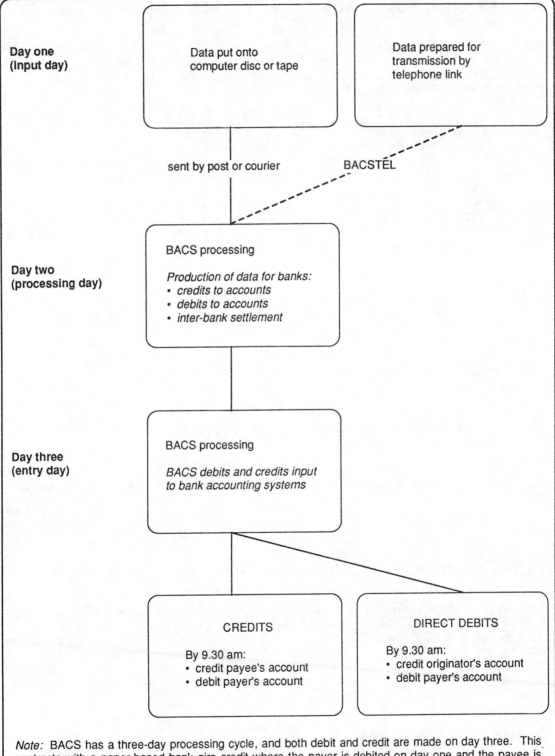

Fig. 10.1 The BACS three-day processing cycle

10.2   Clearing House Automated Payments System (CHAPS)

The CHAPS system is a high value payment clearing system operated electronically. Members of CHAPS are the major London and Scottish Clearing Banks and they provide a 'gateway' into the computer clearing system for their customers, and other banks. The system is available for payments of £7,000 or more (£5,000 or more from February 1990).

Operating the CHAPS system

Payments can be put into the computer system only by a *settlement bank,* i.e. one of the members of CHAPS. A customer wishing to make a payment must, therefore, approach his or her bank. Also, non-settlement banks must route transactions through a settlement bank.

Each settlement bank is able to transmit payments of £7,000 or more (£5,000 or more from February 1990) to the computer systems of other settlement banks who will credit the payee's account that day. Once accepted into the system, payments cannot be stopped and, so, the funds are guaranteed as being cleared and can be used by the payee immediately.

The CHAPS system is widely used for making guaranteed payments and, to some extent, it has taken over from the Town clearing (see chapter 9.5). However, it is used between bank branches throughout the United Kingdom (unlike the Town clearing which is restricted to banks in the City of London). A good example of the use of CHAPS is where solicitors wish to make payment for houses - a guaranteed, speedy means of payment is essential.

Advantages of using CHAPS

The main advantages to a bank customer using CHAPS are:

Same-day transfers
The payee's bank account is credited on the same day as the payer instructs the settlement bank to make the transfer.

Cleared funds
The payment cannot be stopped, once accepted into the system, and so the funds are cleared when received by the payee.

10.3   Electronic Funds Transfer at Point of Sale (EFTPOS)

EFTPOS is a step towards the 'cashless society', where there will be no need to carry around larger sums of money and only small change will be needed. It is a system which allows a retail outlet, using an electronic till, to debit the bank account or credit card account of the purchaser at point of sale and, at the same time, to credit the retailer's bank account. Besides reducing the need to carry so much cash, the system cuts down the paperwork of writing out cheques or filling in credit card vouchers. Examples of bank EFTPOS schemes are 'Connect' and 'Switch'. Schemes operated by credit card companies include Barclaycard's 'PDQ', and Access' 'ACCEPT'.

Operating the EFTPOS system

EFTPOS is operated by means of plastic cards - either *debit cards* issued by banks and building societies, or by credit cards. When goods are to be paid for using this method, the retailer 'swipes' the card through a card 'reader'. The amount to be paid is entered into a computer-linked checkout till. The till prints a sales slip which is signed by the customer to authenticate the transaction; the retailer checks that the signature on the sales slip is the same as that shown on the card.

Alternatively, the transaction can be authenticated by the customer keying in his or her PIN (Personal Identification Number) on a key pad. Details of the transaction are transmitted electronically by means of a computer link to a central computer. The cost of the goods being purchased is checked against the cardholder's bank or building society account, or the available credit in the credit card account. If the transaction is authorised, the customer's account is debited and the retailer's account is credited with the appropriate amount. (Some EFTPOS systems work 'off-line' and are not connected directly to a central computer. Instead, at the end of the day, all the data for the day's transactions is transmitted by a telecommunications link into the bank's computer system, or a magnetic computer disc or tape can be sent to the bank. With this type of system, not all transactions are guaranteed to be paid: higher value items can be returned unpaid by the payer's bank.)

It is only within the last year that EFTPOS systems have been developed on a nationwide basis and, as yet, the system is still in its early days. It is certain to be used increasingly in the future in place of cash and cheque transactions. Developments in card technology are also moving forward - the latest generation of cards, known as *smart cards* (see Chapter 16.9), incorporate a microchip which stores information about the cardholder and his/her account.

Advantages of using EFTPOS

To the customer:
* a convenient way of paying for goods and services
* there is no need to write out a cheque
* goods and services can be bought for any value, subject to the purchaser having sufficient money in his or her bank account

In early EFTPOS schemes, purchasers were reluctant to have their accounts debited instantaneously, so now bank schemes allow a three-day 'clearance' period, similar to cheques.

To the retailer:
* greater efficiency - customers take less time to make payment
* reduced queuing time
* less cash to handle (giving fewer security risks)
* guaranteed payment of lower value transactions once acceptance has been made (but higher value transactions can be returned unpaid by the payer's bank)

After some initial reluctance from retailers concerning who was to pay for the expensive computer-linked tills, EFTPOS has been accepted rapidly by most major retailers. Recent developments include machines at large railway stations to enable travellers to buy tickets and have the cost debited to a bank account or credit card account.

10.4 Automated Teller Machines (ATMs)

For the personal customer, ATMs probably represent the most noticeable change in current account services over the last ten years. Most bank branches now have an ATM installed either outside the premises, or in a card-access lobby, open up to 24 hours a day and seven days a week. A number of 'stand-alone' machines have been installed away from the branch premises, such as in shops or at railway stations. The building societies, too, have developed ATM services.

An ATM operates by the user inserting his or her ATM card (or *cash card,* as they are often known) into the machine, and keying in his or her Personal Identification Number (PIN). This action enables the machine, which is linked to the bank's computer, to 'look up' the account and carry out certain transactions on the instructions of the user operating the machine's keyboard in conjunction with the visual display screen.

The main functions of ATMs are:

- cash withdrawal (the customer keys in the amount required)
- balance enquiries
- statement requests (some ATMs can print the last ten transactions on the account in the form of a mini-statement)
- cheque book requests
- acceptance of deposits of cash and/or cheques for the customer's account (not all machines have this facility)
- carrying out payment of bills (not all machines have this facility)

ATM cards are issued to current account and deposit account holders (cheque book requests and payment of bills are not available to the latter).

The disadvantage of multi-function ATMs is that they are relatively slow to use. To overcome this problem, some banks have installed rapid cash machines which can dispense fixed amounts of money, e.g. £50 or £100 in about fifteen seconds. These machines are usually located inside the bank branch, or in a card-access lobby.

Over the last few years, a number of shared ATM networks have been built up so that a card issued by one bank will operate the machines of another. Shared networks are:

- Midland, National Westminster, TSB, Clydesdale
- Barclays, Lloyds, The Royal Bank of Scotland, Bank of Scotland
- *Link* - Co-op bank, Girobank, plus various building societies
- *Matrix* - a building society network

As a method of funds transfer, ATMs save the customer having to write out a cheque for a cash withdrawal and, where the service is available, enable the payment of bills. Thus, ATMs offer an electronic method of funds transfer.

10.5 Truncation

Truncation is the process whereby the flow of paper is stopped as it enters the banking system and moves no further than the branch where a cheque is cashed or a bank giro credit is paid in. At present truncation is used by some banks on an inter-branch basis for

- cheques which have been cashed under a cheque card agreement*
- bank giro credits for accounts held at other branches of the bank

(* Note: there is no real need for cheques cashed under a cheque card agreement by a branch of the bank to be passed through the clearing system to the account-holding branch: such cheques cannot be stopped by the drawer, who has already received cash.)

Details of these items are input to the bank's computer system by the branch which takes in the cheque or credit, so that the debit or credit to the customer's account at the account-holding branch can be made automatically.

It seems only a matter of time before truncation is used more widely on an inter-bank basis: links between banks' computer systems already exist. They need to be developed further in order to reduce the need for paper-based clearing systems. The Jack Committee (see Chapter 16.5) has recommended that the use of truncation should be developed.

10.6   Home Banking

This is an electronic funds transfer system which the customer uses from home, sending instructions to the bank's computer either by using the 'tones' of a telephone keypad, or by speaking direct to a voice recognition computer. Home banking is discussed more generally in Chapter 11.12 but, for funds transfer, it offers:

- transfers between customer's accounts, e.g. from current to deposit account
- payment of bills for pre-arranged payees, e.g. credit card, gas, etc.

All transfers can be either immediate, or instructions can be given to make payment at a date in the future. For payment of bills, the customer has to complete an authorisation form for each beneficiary, which is lodged with the bank. The authorisation form requires details of the payee and his/her bank account details. Each authorisation is numbered and it is this reference number that is keyed in using the tones of the keypad, followed by the amount that is to be transferred.

A similar service to home banking is offered to business customers and operates through an office computer as a *cash management service*. It can be used for payment of wages and salaries, and for paying suppliers. With this service a telephone link is established with the bank's central computer, and the details of the customer's bank account appear on the computer screen. Transactions can then be effected by means of the computer keyboard.

10.7   Revision points

❏ Electronic systems of funds transfer include:

- BACS, the electronic bulk clearing
- CHAPS, the high value clearing
- EFTPOS, electronic funds transfer at point of sale
- ATMs, automated teller machines
- truncation
- home banking

❏ *Bankers Automated Clearing Services (BACS):*

- electronic funds transfer for credits and direct debits
- input by means of computer discs or tapes, or by BACSTEL
- a three-day payment cycle, with both debit and credit being passed to accounts on day three

❏ *Clearing House Automated Payments System (CHAPS):*

- is a high-value clearing system for payments of £7,000 or more (£5,000 or more from February 1990)
- is operated using the computer networks of the main London and Scottish clearing banks
- provides guaranteed payments
- provides same-day payments

❏ *Electronic Funds Transfer at Point of Sale (EFTPOS):*

- is a computerised system which permits the automatic transfer of funds from buyer to seller at the point of sale
- uses credit cards or debit cards

❑ *Automated Teller Machines (ATMs):*

- provide a range of services which include cash withdrawal, balance enquiries, statement requests, cheque book requests, acceptance of deposits, payment of certain bills
- use a number of shared ATM networks

❑ *Truncation:*

- is the process whereby the flow of paper is stopped as it enters the banking system
- uses the bank's computer system to input debits and credits for other branches
- is at present used on an inter-branch basis for cheques cashed under a cheque card agreement, and bank giro credits
- is likely to develop in the future on an inter-bank basis

❑ *Home banking:*

- uses a telephone to connect with the bank's computer
- provides for transfers between customer's accounts, and payment of certain bills

10.8 Know your *Funds Transfer: Electronic Systems*

Multiple-choice Questions

Choose the *one* answer you think is correct.

1. BACS handles

   A the high value clearing
   B electronic funds transfers for credits and direct debits
   C truncated cheques
   D special presentations

2. Direct debits are

   A originated by the payer's bank and sent through the clearing system to the beneficiary's bank
   B originated by the beneficiary's bank and sent through the clearing system to the payer's bank
   C used for fixed amounts only and for regular payment dates
   D originated by the beneficiary, passed to the bank and sent through the clearing system to the payer's bank

3. CHAPS

   A is a computer system to assist companies to pay bulk salaries
   B is used direct by all major banks and companies
   C deals only with the transfer of large amounts, say £10,000
   D handles credit transfers on behalf of the banks

4. EFTPOS stands for

    A electronic financial transactions for payment of services
    B electronic financial transfer at point of sale
    C electronic funds transfer at point of sale
    D electronic funds transactions for payment of salary

5. Which one of the following services is not provided by ATMs?

    A request for a cheque book
    B cash withdrawal
    C setting up a loan or overdraft
    D statement request

Short Answer Questions

6. What does BACS stand for?

7. You want to pay your insurance premium monthly through your bank account. The premium will vary each year and you do not want the problem of advising the bank of any changes in amounts.

    Which bank service would you use?

8. List *two* safeguards for customers which prevent companies misusing the direct debit system.

9. What does CHAPS stand for?

10. What does PIN stand for?

11. What do SO and DD stand for?

10.9 Essay questions *Funds Transfer: Electronic Systems*

1. 'Moving paper around the banking system is an expensive way of transacting business.' Explain some of the methods and systems that are available to cut down on this movement of paper.

    [question 27, Spring 1987]

2. New employees no longer have the legal right to receive their wages in cash. What methods are open to employers to pay their workers wages and which one would you recommend for large companies?
    Give the benefits associated with your choice.

    [question 7, Autumn 1987]

3.   The manager of the bank branch where you work, Mr Palmer, hands you the following letter
      which has been received this morning:

```
                                                         High Bridge House
                                                         Lower Snodsbury
                                                         Wyvern

          11 August 19-2

          The Manager
          National Bank

          Dear Mr Palmer

          I am concerned about the regular payments made by the bank in respect
          of my National Brittanic accident policy.  Until recently the payments
          were made by standing order and I had to come in each year to increase
          the monthly payment, as the amount covered by the policy increases in
          accordance with the rate of inflation.  Now the company has asked me
          to sign a 'direct debit' authority and they say they will increase the
          amounts automatically.  I am particularly concerned because the form
          they gave me to sign didn't have a money amount indicated.  I really
          don't understand, but I'm sure you could explain it all to me very
          simply.


          Yours sincerely

          Ethel Everard

          Ethel Everard (Miss)
```

The Manager asks you to draft a letter of reply for his approval.

Chapter Eleven
Accounts and Services: Personal Customers

This chapter and the next three chapters look at *bank services* for the personal and the business customer.

Through their various accounts and services, most banks provide four main areas of service:

- *money transfer*   cheque encashment, cheque cards, credit cards, debit cards, smart cards, ATMs, money transmission by standing order and direct debit

- *deposit-taking*   savings and investment

- *advances*   overdrafts, mortgage loans, personal loans, budget accounts, revolving credit (cashflow) accounts, credit cards

- *other services*   safe custody, night safe, foreign services, unit trusts, insurance, investment management, Personal Equity Plans, share dealing, executor and trustee, home banking, bank drafts, estate agency

It is important to be aware of the services offered by banks and, if you work in a bank, the services of your own particular bank. Besides knowing the features of each service, it is important to know the specific group of customers for which each service is aimed, e.g. students, young married couples, elderly people, etc.

This chapter examines the accounts and services offered by banks to personal customers. Chapter 12 considers investments for personal customers; Chapter 13 looks at bank lending to personal customers; Chapter 14 is concerned with the accounts and services offered to business customers.

11.1 Bank Accounts

For personal customers, the main types of accounts offered are:

- current account
- deposit/savings account
- high interest account and term deposits
- personal loans
- budget accounts
- revolving credit (cashflow) accounts
- mortgages

Many customers have more than one account with their bank - e.g. a current account and deposit account, a current account and a personal loan, a current account and a mortgage, etc.

11.2 Current Account

This is the most popular type of account and is used by both personal and business customers. The main features and benefits of this type of account are shown in fig. 11.1.

A current account is easily opened (see Chapter 7.1 for the procedure on opening accounts) and can be for:

- personal customers (usually aged 16 upwards)

    - in a sole name
    - in joint names, e.g. husband and wife, boyfriend and girlfriend, for which a joint account
      mandate must be signed

- business customers

    - in a sole name, perhaps with a trading name, e.g. John Smith trading as Grange Road Stores
    - in the name of a partnership, e.g. Anne Green and Tanya Turner trading as Wyvern Plumbers
    - in the name of a limited company, e.g. Wyvern Hotel Ltd.

- other types of customer, e.g. clubs and societies, local authorities, etc.

For personal customers, current accounts are usually operated by most banks free of charge, provided that the account remains in credit; some types of current account pay interest on credit balances (see below). Current accounts should always be maintained in credit unless overdraft arrangements have been previously made: these arrangements will include an agreed limit on the account beyond which the customer should not go. With overdrawn accounts bank charges are made (on the basis of the bank's published scale of charges) and interest is calculated on the amount of the overdraft on a daily basis. The rate of interest is based on a percentage above the bank's base rate. Bank charges and interest are debited to the account at regular intervals, monthly or quarterly. Bank lending is discussed in more detail in Chapter 13.

Most current account customers are issued with a cheque book, and make use of standing order and direct debit facilities. Other common services include cheque card, ATM card, and debit card. Almost all other services of the bank are available to current account customers.

Interest-bearing current accounts
All the major banks offer accounts which pay interest on credit balances. Examples are Lloyds Bank's Classic account, and Midland's Vector, Orchard and Meridian accounts. Various facilities are offered such as automatic overdrafts and guaranteed loans. Often a fixed monthly charge is made when the account is overdrawn. Many of these accounts have features which will make them attractive to certain types of customer: for example, an account with an automatic overdraft facility may appeal to young married couples who need to anticipate their salaries by overdrawing from time-to-time.

Student accounts
Banks are keen to encourage students to open current accounts and such accounts include a package of facilities which normally include:

- automatic overdrafts - up to a certain limit
- interest paid on credit balances
- cheque card
- ATM card
- debit card
- student advisers - who can assist with the organisation of the customer's finances
- package of 'goodies' - which might include book tokens, discounted travel, etc.

CURRENT ACCOUNT

Features	Benefits
Paying in	
• paying in book	• convenience to customer
• credits in cheque book	• security
• BACS payments to account	• useful for salary payments
• bank giro credits	
Cheque book	• reduces amount of cash needed by customer
	• ease of payment for goods and services
	• useful for postal payments
Cash withdrawals	
• over the counter where the account is held	• speed
• at other branches using cheque card	• convenience
• through ATMs of linked banks	• ATMs available at all hours
Standing orders and direct debits	• automatic payments
	• convenience
	• low cost
	• helps budgeting
Statement of account	• regular advice of balance
	• 'mini' statements from ATMs
	• assists budgeting
Bank charges	• personal customers often receive free banking
	• business customers - fixed charges assist with budgeting
Overdraft facilities	• flexible
	• cheaper than personal loans
	• easily set up

Fig. 11.1   Features and benefits of a current account

The marketing policy operated by each bank is to encourage such accounts. They may well prove to be unprofitable for the bank in the early years, but will be a benefit to the bank in the future when the students move on to well-paid jobs.

Banks will become involved in operating student loans as the Government supplements grants by means of loans (see Chapter 16.2).

Cheque card, ATM card and debit card

Almost all personal customers are issued with these cards as part of their current account facilities. The cards bear an expiry date and, once they have been issued, a new card will be sent automatically to the customer before it expires. Often cards are issued with a renewal date of two or three years. Frequently the three separate functions are put together onto one multi-purpose card - see fig. 11.2.

Cheque card

A cheque card (see also Chapter 3.5) is used to guarantee payment of a cheque, the amount of which does not exceed the cheque card limit (which may be £50, £100 or £250). A cheque card can be used with a cheque to draw cash at other branches, again up to the cheque card limit. Cash can also be withdrawn at other banks, but a charge will often be made for the service.

ATM card

Automated teller machines (see Chapter 10.4) provide banking services which include:

- cash withdrawals
- balance enquiries
- statement requests
- cheque book requests
- paying-in
- payment of bills

In order to ensure security, customers are issued with a Personal Identification Number (PIN). This must be keyed in to the ATM and if the PIN and card do not agree the machine will not operate, and may retain the card.

The main benefit of an ATM card to customers is that they can draw cash at almost any time of the day or night, seven days a week. The increase in shared networks means that a customer is never far from a machine.

Debit cards

Debit cards (see also Chapter 3.6) enable customers to make payment for goods and services from their bank account without the need to write a cheque. Payments are handled by retailers using EFTPOS (Electronic Funds Transfer at Point of Sale) - see also Chapter 10.3. (Retailers without computer-linked checkout tills process debit cards using an imprinter machine - similar to dealing with credit card transactions.)

The main advantages to both customer and retailer are that:

- there is no need to write out a cheque
- goods and services can be bought for any value, subject to the purchaser having sufficient money in his or her bank account

It seems likely that the next generation of debit cards will be *smart cards* (see Chapter 16.9); these are already in use in Europe. Smart cards incorporate a microchip which stores information about the cardholder and his/her account.

Fig. 11.2   A multi-function card

11.3   Deposit/Savings Account

This type of account offers limited banking facilities and is designed as a suitable place for short-term surplus money. Many customers with a current account transfer money to and from a deposit account as required.

Many banks have 'young savers accounts', which are designed to be attractive to the 7-14 years' age group. Features include a high rate of interest, a regular newsletter, and birthday cards. For the 14-18 year-olds, the account is modified and an ATM card is issued.

The main features and benefits of a deposit account are shown in fig. 11.3. Chapter 12.4 will discuss this type of account from a savings and investment viewpoint.

DEPOSIT/SAVINGS ACCOUNT

Features	*Benefits*
Availability	• no minimum age • available to all types of personal and business customers
Amounts	• any amount can be paid in • no minimum/maximum balance
Paying-in	• cash/cheques can be paid in • Bank Giro Credits can be paid direct into the account
Withdrawals	• withdrawals can usually be made on demand, although seven days' notice could be required • cash can be withdrawn at the branch where the account is held, and often at other branches of the bank • some accounts offer an ATM card for withdrawals • withdrawals by cheque can be arranged (but a cheque book cannot be issued)
Statement of account	• issued regularly, half-yearly or yearly • 'mini' statements often available on demand
Interest paid	• interest calculated on daily basis and paid half-yearly or yearly, being either credited to the deposit account or to the customer's current account • interest is paid net of basic rate tax, with no further tax liability for most customers

Fig. 11.3   Features and benefits of a deposit/savings account

11.4   High Interest Account and Term Deposits

High interest account
A higher rate of interest is offered for larger sums of money (often £1,000+), however a period of notice of withdrawal (often one month) is required. See also Chapter 12.4.

Term deposits
Here, the customer deposits a large sum of money (often £2,000+) for a fixed term, e.g. 1, 3, 6, 12 months up to 5 years. Withdrawals are not permitted until the end of the term. Interest rates may be fixed for the term, or vary with money market rates. See also Chapter 12.4.

11.5   Lending

Personal customer lending in the form of current account overdrafts, personal loans, budget accounts, revolving credit (cashflow) accounts and mortgages, are discussed fully in Chapter 13.

11.6   Bank Services

For the rest of this chapter, we shall look at the main personal customers services of:

- credit cards
- foreign travel services
- safe custody
- executor and trustee
- insurance
- home banking
- bank drafts
- estate agency

Investment services such as unit trusts, share dealing, investment management, Personal Equity Plans and insurance company investment products, are discussed fully in Chapter 12.

11.7   Credit Cards

The two main issuing organisations of credit cards (see also Chapter 3.7) in the UK are Visa and Access. Both of these organisations are owned by banks, and cards are issued, upon application, to customers of banks free of charge. Some banks are able to offer both cards to their customers, but others can offer only one. However, a bank customer is not restricted only to the card(s) issued by his/her bank, but can apply to any credit card company for a card (see fig. 11.4).

Fig. 11.4   A credit card

When a card is issued, a credit limit is set on each cardholder's credit card account (which is entirely separate from his/her normal bank account). The limit may be for amounts such as £500, £1,000, £1,500 or higher - it is often a very generous limit.

Goods and services can only be obtained from retailers and other outlets having either the imprinter or computer-linked tills for preparing sales vouchers to record the transactions. Retailers usually display the signs of the credit cards they are prepared to accept. A credit card can be used for ordering and paying for goods by telephone and by post - the card number needs to be quoted.

Most holders of credit cards are issued with a PIN (Personal Identification Number) and this enables the card to be used to draw cash from ATMs both in the UK and abroad. Cash can also be drawn over the counter of branches of the issuing bank.

Each month a cardholder is sent a statement of transactions, and can choose to pay off the balance of the account or to pay part only (subject to a certain minimum amount), carrying forward the remaining balance to next month. Interest is charged after a certain date on balances owing to the credit card company and, by careful timing of purchases, it is possible to obtain up to 56 days' free credit. Note, however, that cash advances incur interest from the date of withdrawal.

In recent years there has been growing concern in the UK at the high rate of interest charged by credit card companies. For example, at the time of writing (Summer 1989), Access is charging a rate of 2% per month, which gives an APR (Annual Percentage Rate) of 26.8%. It is felt that those card users who pay off the balance of their account within the interest-free period are being subsidised by those who incur interest charges. There are two possible ways to reduce the high interest rates charged:

- to reduce or scrap the interest-free credit period
- to make an annual charge for issuing the card (some credit card companies already do this)

It seems inevitable that one or both of these ways will be introduced before too long (see also Chapter 16.7 for comments on the Government's Monopolies and Mergers Commission report on credit cards).

For the customer, the *advantages* of credit cards are:

- a convenient way of paying for goods and services (including buying by telephone or by post)
- they can be used to draw cash at banks and ATMs
- goods and services can be bought for any value, subject to the credit limit on the account
- up to 56 days' free credit can be obtained on purchases (but not on cash advances)
- can be used both in the UK and abroad

The *disadvantages* to the customer are:

- there may be a temptation to buy more than can be afforded
- a high rate of interest is charged on balances owing to the credit card company
- not all businesses are able to accept payment by credit card

In order to encourage holders to use credit cards for more purchases, a number of promotional schemes have been introduced by credit card companies. These include awarding points for every £10 of goods bought - the points are saved up and are used to obtain free gifts from a catalogue. Another promotion awards 'air miles', which can be redeemed by taking a holiday by air.

Another recent development has been the introduction of *affinity cards* under which the credit card company supports a charity, whose logo appears on the card. When the card is used to make purchases, a percentage of the value of purchases is given to the charity by the card company.

11.8 Foreign Travel Services

Travel facilities for personal customers include:

- foreign currency
- travellers' cheques
- Eurocheques
- travel insurance
- credit cards

Foreign currency

All bank branches are able to provide foreign currency to both customers and non-customers. It makes good sense to take some money in the currency of the country to be visited in order to pay small expenses on arrival, e.g. taxi, bus fares, etc. However, not all money should be taken in this form because of the danger of theft or loss.

Not all branches hold stocks of foreign currencies and, therefore, customers should order from the bank a week or so before going abroad. When the currency is supplied, the amount is converted into sterling at the current exchange rate and this amount is debited to the customer's bank account or credit card account. Non-customers pay either in cash or by issuing a cheque backed by a cheque card. A service charge is made for the provision of foreign currency.

Advantage:
- a convenient travel facility - no need to spend time abroad obtaining local currency by means of other travel facilities

Disadvantages:
- danger of loss/theft
- may be bulky to carry
- some countries impose restrictions on the import and export of currency
- not all bank branches hold stocks of foreign currencies, so an order has to be placed beforehand

Unused foreign bank notes (but not usually coins) can be converted into sterling upon return to the UK.

Travellers' cheques

Travellers' cheques (see fig. 11.5) provide a safe way of carrying money abroad (they can also be used in the UK). Banks can supply travellers' cheques in fixed denominations in sterling or other major world currencies, e.g. US dollars. They are also available in the common currency of the European Community - the ECU (European Currency Units).

Travellers' cheques can be cashed at banks throughout the world, and used to pay for holiday expenses in hotels, restaurants, shops, etc. Customers visiting the USA should be advised to take travellers' cheques denominated in US dollars - many US banks will not cash sterling travellers' cheques.

When travellers' cheques are purchased, the customer signs them in one place. When they are cashed the customer countersigns them in the presence of the bank cashier, or hotel clerk, etc., who checks the signatures before making payment. A service charge is made for providing travellers' cheques and, when they are cashed, a charge may be made.

If the travellers' cheques are lost or stolen, it is usually possible to obtain an immediate refund from the local representative of the issuing bank.

Advantages:
- a refund service is generally available if they are lost or stolen
- available in a range of denominations and, therefore, may be less bulky than taking bank notes
- can be cashed at many places other than banks

Disadvantages:
- not as convenient as local currency
- may be problems of encashment in remote areas

Unused travellers' cheques can be cashed upon return and the proceeds paid into the customer's bank account.

Fig. 11.5 A travellers' cheque

Eurocheques

Most banks in Europe (and surrounding areas) are members of the Eurocheque scheme. Under this scheme the customer is issued with the distinctive uniform Eurocheque and supporting cheque card - both of these are common to all participating banks (the only detail that changes is the name of the bank).

With a Eurocheque and card (see fig. 11.6), cheques are written out in the currency of the country where they are being used (up to a maximum of the equivalent of £100, at present, for UK bank customers). They can be used to draw cash from banks, and to pay for goods and services at retail outlets. The normal cheque card procedures apply, except that there is no limit to the number of cheques that can be used for any one transaction.

The cheques are cleared through the international banking system and the sterling equivalent is debited to customers' accounts. A charge is made for issuing a book of Eurocheques and card, and a commission charge is made based on the value of each cheque drawn.

Advantages:
- avoids carrying too much bulky cash or travellers' cheques
- cash can be drawn from banks as and when required
- goods and services can be paid for at retail outlets
- more than one cheque can be issued for each transaction
- cheques are drawn in the currency of the country being visited

Disadvantages:
- danger of loss/theft of cheque book and card
- a limited number of cheques in each cheque book
- facilities not available worldwide

Where a PIN has been issued with a Eurocheque card, cash can be withdrawn from ATMs throughout Europe.

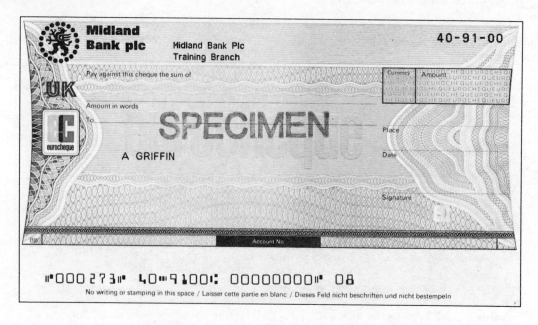

Fig. 11.6   Eurocheque and Eurocheque card

Travel insurance
Banks sell travel insurance to provide cover for:

- emergency medical expenses
- personal accident
- lost/stolen baggage and personal effects
- lost/stolen travellers' cheques and money
- holiday cancellation
- legal costs

Credit cards

When abroad, credit cards can be used in the normal way for the purchase of goods and services abroad, subject to the holder's credit card limit. The credit card voucher is made out in the currency of the country being visited, and is converted into sterling by the credit card company and will appear on the monthly statement.

Cash advances can be obtained from banks abroad which are members of the particular card group; there is usually a service charge made. Cash can also be obtained with a credit card and PIN from ATMs throughout Europe.

11.9 Safe Custody

A customer can deposit documents or valuables for safe-keeping in the bank's safe. A receipt is issued to the customer for each item. The customer can also deposit items in a sealed envelope or locked box. A charge is made based on the size of the item, envelope or box.

With safe custody, the bank enters into a *contract of bailment* with the customer: the bank is the *bailee* and the customer is the *bailor* - see also Chapter 6.4. The bank must exercise a high standard of care with safe custody items. The customer should ensure that items deposited in safe custody are insured against fire, loss or theft.

Some larger bank branches have a *safe deposit,* where the customer rents a small safe.

11.10 Executor and Trustee

Most banks have an executor and trustee department (or company) which offers services for wills and trusts.

When a person dies his/her estate is handled by personal representatives. Where a will has been made, the personal representatives are appointed by the will, and are known as *executors*. Where no will has been made, i.e. the person has died intestate, the personal representatives are appointed by a court, and are known as *administrators*.

In order to deal with the deceased's assets the personal representatives need legal authority granted by a court. For executors, they must obtain a *grant of probate;* for administrators the authority is *letters of administration*.

Many people, when making a will, include a clause in the will appointing the bank's executor and trustee department (or company) to act as executor. The bank can also take on the role of an administrator where a person has died intestate.

Where a will sets up a trust for the benefit of others, such as children, the bank can also handle the trust and make payments to the beneficiaries at the appropriate time.

The advantages of appointing the bank as an executor or a trustee are:

* *experience* - the bank's trustee department deals with many wills each year quickly and efficiently
* *impartiality* - in the event of disputes between beneficiaries of a will, the bank will act impartially
* *continuity* - although anybody can be appointed as an executor or trustee, when the time comes to take on the task they themselves may be elderly and not be able to handle the work; by contrast the bank will always be there and ready to deal with the work

11.11 Insurance and Pensions

Banks offer two main types of insurance:

- life assurance
- general insurance

Insurance (and pensions - see next page) are provided either through an insurance company owned by the bank, or by the bank acting as a broker and dealing with an 'outside' insurance company.

Life assurance

This topic is discussed more fully in Chapter 15, 'Banks and Competiton'. The main types of life assurance policies offered by banks are:

- *Term Assurance*
  This provides life cover for a stated period of years, e.g. 10 or 20 years, and provides a cheap form of assurance. If the life assured does not die within the term, no payment is made by the insurance company. This type of assurance is used for protection of dependants, and common uses include family protection (particularly young married couples with a family), and mortgage protection (in the event of death of the assured, the mortgage will be paid).

- *Whole Life Assurance*
  Here, a specific amount is payable when a person dies, whenever this may happen - this provides a benefit to dependants. Whole life assurance can be *with profits,* i.e. a specific amount is payable plus the benefits of sharing in the profits of the insurance company. A *without profits* does not share in these profits and only the amount of the sum assured is payable; however, the premiums on this type of policy are lower than a with profits policy.

- *Endowment Assurance*
  This type of assurance pays out a specific amount on a fixed future date, or on the death of the assured, whichever occurs first. Endowment assurance is one method used to repay a mortgage (see Chapter 13.9). Both *with profits* and *without profits* endowment assurance is available.

Some types of with profits life assurance policies can be 'unit-linked', i.e. the value of the policy can be linked to particular funds managed by the insurance company. The policy-holder is able to switch between the different funds offered by the insurance company on request.

Banks are also able to offer *regular savings plans* linked to life assurance, and *annuities:* both of these are discussed in Chapter 12.7.

General insurance

The more common types of general insurance offered to personal customers include:

- *House (buildings) insurance*
  Here, the building is insured against fire, flood and structural damage - often buildings insurance can be sold as part of a mortgage 'package'.

- *House contents*
  This insures furniture, carpets, valuables and other contents against fire, theft, flood and other risks. This type of insurance can often be sold at the same time as a mortgage is arranged.

- *Motor insurance*
  This covers cars and other vehicles against third party, fire and theft, or comprehensive risks.

- *Travel insurance*
  This provides cover for personal medical expenses whilst abroad, personal accidents, loss or theft of baggage and personal possessions, including travellers' cheques and money. Most policies also provide cover if a holiday has to be cancelled because of illness or death. This type of policy can be sold when foreign travel facilities are arranged.

- *Card insurance*
  This popular form of insurance provides cover against loss or theft of credit and other cards. It also insures against fraudulent use of cards by others. Other facilities include emergency cash advances in the event of being stranded without money because of loss or theft.

Pensions

Banks are able to give advice on personal pension plans for customers who are:

- self-employed
- not in pensionable employment
- in pensionable employment but wish to top up their firm's pension

Pensions are discussed more fully in Chapter 15.12.

11.12 Home Banking

Although home banking is still in the early days of development, many banks are offering the personal customer a service which uses the telephone to connect to the bank's computer. Instructions are given to the computer either by using the 'tones' of a telephone keypad or, in the latest developments, by speaking directly to a voice recognition computer. Facilities available include:

- balance enquiries

- amendment of standing orders

- ordering cheque books and statements (customers with a fax machine can request a statement to be sent immediately)

- transfers between the customer's accounts, e.g. from current to deposit account

- payment of bills for pre-arranged payees, e.g. credit card, gas, electricity, telephone, community charge, etc. (the bank's computer can also be instructed to make payment at a specified date in the future)

An alternative method of home banking uses a television or computer screen linked by telephone via the Prestel service of British Telecom to the bank's computer. Here, the customer's account can be displayed on the screen and transactions made by means of a keypad.

Home banking is available to current and deposit account customers (and for certain other types of accounts). Although the system offers electronic funds transfer, it has been slow to develop, mainly because few people see the need for the service - most banks have a wide branch network, so there is no difficulty in arranging to visit a branch. There has also been some concern over the security of home banking systems. Nevertheless, all major banks are involved in developments (see also Chapter 16.6) and it may be that this form of banking will become increasingly popular in the future.

11.13   Bank Drafts

A bank draft is a method of payment, similar to a cheque. It is a payment instruction drawn by a branch bank on the head office of the bank and, as a result, is a 'guaranteed' means of payment - virtually as good as cash, but without the problems of security and bulk of cash.

A customer can obtain a bank draft provided he or she has sufficient funds in the account (or an overdraft facility). Common uses of bank drafts are payment of high value items, e.g. purchase of a house, car, etc. - in fact any circumstance when the danger of 'bounced' cheques is to be avoided. With a bank draft the seller need not wait for it to be cleared, as a draft drawn by a major bank is a guarantee of payment.

11.14   Estate Agency

Some banks own chains of estate agents, e.g. Black Horse Agencies belongs to Lloyds Bank. Such banks are able to offer a complete service to house buyers:

*   properties for sale
*   sale of 'old' property, if required
*   mortgage service
*   legal service

11.15   Market Segmentation

In recent years banks have developed a wide range of financial services for the personal customer. To sell these services efficiently and effectively, banks adopt the process of dividing customers into groups - usually on the basis of age. This technique is known as *market segmentation* and means that the bank can prepare a package of services which will appeal to a particular age group.

Some suggested age groups, and the services which may be appropriate are:

*   *age 7-14*   young savers' account
*   *age 15-17*   savings account; card-based current account, perhaps a cheque book issued later
*   *age 18-21*   current account, with cheque book, cheque card, overdraft facility if required, credit card, savings account
*   *age 21-25*   current account with full services, credit card, budget account, revolving credit account, personal loan, mortgage, insurance (house, life, car), savings account, travel services
*   *age 25-45*   as above, plus wills, pension plans
*   *age 45-60*   as above, plus savings and investment
*   *age 60+*   as above, with particular emphasis on financial advice

11.16 Revision Points

❏ The four main services provided by banks are
  • money transfer
  • deposit-taking
  • advances
  • other services

❏ A current account offers
  • cheque book
  • funds transfer by standing order or direct debit
  • overdrafts

  Some types of current accounts for personal customers pay interest on credit balances

❏ A cheque card
  • guarantees cheques up to the cheque card limit
  • allows cash to be drawn by cheque at another branch of the bank up to the cheque card limit

❏ An ATM card provides for
  • cash withdrawals
  • balance enquiries
  • statement/cheque book requests

❏ A debit card
  • allows for goods and services to be bought without writing out a cheque
  • enables goods and services to be bought for any amount, subject to sufficient funds in the bank account
  • can be used for EFTPOS (Electronic Funds Transfer at Point of Sale) transactions

❏ Deposit/savings accounts are used for savings; interest is paid

❏ Credit cards
  • allow goods and services to be paid for
  • provide for cash advances
  • give up to 56 days' interest free credit (not for cash advances)
  • can be used in ATMs (with a PIN)

❏ Foreign travel services include
  • foreign currency
  • travellers' cheques
  • Eurocheques and Eurocheque card
  • travel insurance

❏ Safe custody is where a bank keeps items for safe keeping on behalf of customers

❏ Executor and trustee offers services for wills and trusts

❑   Life assurance is provided by banks in the form of
  • term assurance
  • whole life assurance
  • endowment assurance

❑   General insurance can be provided for
  • buildings
  • contents
  • motor
  • travel
  • card

❑   Home banking uses telephone lines to enable banking transactions to be made from home

❑   Bank drafts are
  • a payment instruction, similar to cheques, drawn by a branch bank on its head office
  • a secure means of payment for high value items requiring guaranteed funds, e.g. purchase of a house, car, etc.

❑   Some banks own estate agents, and are able to offer a complete service to home buyers

❑   Market segmentation is the technique whereby banks target particular services at customers of a particular age group

11.16   Know your *Accounts and Services: Personal Customers*

Multiple-choice Questions

Choose the *one* answer you think is correct.

1.   'A customer uses a card which is placed into a machine in a shop; after authorising the transaction by signing the sales voucher, the customer's bank account is debited, and the bank account of the retailer is credited'. Which type of card is being described here?

  A   Charge card
  B   Credit card
  C   Debit card
  D   Cheque card

2.   What is the maximum period of 'free credit' a customer can obtain when using a credit card in the UK?

  A   14 days
  B   28 days
  C   30 days
  D   56 days

3. A customer deposits a locked box in safe custody. The bank and customer enter into:

   A a joint and several liability
   B the legal relationship of principal and agent
   C a special relationship
   D a contract of bailment

4. You are selling your motorcycle for £650 to someone you do not know. Which of the following would guarantee you payment?

   A Cheque
   B Credit card
   C Bank draft
   D Bank giro credit

Short Answer Questions

5. List *three* features of a current account.

6. List *three* features of a deposit account.

7. For what reasons do banks encourage students to open accounts?

8. What type of bank account allows the customer to make withdrawals of any amount (subject to balance) on demand?

9. Other than cash withdrawals list *two* services that are provided by automated teller machines?

10. What bank service would you offer to a salesman who travels widely and wishes to pay hotel bills and buy petrol?

11. Give *two* reasons for taking travellers' cheques on holiday.

12. Other than travellers' cheques, state *two* other methods by which a UK bank customer, planning to visit France, can obtain cash while abroad.

11.17 Essay questions *Accounts and Services: Personal Customers*

1. Competition for the personal customer market has increased dramatically over the past five years. Describe briefly six bank services that are likely to be of greatest use to personal customers.

   [question 5, Autumn 1987]

2. You have been invited to the local college to talk to students about bank services that could be useful to them.

   What services would you talk about and what customer benefits would you mention? You have just 20 minutes for the talk and can only cover the main services.

   [question 26, Spring 1987]

3.   You are asked to visit a local store to give a half-hour talk to a group of 16-year-old school leavers who have just joined the company. Your brief is to explain to them which bank accounts and related services would be useful to them over the next three or four years so as to help them to make deposits and transfer money. Prepare notes for your talk, listing appropriate accounts and services and explaining their benefits.

[question 6, Spring 1989]

4.   A recent public opinion survey indicates that most people prefer shopping with cash.

Nearly three out of four people, 73 per cent, said they preferred to pay amounts of more than £10 in cash; 18 per cent said cheque and over 8 per cent preferred credit card.

The survey, also asked people to respond to the statement: 'I feel happier paying by cash when I shop' and 76 per cent of people either agreed or strongly agreed with the statement. Only 10 per cent disagreed with it.

This survey seems to prove that people prefer cash.

How would you convince the 73 per cent who prefer to pay cash for purchases of over ten pounds that cheques and credit cards have advantages over cash? Draft a report outlining your proposals.

[question 7, Spring 1988]

5.   Computers are playing an important role in allowing bank services to be delivered away from the bank counter. What services are provided, and how have they improved service to the customer in *each* of the following cases?

(a) When a customer wants to withdraw cash, order a statement, or cheque book, or check on his balance.

[7 marks]

(b) When a customer wants to transact 'banking business' from home.

[6 marks]

(c) When a customer wants to pay for his purchases and have the cost immediately debited from his bank account while at the store.

[7 marks]
[question 7, Spring 1989]

6.   Automation and technology are playing an increasing role in providing and delivering banking services to customers.

Outline *three* examples of how technology has improved service to personal customers to allow their finances to be managed and transferred effectively.

[question 5, Autumn 1988]

7.   **Case Problem Questions**

Note: This chapter and later chapters include a number of 'Case Problem' questions. In examinations to date, there has always been one question which comprises four different case problems, with five marks being awarded to each problem. Sometimes, the four problems within a question are on a similar topic, e.g. bank services, or investments; on other occasions the problems are on different topics. We have sorted the various case problems from past examination questions into appropriate topics.

What particular financial service or services would you suggest for the following? State the benefits to the customer to help explain your choice.

(a)   Dave England has a need for a bank account service even though his lifestyle is such that he writes very few cheques. In fact he only resorts to using a cheque for large amounts and only does this three or four times a year. Dave often leaves a balance in his cheque account of several thousand pounds to cover these cheques, although the loss of interest does annoy him.

What service could you offer Dave and what are its main features?

[5 marks]
[question 9d, Spring 1989]

(b)   Ray and Sally Pegg have just moved into their first house and are surprised at the number of bills that they have to pay.

The bills are a regular source of arguments, not because they cannot pay but because Sally says that Ray should remember and Ray thinks that Sally should do the paying.

Only yesterday they had to pay to have their telephone reconnected; last month it was the gas.

How should the Pegg's pay their regular bills and what advantages would there be?

[5 marks]
[question 9d, Spring 1988]

(c)   Agatha Marple is aged 50 and wants to open an account(s) which would allow her to save money. She worries about carrying money around in her purse when she goes shopping. She has about £2,000 in a tin under the bed which could go into the account.

What account(s) should she open and how will it/they help her?

[5 marks]
[question 9c, Autumn 1988]

(d)   Mark Polo is a sales representative who has to travel throughout the UK. He spends a lot of time away from home and drives about 20,000 miles a year in his company car.

What *two* banking services would be most suitable for him on his travels? Give examples of how he would use them to support your choice.

[5 marks]
[question 9b, Autumn 1988]

(e)   Rita Taylor is going to Italy on holiday and she expects to spend around £450 during her fortnight's stay. She is worried about the amount of bagsnatching that she has heard goes on.

How would you recommend that she takes her spending money, explaining the benefits?

[5 marks]
[question 9c, Spring 1988]

(f)   Glen Hateley is going to work in France for four weeks. He will be living in a small guest house in a village and will travel daily to work in the nearby town. How would you suggest that he takes his funds to combine security with convenience?

[5 marks]
[question 9a, Autumn 1988]

Chapter Twelve
Investments for Personal Customers

Banks are frequently asked to advise their customers on savings and investment. Banks can help their customers in the following ways:

- depositing funds in a bank account
- managing unit trusts which the customer can purchase
- providing facilities for the purchase or sale of stocks and shares
- acquiring insurance company investment products on behalf of the customer
- providing investment management services, including *Personal Equity Plans*

When giving investment advice, the requirements of the Financial Services Act 1986 must be considered; this authorises and controls those who give investment advice (see Section 12.2).

Most bank staff will also be aware of the savings and investment services offered by competitors to banks (see Chapter 15).

12.1 Savings and Investment

Savings can be defined as *setting aside sums of money regularly over a period of time in order to accumulate a lump sum of money.*

Investment can be defined as *placing a lump sum of money in one or more investment schemes in order to achieve an increase in the value of that money (capital growth), or the receipt of income.*

It is impossible to decide a certain money amount and to say that anything below that amount is savings, and anything above is investment. Much depends on the circumstances of the individual, and savings, although regular, need not be on a monthly basis, and the amount saved could vary.

12.2 Financial Services Act 1986

Scope of the Act
The aim of this Act is to regulate the way in which investment advice is given, and to protect the investor from unauthorised financial advisers. The main points of the Act are:

- investment business is defined as dealing, arranging deals, managing and advising on any investment product (bank deposits are excluded from the definition)

- all firms engaging in investment business are required to be authorised to do so

- the power of authorisation is given to a special agency - the Securities and Investments Board (SIB) - and through SIB to a number of Self-Regulatory Organisations (SROs) recognized by SIB, and other regulatory organisations such as the Bank of England and the International Stock Exchange.

Authorisation under the Act

The Securities and Investments Board acts as an overall 'watchdog', but various Self-Regulatory Organisations have been set up to cover particular aspects of the investment business. Examples of SROs are:

- IMRO (the Investment Management Regulatory Organisation), which covers firms involved with investment management - including unit trusts, investment trusts and pension funds

- FIMBRA (the Financial Intermediaries, Managers and Brokers Regulatory Association), which deals with firms of independent intermediaries who provide investment advice

- LAUTRO (the Life Assurance and Unit Trust Regulatory Organisation), which covers insurance companies, and the marketing of life assurance and unit trusts

The notepaper of a firm that gives investment advice states the name of the SRO to which it belongs; for example, most banks are members of IMRO.

Each SRO establishes its own rules and members must abide by these. In particular, people running investment firms must be judged to be 'fit and proper' before they can be issued with a licence to operate by the SRO. They must prove that they have sound financial resources and are of good character.

'Polarisation'

A requirement of the Act is that investors must know whether an adviser is either:

- offering an independent service, i.e. giving advice on a whole range of services available on the open market, *or*

- selling the products of only one company, i.e. a tied agent or company representative, selling only 'in-house' investment products

'Polarisation' is the word that has come to be used to describe this choice, meaning that an adviser must be at one pole or the other - either independent, or selling 'in-house' products: there can be no middle course. The Act requires that the customer must be advised whether independent advice is being given, or whether the adviser is a 'tied agent' selling 'in house' products. From the investor's viewpoint, it would seem that a better service is likely to be provided by the independent adviser who has to keep up-to-date on all the products available in the market, and who has to 'shop around' for the best product to suit the investor's needs. By contrast, the tied agent or company representative can sell only the products of one company. At the time of writing (Summer 1989) Barclays, Lloyds, Midland and TSB banks act as 'tied agents'. National Westminster Bank and The Royal Bank of Scotland act as independent advisers. Most of the building societies are 'tied agents'.

A way round the problem of 'tied agents' is to introduce customers to a subsidiary company within the bank group which can offer independent advice. Often such a subsidiary company will be a member of FIMBRA.

Giving investment advice

It is important to realise that the only people who can give investment advice within a firm are those who are authorised by the firm. For example, in a bank, members of staff can discuss the features of different types of deposit and savings accounts but, if the customer requires advice about any other form of investment, e.g. life assurance, unit trusts, it can be given only by those staff authorised by the bank as *company representatives*.

The basic rules for giving investment advice are:

- *know the customer* - the adviser must find out all the relevant details about the customer's financial situation

- *best advice* - the product recommended must be the best one available

- *suitability of investment* - recommendations must be appropriate to the customer's circumstances

Compensation fund

The Securities and Investments Board operates a compensation scheme which gives compensation where a firm giving investment advice has gone into liquidation and an investor loses money. The scheme pays out:

$$
\begin{array}{lll}
100\% \text{ of first } £30,000 & = & £30,000 \\
90\% \text{ of the next } £20,000 & = & \underline{£18,000} \\
& & £48,000 \text{ maximum}
\end{array}
$$

£48,000 is the maximum amount that can be paid out to an invidual investor. No compensation is given if money is lost because of the fall in value of investments.

12.3   Gross Interest and Net Interest Rates

Interest received by investors is considered by the Inland Revenue to be part of income, and is therefore subject to income tax. It is important when comparing savings and investment schemes, to know whether the interest paid is gross or net of tax.

Gross interest rate is interest before deduction of income tax
Net interest rate is interest after deduction of income tax at the basic rate (currently 25 per cent)

Banks and building societies pay interest to personal customers *net* of tax; certain other customers, such as limited companies, clubs, charities and overseas residents arc paid interest *gross* of tax. Thus, personal customers have no further liability for income tax on interest received, unless their income is such that they pay tax at the higher rate (currently 40 per cent).

The tax deducted by banks and building societies is called *Composite Rate Tax* (CRT). This is at a slightly lower rate than basic rate income tax, e.g. if income tax is 25 per cent, composite rate tax might be 22 per cent. The lower rate allows for the fact that some depositors are non-tax payers and represents the average rate for all depositors.

When a bank or building society has paid interest net of tax, the depositor cannot reclaim the tax deducted. For this reason a bank or building society account is not the best place for a non-tax payer to save or invest. An account that pays interest gross may be a better choice, e.g. a National Savings Bank Investment Account (see Chapter 15.5), or certain of the National Savings schemes (see Chapter 15.6).

12.4   Bank Accounts for Savings and Investment

Banks offer the following types of accounts for savings and investment (although the names given to them by individual banks may vary):

- deposit/savings account
- high interest account
- term deposit

The main features and benefits of these accounts have already been discussed in Chapter 11.3, and each type of account can be opened by any customer, e.g. individuals, husband and wife, clubs and societies, and businesses.   From a savings and investment point of view these accounts are appropriate for different circumstances.

Deposit/savings account

- This account is suitable for short-term savings, e.g. saving for a holiday, or to buy Christmas presents, or as a temporary place in which to put surplus funds before making other investment decisions.
- Withdrawals can be made on demand, although seven days' notice may be required.
- A 'reasonable' rate of interest is paid, net of tax.

High interest account

- This type of account features a minimum balance (often £1,000+).
- A rate of interest higher than that on a deposit/savings account is paid.
- A period of notice of withdrawal is required (often one month).
- The account is most suitable for surplus funds which the investor may need to draw against and does not wish to invest long-term.
- Some banks offer a higher interest account for regular savings, e.g. the customer agrees to save a certain amount (usually between £20 and £200) each month for a minimum time (often one year).

Term deposit

- This type of deposit is where a large sum of money (often £2,000+) is deposited with the bank for a fixed term, e.g. 1, 3, 6, 12 months up to 5 years.
- The money cannot be withdrawn before the end of the fixed term, nor can amounts be added to the balance.
- Interest rates are either linked to money market rates, or may be fixed for the period of deposit.
- Only suitable for funds which will not be needed during the term of the deposit.

12.5   Unit Trusts

These provide a way for a saver to invest in stocks and shares indirectly.   Investors contribute money to form a pool of money, which is then invested on their behalf by the *unit trust managers*.

Parties involved in unit trusts

There are three parties involved in unit trusts:

- unitholders
- unit trust managers
- trustees

The *unitholders* are the individual investors who contribute their money to the pool of money. They are allocated a certain number of units in the trust, which they can sell at any time; they can also add to their investment at any time by buying more units (subject to minimum amounts).

The *unit trust managers* promote the trust by advertising it and selling units to the public. The managers decide the investment policy of the trust, and use their investment expertise to decide which shares to buy and sell, and when. They make a market in the unit trust, i.e. will sell to, and buy back, units from the unitholders. The managers aim to make a profit from the trust by charging for their services. Unit trust managers are financial institutions such as banks, insurance companies, and professional savings companies.

The *trustees* safeguard the interests of unitholders by watching over the actions of the unit trust managers. In law, every unit trust must have a trust deed which governs the running of the trust and the role of the trustees, managers and unitholders. The trustees must be independent of the managers - often a bank or an insurance company is the trustee - and be approved by the Department of Trade. The trustees are the legal owners of the assets of the trust, which are held on trust for the unitholders. The trustees will not interfere with the day-to-day management of the trust, unless the managers go outside the terms specified in the trust deed.

Advantages of unit trusts

From the unitholder's viewpoint, unit trusts offer the following advantages:

- an easy method of investing in stocks and shares indirectly
- potential for capital growth, and/or income
- smaller investments accepted (often the minimum lump sum accepted is £500)
- risk is less because the unitholder's money is spread over all the shares owned by the unit trust (the trust's *portfolio* of shares)
- the investment expertise of the unit trust managers
- there is always a market in the unit trust - the managers buy back from, and sell to, the unitholders
- wide choice of different types of unit trusts (see below)

Offer and bid prices

The value of units in a trust varies with changes in the value of the stocks and shares owned by the trust. For example, the units might have been issued originally by the managers at 50p each: a rise in stock market prices might increase the value to 60p, but a fall might reduce the value to 40p. Prices of unit trusts appear in most daily newspapers, and these usually show two prices:

- *offer price,* i.e. the price at which the public may buy from the unit trust managers
- *bid price,* i.e. the price at which the unit trust managers will buy units back from the unitholders

An investment in a unit trust should always be regarded as long-term and, unlike the other savings and investment schemes considered so far in this chapter, it is possible to lose money with unit trusts (and indeed with any investment in stocks and shares). All unit trust advertisements must contain wording similar to the following:

> *The price of units and the income from them can go down as well as up. Past performance is no guarantee of future returns.*

Types of unit trusts

For the potential investor, there is a wide choice of different unit trusts. Each trust will state its investment strategy, and there are initially three different strategies:

- *capital growth* - to increase the value of units over time
- *income* - to provide a regular income for the unitholder
- *mixed* - to provide a degree of capital growth, with some amount of regular income

In order to achieve one of these objectives, the unit trust managers will invest the unitholders' funds in particular types of shares. For example, to achieve a high income the managers will buy shares which are likely to pay high dividends so that large distributions of income can be made to unitholders.

The unit trust managers must also make the choice between:

- *general unit trust,* which invests generally in shares with no particular emphasis on industries

- *specialist unit trust,* which invests in particular shares such as those of small companies, overseas companies, particular overseas stock markets (e.g. Japan, Germany, USA, etc.) or in the shares of one particular sector (e.g. oil and energy companies, gold mining companies, financial institutions, etc.)

The unit trust managers may also decide to offer two different types of units to the unitholders:

- *ordinary (or income) units,* from which the unitholder receives distributions from the income of the trust

- *accumulation units,* where no distributions are paid to unitholders, but the income received is retained in the trust to increase the capital value of units

It is also possible for distributions to be applied automatically towards the purchase of additional units.

Methods of investment in unit trusts

There are three main methods of investing:

- *Lump sum,* which can be invested directly with the unit trust managers, or indirectly through an intermediary such as a bank, stockbroker, or financial intermediary. The investor receives a *contract note* which shows the number of units purchased and the price. Once the amount of the contract note has been paid, the investor receives a certificate for the units, or a statement of units held (not all unit trust managers issue certificates). The minimum lump sum varies with each unit trust manager, but £500 is a common amount.

- *Savings plans,* paid monthly to the unit trust managers. A certificate or statement will be issued at the end of the financial year, showing units held. The minimum monthly payment for savings plans can be as low as £25.

- *Share exchange schemes,* where an existing shareholder can 'trade in' shares in exchange for units in the trust. Often the unit trust managers will offer low-cost share dealing in such circumstances.

Unit trusts can also be linked to other investment and financial schemes:

- life assurance policies (see Chapter 12.7)
- investment bonds (see Chapter 12.7)
- mortgages (see Chapter 15.2)
- pension plans (see Chapter 15.12)

Banks and competitors

Banks are only one group of financial institutions which provide unit trusts: the other major groups are insurance companies and professional savings companies. Banks can act in two roles in unit trusts - managers and trustees - but they cannot be both in the same unit trust. It is in their role as managers that they should be considered on their investment performance.

12.6   Share Dealing Service

All bank branches can buy or sell shares on behalf of customers. The buy or sell transaction is usually placed through the bank's own investment bank (see Chapter 4.6) which handles the stock exchange transaction. After the transaction has been made, the customer receives a *contract note* which shows the number of shares bought or sold, the price, dealing charges, and the net amount. The minimum dealing cost for a transaction is around £20, so it is uneconomic to invest less than about £1,000 in any one share.

Most share transactions are processed over a computer terminal in the branch to the bank's investment bank. With shares in the largest companies quoted on the Stock Exchange, some banks offer *touch-screen dealing* whereby the customer can see the price at which the shares are trading and then, if appropriate, can make an immediate purchase or sale. This facility is also offered for major new issues of shares (when the shares are first quoted on the Stock Exchange). Using such systems the contract note is printed immediately.

Like unit trusts, shares can go up or down in value but, unlike most unit trusts, the variation can be more dramatic. Whilst shares do give an investor the freedom to make his or her own investment decisions and may offer the potential of considerable capital growth, the problems of owning shares can be summarised as:

- *risk,* the danger of investing too much in one share which may go down in value

- *expense,* the costs of buying and selling shares are quite high, and the price of shares needs to increase quite considerably to cover the costs

- *monitoring of performance,* the investor needs to be reviewing progress of the shares on a daily basis, reading the financial pages of newspapers, and making buy and sell decisions

Shares should normally be considered as a long-term investment but, in an emergency they can be sold quickly - the money being received within a week or two. Ideally an investor should aim to build up a small portfolio of shares in order to minimise the risk of one share falling in value.

Bank staff in 'High Street' branches should not give advice to customers about when to buy or sell shares. Advice can be obtained for the customer from the bank's investment bank and passed on to the customer without comment.

In order to reduce these risks investors can consider:

- *unit trusts* (see above - Section 12.5)

- *investment trusts,* (see Chapter 15.11) which operate in a similar way to unit trusts by pooling the resources of their investors in order to purchase shares, but are themselves companies quoted on the Stock Exchange

- *investment management services,* provided by banks, including Personal Equity Plans (see Sections 12.8 and 12.9)

12.7   Insurance Company Investment Products

The investment products available from insurance companies include:

- endowment assurance
- regular savings
- investment bonds
- annuities

Banks provide these services to their customers either directly through the bank's own insurance company, or by the bank acting as a broker - an intermediary - between customer and insurance company. Insurance companies are competitors of banks and their full range of services is detailed in Chapter 15.8.

Endowment assurance

An endowment assurance policy is a life policy for long-term regular savings of perhaps 20 or more years' duration. A fixed amount of money - the *sum assured* - is paid at the end of a certain time period, or on death of the life assured, whichever occurs first. Most endowment policies are 'with profits', i.e. they share in the profits of the insurance company which will be added to the sum assured. An endowment policy can also be 'unit-linked', i.e. the regular premiums are invested in a fund similar to a unit trust, managed by the insurance company, although here the amount paid out will vary with the value of the fund.

An endowment policy can also be used in connection with a mortgage (see Chapter 13.9).

Regular savings

Insurance companies offer regular savings policies for those who wish to accumulate a lump sum of money. The term of these policies is usually shorter than an endowment policy, but generally will be for 10 years or more. Regular premiums are paid, a part of which goes to provide life cover in the event of the early death of the policyholder. Most of the premiums go towards building up the lump sum. As with endowment assurance, the policy can be 'with profits' or 'unit linked'.

Investment bonds

For the investor with a lump sum of money available (often a minimum of £1,000), insurance companies offer investment bonds. Most of the lump sum is placed in a unit trust or an investment fund managed by the insurance company. The period of the bond is usually five years or more. The bond is organised in such a way that the lump sum originally invested is guaranteed to be repaid in the event of death of the investor or at the end of the term of the bond. With the lump sum being placed in a unit trust or an investment fund, there is a good chance of capital growth, but there is the guarantee of being paid at least the original investment.

While most investment bonds are designed for capital growth, some bonds can provide the investor with a regular income - either annually or quarterly.

Annuities

With an annuity an investor - the annuitant - pays a lump sum of money to an insurance company and then receives a regular income until death. Thus an annuity operates in reverse to a life policy: a lump sum now is exchanged for regular income in the future. This solves the problem for many older people of making their savings last for the rest of their lives. The insurance company takes the 'risk' that the investor will live to a 'ripe old age' or will die early before many payments have been made. The amount paid out under the annuity will vary with the age, sex and health of the investor: annuities are a suitable investment only for people requring an income during retirement.

There are several different types of annuity:

* *Immediate annuity.* This starts to pay a regular income from the date of purchase.

* *Deferred annuity.* This starts at a future specified date and gives the investor the opportunity to invest now for future income - as the insurance company has the use of the money before payments start, the income will be higher than an immediate annuity.

* *Reversionary (or joint-life) annuity.* Here the annuity is paid on the lives of two people until the death of the last survivor. Thus a husband might take out a reversionary annuity jointly with his wife: the regular income will continue to be paid until the second death.

* *Guaranteed annuity.* For most annuities, once the lump sum has been paid at the start, everything is lost if the annuitant dies shortly afterwards. However, a guaranteed annuity will make a certain number of payments - in the event of the early death of the annuitant, payments are made to the beneficiaries of the annuitant's estate.

- *Temporary annuity*. While most annuities continue to pay until the death of the annuitant, a temporary annuity is arranged at the outset for a fixed time period - perhaps five or ten years.

The amount of the regular income of an annuity can also be increased with inflation, but this means that lower payments will be received initially.

12.8   Investment Management Services

For investors with large sums of money available (either in cash or already invested) banks can offer an investment management service, usually through the bank's investment bank or trust company. The amounts vary from bank to bank, but usually a minimum sum of £50,000 available to invest in stocks and shares is required. Below this amount, the bank might be prepared to manage investments in unit trusts on behalf of the customer.

The investment management service discusses with the customer his or her financial position and will then draw up an investment strategy. The investments are then managed on a day-to-day basis. Customers can choose whether to allow the bank to make investment decisions at its own discretion, or to ask the bank to refer decisions to them for approval.

The service is available only to long-term investors and is not for speculators seeking short-term gains and wishing to make frequent changes in investments. The bank makes a charge for the service based on the value of the customer's investments.

The advantages to the customer of using the investment management service are:
- the investment expertise of professional managers
- day-to-day supervision of the customer's investments
- an investment policy tailored to meet the requirements of the customer

12.9   Personal Equity Plans (PEPs)

Personal Equity Plans are a Government scheme to encourage investment in UK companies. Investors are allowed to invest a maximum of £4,800 (limit set in 1989), in each tax year (6 April - 5 April) directly in shares of UK companies. (Up to £2,400 can be invested in unit trusts which invest mainly in the UK.) The advantage of PEPs is that there is no tax to pay on the income from the investments or any capital gains made.

PEPs are managed by banks and other financial institutions who provide professional expertise at reasonable cost. Like other investments in shares, PEPs should be regarded as a long-term investment. Investment can be made either by means of a lump sum, or by a monthly savings scheme.

12.10   Revision Points

❑   Saving is *setting aside sums of money regularly over a period of time in order to accumulate a lump sum of money.*

❑   Investment is *placing a lump sum of money in one or more investment schemes in order to achieve either capital growth or income.*

❏ The Financial Services Act 1986 regulates the giving of investment advice: the Securities and Investment Board (SIB) and Self-Regulatory Organisations (SROs) control those who give advice.

❏ Gross interest rate is interest before deduction of income tax.

❏ Net interest rate is interest after deduction of basic rate income tax.

❏ Banks offer savings and investment facilities through:

  • *deposit/savings account,* for small amounts of money, regular savings
  • *higher interest account,* for larger amounts of money, notice of withdrawal may be required
  • *term deposit,* for large amounts of money for a fixed term

❏ Unit trusts pool the money contributed by investors and buy shares. The unit trust managers provide professional investment expertise.

❏ Unit trusts provide for:

  • capital growth
  • income
  • mixed

  A general unit trust invests in a wide range of shares, while a specialist unit trust invests in particular industries or stock markets.

❏ A share dealing service is offered by banks to enable customers to buy or sell shares.

❏ Banks provide insurance company investment products such as:

  • *endowment policies,* for long-term regular savings, either with profits or unit-linked
  • *regular savings policies,* for regular savings, often unit-linked
  • *investment bonds,* for lump sum investments with guaranteed repayment of capital
  • *annuities,* which pay a regular income in exchange for a lump sum investment

❏ The investment management service is offered by banks to their more wealthy customers.

❏ Personal Equity Plans (PEPs), which are managed by banks and other financial organisations, offer investment in shares and unit trusts. The Plans are completely free of tax. The maximum amount that can be invested by an individual is currently £4,800 in any one tax year.

12.11 Know your *Investments for Personal Customers*

Multiple-choice Questions

Choose the *one* answer you think is correct.

1. Banks pay interest to the majority of personal customers net of
   A Composite Rate Tax
   B Annual Percentage Rate
   C Higher Rate Tax
   D Value Added Tax

2. Which type of bank account will offer the highest interest rates for a sum of money which will not be needed for six months?

   A Deposit account
   B Interest-bearing current account
   C Savings account
   D Term deposit account

3. The people who supervise the operation of a unit trust are known as

   A unitholders
   B trustees
   C professional savings companies
   D unit trust managers

4. Which of the following is *not* an annuity?

   A Endowment
   B Reversionary
   C Guaranteed
   D Deferred

5. PEP stands for

   A People's Endowment Policy
   B Personal Executive Pension
   C Personal Executor Planning
   D Personal Equity Plan

Short Answer Questions

6. Distinguish between savings and investment.

7. Give *two* reasons why people save.

8. What is the name of the Act which regulates the giving of investment advice?

9. What does SIB stand for?

10. What is meant by 'polarisation'?

11. What type of bank accounts would you recommend for each of the following:
    - £250, which will be needed in six months' time to pay for a holiday
    - £5,000, which may be needed at some time in the future
    - £10,000, which will not be needed for the next 12 months

12. What are the *three* different strategies which might be adopted by the managers of a unit trust?

13. Distinguish between the bid and offer price of a unit trust.

14. For the smaller investor, what are the problems of owning shares?

15. What are the advantages of a customer using the bank's investment management service?

12.12 Essay questions *Investments for Personal Customers*

1. (a) Why do people save?

    [8 marks]

    (b) What types of bank account are available to help savers?

    [12 marks]
    [question 8, Autumn 1988]

2. Two of your customers have spoken to you about their financial position:

    Customer A is a teacher aged 27, married, with one child who is two years old. He has a gross income of £12,000 a year. His wife is not working. After mortgage and hire purchase commitments, together with day-to-day living expenses, he feels he can set aside £50 each month for investment.

    Customer B is a steelworker aged 59, who has been offered early retirement with a lump sum payment of £20,000 which he intends to invest. His wife, who is 55 years old, has a part-time job as a school meals assistant earning £45 a week. He has a daughter who is married to a chartered accountant and they have a two year old son.

    Outline the investments which would be suitable for:
    (a) Customer A, and (b) Customer B.

    [The Chartered Institute of Bankers' specimen paper]

3. Outline the scope and requirements of the Financial Services Act 1986. What is the effect on banks with regard to the giving of investment advice?

4. A customer seeks your advice. She has recently inherited £25,000 and wishes to invest it. She would like to put the money into stocks and shares but feels that she doesn't know enough about 'the City' to risk her money in a few shareholdings. Suggest a method of investing in stocks and shares offered by your bank, which spreads the risks and gives professional investment management. Explain the general features of the investment scheme.

Chapter Thirteen
Bank Lending to Personal Customers

One of the main functions of a bank is to lend or advance money to its customers. The interest charged on loans and advances is a major source of bank profits. In this chapter we shall look at the main forms of lending for personal customers (lending services for business customers are considered in Chapter 14). We will also look at the *principles of lending* which are considered whenever a loan or advance is made.

13.1   Different Forms of Lending to Personal Customers

Banks lend or advance money to personal customers for a variety of purposes and the main forms of lending are:

- current account overdrafts
- personal loans
- budget accounts
- revolving credit (cashflow) accounts
- credit cards
- mortgages
- bridging loans

We will consider each of these in more detail later in this chapter. Note that most of the forms of lending described in this chapter are normally available only to current account customers.

13.2   Principles of Lending

Whenever a customer wishes to borrow there are always a number of lending points to consider: *integrity, purpose, amount, repayment, terms, security*. The lending questions for each of these points are shown in fig. 13.1, and satisfactory answers will be required by the bank before the lending can be agreed.

The principles of lending are important for all forms of bank lending and, in an interview with a customer, the loans officer would consider each of the points. However, many forms of personal lending do not require an interview - instead the customer completes an application form which is taken or sent to the bank where it is credit-scored (see page 158), and the customer advised whether or not the loan can be granted. The application form itself incorporates the principles of lending.

I **ntegrity**

- What is the *character* of the customer? How long has customer banked with us? Account conducted satisfactorily? Any previous lending? If so, satisfactorily repaid?

- What *capital* is the customer contributing? (most forms of lending require the customer to make a contribution)

- Has the customer the *capability* to stick to an agreement made with the bank?

P **urpose**

- For what purpose will the loan be used?

- Is the purpose legal?

- Is the purpose within bank and government guidelines?

- Are there any technical problems?

A **mount**

- How much is the bank to lend?

- How much is the customer putting in?

- Is the amount requested too little/too much?

R **epayment**

- What is the source of repayment?

- Can the customer afford the repayments? (check income and expenditure)

T **erms**

- What is the period of the loan?

- Is the term correct for the purpose of the loan?

- What interest rate and other charges will the bank apply?

S **ecurity**

- Is the bank lending secured or unsecured?

- If lending is secured, what security is available? (acceptable security would be life policies, deeds of a house, guarantees, stocks and shares)

Note: The principles of lending can be remembered easily using the word IPARTS

Fig. 13.1 Principles of lending: questions

For personal lending, security may not always be required. However, it is often taken by a bank as possible insurance should the customer be unable to repay lending. The best type of security is one that is not likely to fall in value and which is easy to realise should the need arise. The types of security commonly acceptable to banks are life policies, the deeds of property, e.g. a house, guarantees, and stocks and shares.

Credit scoring

Credit scoring is used to assess the creditworthiness of customers. The technique involves awarding points to answers given to questions on an application form. Typical questions include:

- married or single
- age
- occupation
- number of years at present address
- whether a houseowner or tenant
- length of time with current employer
- current salary

Each answer is awarded a number of points. For example, a houseowner will score higher points than a tenant. Certain questions will carry a higher weighting than others. For example, occupation and length of time with current employer will be one of the most highly weighted questions, while marital status, i.e. whether married or single, will be less important. All answers are scored in this way and, if the total is higher than a certain figure, the application is approved.

Banks use credit scoring for a number of purposes, including opening a current account, applications for cheque cards and credit cards, and for applications for personal loans (see fig. 13.2). The advantage of credit scoring is that any member of bank staff can credit score applications - usually by operating a computer programme - without having to apply subjective judgements. Often provision is built in for marginal applications to be referred to supervisory staff. Credit scoring cannot be used for complex bank lending proposals.

13.3   Borrowing by Minors

Care should be taken when a bank lends to a minor (see Chapter 7.3), i.e. a young person under the age of eighteen. Under the terms of the Minors' Contracts Act 1987, loans to minors are valid (i.e. they are legal) but are unenforceable (i.e. the bank cannot take the minor to court to seek repayment). The remedy open to a bank is to take the minor to court to recover the items bought with the loan (a bit difficult if the loan was to pay for a holiday!).

When a minor is granted a loan, the bank will usually take a *guarantee* from an adult as security. The guarantee can be enforced against the adult if the minor does not repay the loan.

13.4   Current Account Overdrafts

An overdraft on a current account is a convenient form of bank lending for both customer and bank, being simple and easy to arrange. A limit, e.g. £100, £500, etc. is agreed, beyond which the customer should not draw. The overdraft is created by the customer drawing cheques or other payments from the account.

Uses
- short-term requirements, e.g. temporary emergency, purchase of an item which is to be repaid quickly
- anticipation of salary
- student overdrafts

Rates
- the rate of interest charged is usually around five percentage points above the bank's base rate, e.g. if base rate is 10%, then the overdraft will be charged at 15%
- unauthorized overdrafts are charged at between 12% and 14% over the bank's base rate

Terms
- any amount, subject to lending constraints, can be borrowed on overdraft
- interest is charged on the amount borrowed (calculated on a daily basis and debited to the account monthly or quarterly)
- an overdraft limit is agreed for a particular time period, e.g. one month, six months, a year, and may be renewed if still required
- security might be required, although personal lending for relatively small amounts is often unsecured

A number of interest-bearing current accounts (see Chapter 11.2) also include, as part of the 'package', an automatic overdraft facility which does not need to be arranged separately. For example, Lloyds Bank's 'Classic' account automatically allows overdrafts of up to £100 without charging interest; overdrafts beyond £100 can be arranged at the standard personal overdraft rate.

An alternative to a *short-term* bank overdraft could be the use of a credit card (see Chapter 13.8), provided the transaction is within the cardholder's limit. Although the interest rate charged is higher, it might be possible to use the 56-day free credit period to advantage.

13.5 Personal Loans

With a personal loan, a customer borrows a fixed amount of money for an agreed period of time at an interest rate which is fixed at the time the loan is arranged. Regular repayments (usually monthly) incorporate the interest payments.

Uses
- purchase of consumer durables, e.g. car, furniture, television, etc.
- to pay for a holiday
- to pay for home improvements

A personal loan is different from hire purchase (see Chapter 15.4) because the goods bought with the loan belong to the bank customer in the same way as if cash had been used to buy them. (With hire purchase, the goods belong to the hire purchase company until the final payment.)

Rates
- interest rate is fixed for the period of the loan
- interest is calculated on the original amount of the loan (i.e. *not* on the loan amount outstanding on a daily basis) and the Annual Percentage Rate (APR) of charge is quoted to the customer

Terms
- personal loan amounts range from a minimum of £250 up to £10 000
- loans can be arranged for periods from one year up to five years, although a loan for a holiday would usually have a maximum repayment period of twelve months
- no security is required

To obtain a personal loan, the customer completes an application form (see fig. 13.2). When completed, the form is credit-scored (see Section 13.2) by inputting the customer's answers to the bank's computer. A credit reference agency may also be used to check the name of the applicant and to ensure that no court judgements have been made against the customer. If the loan is approved, a personal loan agreement is completed by the bank and signed by both bank and customer, each keeping a copy. The amount of the loan is then credited to the customer's current account and debited to a personal loan account in the customer's name. The customer can then buy the goods, paying by cheque, for which the loan was agreed. Repayments will commence on a monthly basis by debit to the customer's current account and credit to the personal loan account.

Most bank personal loans include life cover. This ensures that, if the customer dies during the period of the loan, the amount of the loan will be repaid by insurance. For a small increase in the monthly repayments, the customer can insure against accident, sickness and unemployment - if any of these occur during the loan period, repayments will continue to be made through the insurance.

Banks normally offer personal loans only to their existing customers, but other organizations, e.g. finance companies and retailers (see Chapter 15.7), offer them to the general public.

An alternative to a personal loan is a hire-purchase agreement (see Chapter 15.7), which can often be arranged through a finance company at the store or outlet where the goods are purchased (not at a bank). A personal loan is to be preferred though, because the borrower owns the goods from the start; also, personal loan interest rates are usually slightly cheaper than hire-purchase.

13.6   Budget Accounts

A budget account is a separate account opened in the name of the customer. It is used to spread the cost of bills evenly over a year. The customer totals bills such as telephone, electricity, gas, water, community charge, car tax, car insurance, etc. which are expected during the year (a budget schedule form - see fig. 13.3 - can be used). This total is divided by twelve to give the amount of the monthly transfer from the customer's current account to the budget account. As each of the specified bills falls due the customer settles them by payment from the budget account (a special budget account cheque book is issued). This means that the budget account could be overdrawn at certain times of the year, but have a credit balance at other times. At the end of the twelve months the balance of the budget account should be approximately nil. The account is then reviewed by the bank and the customer is asked to complete another budget planner for the forthcoming twelve months.

Uses
• to spread the cost of bills evenly over a twelve-month period

Rates
• the rate of interest charged is around five percentage points above the bank's base rate
• some banks charge an overall fixed operating fee

Terms
• interest is calculated on a daily basis on the amount that the account is overdrawn and is debited either to the budget account or to the customer's current account
• the account operates for twelve months after which it is reviewed and usually renewed

MIDLAND PERSONAL LOANS

Application Form

PLEASE COMPLETE IN BLOCK CAPITALS, WRITE 'NONE' WHERE APPROPRIATE AND TICK ☐ WHERE APPLICABLE.

Personal Details

Surname _____ Mr/Mrs/Miss/Ms

Forename(s) _____

Postal Address _____
Postcode _____

Date moved to present address Month ___ Year ___

Previous address (if at present address less than 2 years) _____
Postcode _____

Date moved to previous address Month ___ Year ___

Tel. No. Home _____ Business _____

Date of birth _____

Marital status: Married ☐ Single ☐ Separated ☐
Divorced ☐ Widowed ☐

Number of children ___ Ages ___

Your Home

Are you: An owner occupier ☐   A tenant ☐
Living with parents ☐   Other ☐

If an owner occupier:

Market value of residence £ _____

Amount outstanding on mortgage(s) £ _____

Your Job

Employer's name _____

Address _____ Postcode _____

Employer's business _____

Your occupation _____

Is your position pensionable? Yes ☐   No ☐

Date started in present employment Month ___ Year ___

Date started in previous employment Month ___ Year ___

How paid: Cash ☐ Cheque ☐ Other means ☐

Direct credit to your bank account ☐

When paid: Weekly ☐ Monthly ☐ Fortnightly ☐ Otherwise ☐

Your Monthly Income

Monthly earned income after deductions of tax and national insurance £ _____

Wife/husband's monthly income after deductions £ _____

Any other regular income £ _____

Total net monthly income £ _____

Your Monthly Outgoings

Mortgage/Rent, Rates and other loan repayments (from previous page) £ _____

Total of all instalment credit and other loan repayments £ _____

Other regular commitments £ _____

Total regular outgoings £ _____

Your Bank

Date you first opened a Midland Current Account Month ___ Year ___

Name of present branch _____

Current Account no. _____

Other accounts held (please specify) _____

Name & branch of bankers if not a Midland customer _____

Cards issued:
Cheque Card ☐
Midland Access ☐
Other Access ☐
Visa ☐
Other ☐

Balance / Limit £ / £ ...

Personal Loan Details

Amount required £ ___ over ___ months

Purpose of loan _____

Total expenditure of which the loan forms part £ _____

Insurance Protection Details

Unemployment, Accident, Sickness and Death Cover. WE RECOMMEND THAT YOU TAKE OUT INSURANCE PROTECTION

If you do NOT require cover please tick here ☐
Where insurance cover is taken out the premium (rounded down to the nearest £10) will be added to your loan unless you advise us otherwise. For joint accounts, cover will apply only to one borrower, please name the person to be covered _____

Details of instalment credit and loans from Banks, Finance Companies, Retailers & Credit Cards

Company	Monthly Repayment	Date of Final Repayment
	£	£
	£	£
	£	£
Total £		

(carry forward to Your Monthly Outgoings)

Declaration

I/We confirm that the above information is correct to the best of my/our knowledge and belief, and agree that the Bank may make any enquiries it thinks fit regarding this application.

Applicant's Signature(s) _____ Date _____

FOR BANK USE ONLY				
D.C.	C.R.S.	V.R.S.	C.S.	B.B.E.
S.O.	£	DATE	R.N.	

Fig. 13.2   A personal loan application form

BUDGET SCHEDULE –
CUSTOMER COPY

	Estimated Annual Expenditure	Estimate of when payable
Mortgage/Rent	£	
General Rates	£	
Water Rates	£	
Electricity	£	
Gas	£	
Telephone	£	
TV Licence	£	
Car Road Tax	£	
Insurance – Car	£	
– House	£	
– Other	£	
Holidays	£	
Christmas	£	
Annual Subscriptions	£	
Decoration and repairs	£	
Contingency/Emergency	£	
Other Items	£	
	£	
	£	

Total Expenditure for year: £

Divide by 12 to calculate
your monthly transfer   £

First transfer date   _____

Title of Account   _____

I confirm that the Bank has
agreed/renewed the facility
as requested

Manager

Fig. 13.3   A budget schedule form for use with budget accounts

13.7 Revolving Credit (Cashflow) Accounts

This is an account into which the customer makes fixed monthly payments; the customer is able to draw on the account to create a maximum overdraft at any one time of twenty-five (sometimes thirty) times the monthly payment. For example, a monthly payment of £10 gives a maximum overdraft of £250. The account is highly flexible because the money can be used for any purpose and the account can be drawn against at any time provided the maximum overdraft is not exceeded.

Uses
- any purpose, e.g. to pay bills, to purchase consumer goods, to pay for holidays, etc.

Rates
- the rate of interest charged is usually around five percentage points above the bank's base rate

Terms
- maximum overdraft is a multiple (usually twenty-five or thirty times) of the monthly repayment
- interest is charged on the amount borrowed (calculated on a daily basis) and is debited to the account
- the account will be reviewed annually and, provided it has been conducted satisfactorily by the customer, will be renewed

To open a revolving credit (cashflow) account, the customer completes an application form, similar to a personal loan application. It is then credit-scored and, if satisfactory, the account is opened for the customer and a special cheque book and debit card issued. A monthly standing order to transfer repayments from the customer's current account to the revolving credit account is taken.

Some credit card companies offer a similar type of revolving credit account, e.g. Barclays' 'Assent'. Here the account is card-based, i.e. no cheque book is issued; instead the customer has a card to charge purchases to the account. Monthly payments into the account are by direct debit from the customer's bank account.

13.8 Credit Cards

The use of credit cards has already been discussed in Chapter 11.7. They represent a form of bank lending via the credit card company to personal customers.

The cards are issued, upon application, by banks (and also building societies and retail groups) which operate credit card companies. Application forms are usually credit-scored to decide whether a card can be issued. A credit limit is set on each cardholder's account - limits are often £500, £1,000, £1,500 or more. The credit card company will consider increasing a customer's limit on request, and may also do so from time-to-time automatically. Goods and services are purchased using the credit card, or cash can be withdrawn from banks and ATMs (a PIN - Personal Identification Number - is required for the latter). The cardholder can decide, upon receipt of the monthly statement, whether to pay off the whole balance, part of it, or a certain minimum amount. Thus credit cards can be used to spread the cost of purchases over a number of months.

Uses
- short-term finance for purchase of goods and services, provided the supplier is prepared to accept payment by credit card
- cash can be drawn from banks and ATMs

Rates
- interest is charged at a certain percentage each month, but rates are much higher than overdrafts, e.g. 2 per cent per month is equal to an APR of 26.8 per cent

Terms
- goods and services can be purchased, and/or cash withdrawn up to the cardholder's credit card limit
- purchases can be interest-free for up to 56 days
- for cash withdrawals, interest charges commence immediately
- a minimum repayment - shown on the statement - must be paid each month
- no security required

13.9 Mortgages

Banks lend money for the purchase of property, e.g. a house or flat, by means of a mortgage. This is one form of personal lending where security is *always* taken, the security being a mortgage over the property purchased. A mortgage gives the bank the right to sell the property if the customer is unable to maintain loan repayments. The maximum amount of the mortgage will be 90% - 95% of the purchase price for first-time buyers, and up to 80% for second-time buyers (the lower percentage is because there will be a profit on the sale of a previous house, part of which should be put into the new house). The amount that a bank will lend is based on the gross annual income of the borrower(s): often up to three times the income, plus the annual income of a joint borrower, will be lent. Repayment comes from the customer's regular income. Mortgages are long-term lending, typically for between twenty and thirty years. Almost any amount can be lent on mortgage, the most important consideration being the customer's ability to make repayments: most mortgages are for amounts between £10 000 and £200 000.

Uses
• property purchase, e.g. house or flat
• major extensions to property

Rates
• mortgage rates are advertised by banks, they are not directly linked to the bank's base rate

Terms
• the maximum amount that a bank will lend to a customer is often three times the customer's gross annual income, plus the annual income of a joint borrower
• up to 95% of the purchase price of a property is lent
• interest is charged on the amount borrowed (calculated on a daily basis) and is debited to the account
• security is taken, being a first mortgage of the property

Types of mortgage

Repayment mortgage
With this type of mortgage the borrower makes monthly payments which meet both interest and repayment of the capital or principal sum borrowed. In the early years of such a mortgage, most of the payments go towards the interest and only a little towards repayment of capital; in later years, as the amount of the loan reduces, less goes towards interest and more in repayment of capital.

Endowment mortgage
Here, the borrower takes out an endowment assurance policy (see Chapter 12.7). During the term of the mortgage the borrower pays the monthly premiums on the insurance policy and pays the interest on the loan. No capital is repaid during the term of the mortgage but, at the end of the mortgage period, the endowment assurance policy matures, and the proceeds are used to repay the capital sum.

There are two other types of mortgage which operate in a similar way to the endowment mortgage, i.e. only interest is paid during the term of the mortgage, and the capital sum is repaid in a lump sum at the end. One is a *unit-linked mortgage,* which is the same as an endowment mortgage except that monthly payments, instead of going into an insurance policy, are invested in a fund or funds similar to unit trusts. The funds are more closely linked to movements in the Stock Exchange and there is scope for considerably better results than with an endowment assurance policy; equally, though, the risks are greater. The other type of mortgage is a *pension mortgage,* where the capital is repaid at the end of the term from the lump sum received from the borrower's pension plan on retirement.

At present the Government gives a tax allowance on interest paid on the first £30 000 borrowed on a mortgage: the allowance scheme is called MIRAS (mortgage interest relief at source). With a repayment mortgage, the capital sum reduces through the mortgage term and, therefore, the interest is less, so that less tax relief is available. With endowment, unit-linked, and pension mortgages, the capital sum remains outstanding for the term of the mortgage; therefore the interest will be greater than with a repayment mortgage, and so more tax relief will be available.

Most mortgages include life cover (see Chapter 15.8) so that, if the borrower dies, the loan outstanding will be repaid from an insurance policy.

13.10   Bridging Loans

In connection with house purchase, banks are often involved in providing bridging loans to customers. Bridging loans enable a person to pay for a new house before the sale proceeds of the old house are received; the loan is repaid upon receipt of the money from the old house. Bridging loans are normally very short-term, e.g. a matter of days, and interest is charged on a daily basis on the amount borrowed at a rate which will be around five per cent over the bank's base rate. As bridging loans are normally short-term in nature and the bank will not receive much interest, it is also usual to charge an *arrangement fee* for providing the loan.

13.11   Consumer Credit Act

All forms of lending to individuals (including societies, sole traders and partnerships, but not limited companies) up to £15 000, are controlled by the *Consumer Credit Act 1974*. The Act covers *regulated agreements,* and requires that the borrower must be given written details of his or her rights and duties (overdrafts on current accounts are excluded from this requirement). The details to be given include:

- a statement that it is a 'credit agreement regulated by the Consumer Credit Act 1974'
- the amount of credit, or the credit limit
- the timing and amount of repayments
- the Annual Percentage Rate (APR) of charge
- the cash price, total charge for credit, and total amount payable
- the signature of both borrower and lender

A further aspect of the Consumer Credit Act is that, under certain circumstances, when goods have been bought with a credit card, the credit card company can be held liable to the purchaser for faulty goods. This is known as a *connected lender liability* and applies only to:

- goods and services with a cash price of more than £100, but less than £30,000 per single item, and
- where the items have been bought with a credit card

Under these circumstances both retailer and credit card company have *joint and several liability* to the purchaser for the cost of faulty goods and services.

13.12 Revision Points

❑   Interest charged on loans and advances is one of the main sources of bank profit.

❑   The principles of lending (which apply to all lending situations) can be summarized by the word IPARTS:

Integrity
Purpose
Amount
Repayment
Terms
Security

❑   Credit scoring is used to assess the creditworthiness of customers by awarding points to answers given to questions on an application form.

❑   The main forms of bank lending to personal customers include:

- *current account overdrafts*
  - used for short-term requirements; anticipation of salary; student overdrafts
  - interest charged at around five percentage points above base rate
  - interest charged on amount borrowed
  - overdraft limit agreed for a particular time period, and may be renewed

- *personal loans*
  - used to purchase consumer durables; pay for a holiday; pay for home improvements
  - interest rate fixed for the period of the loan
  - Annual Percentage Rate (APR) of charge quoted to the customer
  - amount of personal loans from £250 up to £10,000
  - period of loan from one to five years
  - application forms usually credit scored
  - monthly repayments

- *budget accounts*
  - used to spread the cost of bills evenly over a twelve-month period
  - interest charged at around five percentage points above base rate
  - some banks charge an overall fixed operating fee
  - the account operates for twelve months, after which it is reviewed and usually renewed

- *revolving credit (cashflow) accounts*
  - used for any purpose, e.g. to pay bills, to purchase consumer goods, to pay for holidays, etc.
  - interest charged at around five percentage points above base rate
  - monthly payments
  - maximum overdraft is a multiple (usually twenty-five or thirty times) of the monthly repayment

- *credit cards*
  - short-term finance for the purchase of goods and services
  - cash withdrawals from banks and ATMs
  - credit card limit established
  - interest charged monthly on outstanding balance
  - a minimum repayment must be paid each month

❏ Mortgages are loans for the purchase of property.

- maximum amount of a mortgage will be 90%-95% of purchase price
- up to three times the gross income of the borrower will be lent
- the bank always takes security - a first mortgage of the property
- types of mortgage
  - repayment
  - endowment
  - unit-linked
  - pension

❏ All forms of lending to individuals (including societies, sole traders and partnerships, but not companies) up to £15 000 are *regulated agreements,* under the Consumer Credit Act 1974.

❏ The borrower must be given written details of his/her rights and duties for all regulated agreements (except for overdrafts).

13.13 Know your *Bank Lending to Personal Customers*

Multiple-choice Questions

Choose the *one* answer you think is correct.

1. Which of the following would you *not* accept as security for a loan?

    A Land
    B Gold and diamonds
    C Life assurance policy
    D Stocks and shares certificates

2. Under a credit scoring system, which one of these points is likely to be weighted most favourably?

    A Nature of property occupied, and whether owned or rented
    B Marital status and dependants
    C Age
    D Occupation and length of time in present employment

3. Which of the following would be a cost-effective alternative to an overdraft for someone wanting to cover expenditure of £500 for five weeks?

    A Credit card
    B Personal loan
    C Budget account
    D Secured loan

4. A customer wishes to borrow £4,000 from the bank to assist with the purchase of a car costing £8,000. Assuming that the bank is prepared to lend, which facility is most likely to be offered?

    A Budget account
    B Personal loan
    C Revolving credit account
    D Overdraft

5.   A budget account

    A is used to spread the cost of household bills throughout the year
    B is used to make monthly standing order payments, such as mortgage, insurance and hire
       purchase
    C offers high rates of interest to regular savers
    D can be used as an alternative to a personal loan account

6.   An account where a customer can overdraw up to a certain limit for any purpose dependent
     on a fixed monthly payment is

    A a personal loan
    B a budget account
    C an overdraft
    D a revolving credit account

7.   The short-term bank loan often used to cover the period between buying one house and
     selling another is called a

    A personal loan
    B revolving credit account
    C home improvement loan
    D bridging loan

8.   The Consumer Credit Act regulates loans up to what amount?

    A £5,000
    B £10,000
    C £15,000
    D £20,000

Short Answer Questions

9.   List *two* factors which a bank would consider when making a loan.

10.   Give the words for each letter of 'IPARTS'.

11.   Why do banks often take security for loans?

12.   Define credit scoring in not more than 25 words.

13.   Give *two* examples of the types of lending for which an overdraft on current account is most
      appropriate.

14.   What bank service would you offer to a 25 year old wishing to buy a car?

15.   What does APR stand for?

16.   A customer requires a personal loan to pay for a holiday. What maximum repayment period
      would you agree?

17.   What is the purpose of a revolving credit account? How does it differ from a budget
      account?

18.   Name *two* different types of mortgage.

19.   To what types of customer does the Consumer Credit Act apply?

13.13 Essay questions *Bank Lending to Personal Customers*

1. *Note: This question is not solely concerned with bank lending; instead it brings together all aspects of personal customer services, covered in this and the previous two chapters.*

    Suggest the bank services which you could offer to Eric in the seven stages of his life:

    (1) little Eric is only 8 years old

    (2) Eric is 15 and at high school

    (3) Eric is 18 and going to university in October

    (4) Eric is 24, a qualified accountant, and is getting married to the lovely Erica; they are setting up home

    (5) Eric and Erica have two children, aged 3 and 6, and want to provide for them in the future

    (6) Eric and Erica are about to retire, and have paid off their mortgage

    (7) Eric, alas, has died

2. What are the main principles of lending? What points would the lending officer be looking under each principle when considering a loan request?

3. A customer tells you that she is moving house shortly. She enquires about:

    (1) the different types of mortgages offered by the bank
    (2) financing the short-term 'gap' between buying her new house and receiving the money from the sale of her old house

    What advice would you give her?

4. Obtain leaflets from your bank on:

    • personal loans
    • budget accounts
    • revolving credit (cashflow) accounts

    Compare the features of each, contrasting uses, rates and terms.

5. What forms of lending would you offer to the following customers?

    (a) John, aged 17, wishes to buy a motorbike costing £750

    [5 marks]

    (b) John and Julie, both aged 22, just married, wish to buy a house

    [10 marks]

    (c) John and Julie, aged 35, are moving house

    [5 marks]

6.   ***Case problem questions***

What particular financial service or services would you suggest for the following? State the benefits to the customer to help explain your choice.

(a)   Donna Wright has just started work in London and, although she is earning £15,000 a year, she knows that she does not manage money well. Once she has paid her monthly accounts she tends to spend the rest on having a good time, leaving little cash available to pay for irregular items such as car tax and insurance, annual subscriptions, holidays, and maintenance contracts on her many electrical appliances.

What account would help her to manage her finances and how would it help her to stop running out of money?

[5 marks]
[question 9d, Autumn 1988]

(b)   George Williams is aged 19 and has just started a new job in London and he travels daily by British Rail. His daily fare is £6 but if he could afford £920 he could buy an annual season ticket which would give him an annual saving of £470. He has £120 of his own which he could use.

George has had a bank account for two years and he has his wages paid into the account.

What alternatives are available to George? Give the advantages and disadvantages in note form only.

[5 marks]
[question 9a, Spring 1988]

(c)   Jean and Billy Slocombe are buying their first house, having recently been married on Jean's 21st birthday. Jean is a supervisor in a high street retailer and hopes to progress to a management position.

Billy is 25 years old and works as a computer analyst in the local university.

The house, which is terraced, cost £50,000 and both Jean and Billy have set themselves a couple of 'housing' targets: namely to move up market over the years and eventually buy a detached house, and to be clear of their mortgage payments by the time Billy is 50.

[5 marks]
[question 9b, Autumn 1987]

(d)   Jane and Peter Fitzgerald are a newly married couple who are hoping to buy their own house. They are both aged 22 and work for the local council. They will be able to save £150 a month for the next year or two, which they hope will give them a deposit for their house.

[5 marks]
[question 28c, Spring 1987]

Chapter Fourteen
Accounts and Services: Business Customers

In this chapter we shall look at the bank services for the business customer, i.e. sole traders, partnerships and limited companies. We will consider:

* general bank services for the business customer
* forms of business lending
* other forms of finance for business
* other services for the business customer

14.1 General Bank Services for the Business Customer

Many bank services which are suitable for personal customers are used by business customers. These include:

* current accounts
* deposit accounts
* funds transfer - cheques, bank giro credits, BACS, bank drafts

These services are not discussed in this chapter - please refer to the appropriate section in the book.

More specialist business services include:

* advisory services
* international services
* insurance
* computer services
* night safes

These are detailed later in this chapter.

14.2 Business Lending

With lending to businesses, the same principles of lending are used as for personal customers (see Chapter 13.2). To recap, the principles of lending are:
  I ntegrity
  P urpose
  A mount
  R epayment
  T erms
  S ecurity

Most business lending propositions require the approval of the branch manager, assistant manager, or senior lending officer and will usually be subject to a lending interview with the business customer. Very few business lending propositions can be credit scored.

Often security will be taken from business customers to provide the bank with some 'insurance' should the lending not be repaid. Such security often takes the form of:

- land and buildings
- life policies
- stocks and shares
- guarantees

Remember that banks do not lend on security - the lending proposition should 'stand up in its own right', but the security forms a safeguard for the bank.

The requirements of the *Consumer Credit Act 1974* (see Chapter 13.11) apply to lending up to £15,000 to sole traders and partnerships (but not limited companies). Above this amount, and for lending to limited companies, the Act does not apply.

14.3 Forms of Business Lending

There are two main forms of business lending:

- overdrafts
- business development loans

Overdrafts

As with personal customers, businesses use an overdraft as a flexible and cheap form of short-term finance. In fact, overdrafts are the most common form of business finance.

Uses
- to provide working capital, i.e. to finance the day-to-day expenses of running the business such as paying suppliers (creditors) for purchases of stock, allowing customers (debtors) time to pay, payment of the running costs of the business

- short-term requirements for the purchase of a specific item, e.g. the purchase of new office equipment (such items are financed on a longer-term basis by means of a business development loan, or hire purchase, or leasing [see Section 14.4])

- seasonal requirements, e.g. a shop stocking up for Christmas

Rates
- a rate of three to five per cent over the bank's base rate would be usual, although a good business customer borrowing larger amounts might be able to negotiate a rate as low as one per cent over base rate

- often a fee will be charged for arranging an overdraft facility, and for committing the bank's money

Terms
- any amount can be borrowed on overdraft

- interest is charged on the amount borrowed (calculated on a daily basis) and charged to the account monthly or quarterly

- an overdraft limit is agreed for a particular time period, e.g. one month, six months, a year, and may be renewed if still required

- security is often required, although it is not essential

Business development loans

These are loans for a specific time period and for a fixed amount of money. Different banks will give them different names such as 'business loans' and 'medium-term loans'. Regular repayments are made (often on a monthly or quarterly basis), which incorporate the interest payments. The amount of the loan is credited to the customer's current account and debited to a loan account.

Uses
- purchase of specific assets, e.g. machinery, office equipment, motor vehicles

- purchase or extension of business premises

- purchase of a business

- provision of additional working capital

Rates
- interest rates of about two-and-a-half to five per cent over the bank's base rate are charged

- some business development loans can be arranged at a rate of interest fixed throughout the term of the loan

Terms
- business development loans are available for amounts from £5,000 upwards

- security invariably required for this type of loan

- loans can be arranged for between one and twenty years, although most would be between three and ten years

- a capital 'holiday' can often be arranged for the first year or two of a loan, during which time capital repayments need not be made (although interest must be paid during this time)

- a fee for arranging the loan is charged (often one per cent of the loan amount)

Other forms of business lending

Most banks provide loan facilities which provide finance for particular types of business, or for specific purposes. Some examples of these are:

- **Farmers' loans**, which assist farmers with their seasonal requirements, e.g. they can be used to finance the time period between sowing seed and harvesting and selling the crops.

- **Franchise loans**, which allow the purchase or development of a franchise. (A franchise is where the owner of a franchise sells the rights to market a product in a certain area - examples are some fast-food shops, instant-print shops, etc.).

- **Commercial mortgages**, which enable the purchase of business premises over a period of up to 25 years.

- **Small Firms Loan Guarantee Scheme,** under which banks provide finance up to £100,000 to new and existing small businesses, supported by a guarantee from the Department of Employment, the guarantee covering 70 per cent of the amount advanced.

14.4   Other Forms of Finance for Business

Industrial hire purchase

- Businesses often use hire purchase to enable them to finance the acquisition of assets such as motor vehicles, machinery, office equipment. Hire purchase operates in the same way as for personal customers, i.e. an initial deposit is paid, and payments are made at regular intervals - often monthly - for a period of time, usually between three and five years.

- With hire purchase, a business obtains the use of an asset without a major outlay of cash.

- Finance companies (see Chapter 15.7), some of which are wholly or partly owned by banks, provide hire purchase.

- Legal ownership of the asset remains with the finance company until the last payment is made, at which point it passes to the business.

Leasing

- Another method for a business to finance the acquisition of assets such as motor vehicles, etc., without a major outlay of cash.

- A leasing company, which is a finance house (see Chapter 15.7) - perhaps partly or wholly owned by a bank, buys the asset.

- The asset is then *rented* to a business for a period of time - often up to five years for a *finance lease*.

- Shorter-term leases - called an *operating lease* - can be arranged; these often include repair and maintenance of the asset.

- Rental payments are made on a regular basis - often monthly or quarterly.

- Ownership of the asset remains with the leasing company, although the terms of a lease may give the business an option to purchase at the end of the lease.

Factoring

- Factoring provides finance to a business by using the amounts owed to a business by its debtors.

- Factoring companies, some of which are wholly or partly owned by banks, will:
  - provide finance against debtors
  - manage the debtors of a business (i.e. handle the book-keeping records of sales made)

- A commission fee of between 0.75% - 2% of the business' total sales is charged for the service.

- Interest is charged on amounts advanced at interest rates slightly higher than a bank overdraft.

- The amount advanced will be up to 80% of the invoice amount, with the balance (less commission fee and interest) being paid at an agreed date in the future - often in three months' time.

- Factoring is only suitable where a business sells to other businesses - it cannot be used for a shop selling to the general public.

- Normally only available for businesses with sales of more than £250,000 each year.

14.5   Other Services for the Business Customer

In this section we will consider the other main services offered by banks to their business customers:

- advisory services
- international services
- insurance
- computer services
- night safes

Advisory services

Business customers often turn to a bank for assistance on a wide range of issues, and the role of a bank's business manager is to become involved in the financial activities of this important group of customers. Advice may be sought on:

- buying assets such as motor vehicles, machinery, etc.
- buying new premises
- purchase of a new business
- expansion of an existing business
- the financial implications of a new product
- seeking new markets for the firm's products and making *status enquiries* to check on the credit-worthiness of potential new customers

Many banks provide a specialist *business advisory service* for their small and medium-sized business customers. The service is operated by managers who are specially trained to provide advice and guidance on a range of financial planning and control systems. They will spend a number of days (usually from 2 - 5 days) at the premises of a business customer and will prepare a report for the owner(s) of the business.

International Services

Banks provide services to business customers involved in international trade as either exporters or importers. The main services are:

- **Foreign exchange**
  Banks can buy and sell foreign currencies in exchange for sterling to enable a business to export (sell) goods and import (buy) goods priced in foreign currencies.

- **Documentation**
  The exporter (seller) or importer (buyer) will seek advice from his/her bank about the appropriate documents for an international transaction.

- **Methods of payment**
  Banks are involved in *documentary credits* under which an importer's (buyer's) bank guarantees payment to the exporter (seller) in another country. They also handle *collections,* by means of which an exporter asks his/her bank to deliver the documents of the export transaction to the importer's bank, which hands over the documents against payment or a signed promise to pay in the future (usually in the form of a bill of exchange).

- **Methods of settlement**
  Banks are able to make settlements of amounts owing between importer and exporter by means of:
  - telegraphic (or cable) transfer
  - mail transfer
  - bank draft

  Telegraphic transfer and mail transfer usually pass through an international settlements system operated by banks called SWIFT (Society for Worldwide Interbank Telecommunications)

- **Finance**
  Special finance facilities are offered by banks to their export/import customers.

- **Advisory**
  Banks can:
  - provide information about selling to particular overseas markets
  - obtain the names of potential buyers or agents abroad
  - obtain the names of potential sellers abroad
  - undertake status enquiries on overseas companies

Insurance

Banks can provide for the special insurance needs of business customers. A business will often seek insurance cover for the following:

- *Fire and theft* - covering the business premises and stock

- *Loss of profits* - provides cover where serious disruption is caused to the business after a major disaster, such as a fire or a flood

- *Employers' liability* - insures against the employer's liability for accidents to employees at work

- *Public liability* - to cover possible claims for damages from the public

- *'Keyperson' insurance* - to cover against the death, illness or injury of employees or owners who are especially important to the continued running of a business

Computer services

Most banks offer computer services to their business customers; such services include:

- *Payroll* - calculation and processing of employees' weekly or monthly pay

- *Accounting* - handling the accounting records of a business, especially debtors (customers who owe money to the business) and creditors (suppliers to whom the business owes money)

- *Cash Management Services* - a facility by which business customers can use their own computers to obtain balances of their accounts by means of a telephone link to the bank's computer, and can authorize payments to be made (see also Chapter 16.6 - 'home banking')

Night safes

- Most bank branches have a night safe installed, the entrance to which can be seen on the outside wall.

- A night safe provides a facility for business customers to deposit money in a secure place outside banking hours. Thus it is an ideal method of depositing takings received by shops and other businesses after the banks have closed.

- Special wallets or bags are provided by the bank, together with a key to open the night safe. The wallets drop down a chute into a separate safe in the branch premises.

- Wallets can be either opened by bank staff and the amount credited to the customer's account, or they can be collected, unopened, by the customer.

- A charge is made by the bank for providing night safes.

14.6 Revision Points

❏ Business customers make use of general bank services such as:

- current accounts
- deposit accounts
- funds transfer

❏ Lending to business customers is usually subject to a lending interview; the principles of lending - IPARTS - will be followed.

❏ Business lending is carried out by means of:

- overdraft
- business development loan
- specialist forms of lending, such as farmers' loans, franchise loans, commercial mortgages, Small Firms Loan Guarantee Scheme

❏ Other business financial services include:

- *industrial hire purchase,* for the acquisition of assets such as motor vehicles, machinery, etc.
- *leasing,* which is the 'rental' of assets such as motor vehicles, machinery, etc.
- *factoring,* which is the provision of finance against the debtors of a business

❏ Other services include:

- advisory services
- international, especially foreign exchange, documentation, methods of payment, methods of settlement, finance, advisory
- insurance, especially fire and theft, loss of profits, employers' liability, public liability, 'keyperson'
- night safes

14.7 Know your *Accounts and Services: Business Customers*

Multiple-choice Questions

Choose the *one* answer you think is correct.

1. A company customer requires finance for working capital. The bank will provide this by means of

   A an overdraft
   B a business development loan
   C a commercial mortgage
   D industrial hire purchase

2. A business customer of your bank obtains finance against its debtors; it is using

   A business development loan
   B leasing
   C factoring
   D hire purchase

3. A business that has the use (but not the ownership) of a vehicle upon payment of a sum of money on a regular basis over a long period of time is using the finance service of

    A factoring
    B leasing
    C hire purchase
    D overdraft

4. Cash management services provide businesses with
    A high rates of interest for large fixed-term deposits
    B computer access into the bank's computer so that the customer's balance can be obtained
    C cash withdrawal facilities at all branches of the bank
    D advice on investments

Short Answer Questions

5. Give *two* examples of the types of business lending for which an overdraft is appropriate.

6. Give *two* examples of the types of business lending for which a business development loan is appropriate.

7. State *two* features of the *Small Firms Loan Guarantee Scheme*.

8. Explain leasing in not more than 25 words.

9. What are the two main types of lease?

10. List *two* services of a factoring company.

11. List *four* international services provided by banks to exporters and importers.

12. State *three* types of insurance that a business customer will use.

14.8 Essay Questions *Accounts and Services: Business Customers*

1. Obtain leaflets from your bank on:
    • business overdrafts
    • business development loans

    Compare the features of each contrasting *uses, rates* and *terms*.

2. Explain the features and uses of:
    • industrial hire purchase
    • leasing
    • factoring

3. A 'Hi-tech' firm employing 500 staff wishes to pay its staff monthly into a bank account rather than by cash as at present. What methods of payment are open to it and what advantages are there for both firm and employee in using such methods?

    [The Chartered Institute of Bankers' specimen paper]

4. You receive the following letter from a large and important customer. Draft a suitable letter in reply.

```
Dear Sir,

You will no doubt be aware of some of the problems that my monthly
paid staff are experiencing when they come into your branch with their
salary cheques on payday.

They are having to queue for most of their lunchtime to pay in their
cheques and this is causing great inconvenience not to mention the
work I lose when they are late back from lunch.  Are there any
alternatives?  How do they work, and are there any advantages to me?
You will also have heard about the wages snatch at my factory when
£10,000 was stolen.

Despite my attempts to get those employees who at present insist on
receiving their weekly wages by cash to switch over to payment by
cheque they cannot understand how the system moves money from one
account to another.

Could you suggest some ways that I could improve my payments system to
both groups?

Yours faithfully

D. Molytshun

Managing director - Earth Movers UK plc
```

[question 6, Spring 1988]

5. Summarise, under *six* headings, the international services that are offered by your bank to business customers.

6. *Case problem questions*

What particular financial service or services would you suggest for the following? State the benefits to the customer to help explain your choice.

(a) Terry Daley started up in the building business some ten years ago and formed a small private company about three years ago.

He now wants to diversify his activity into the construction of swimming pools and large ornamental ponds. He has looked into the market and there is enough business to justify the acquisition of a small JCB 'digger' to excavate the ponds/pools.

Terry neither wants to tie up his capital in the purchase of the machine nor to worry about the maintenance and repair of the digger. *[5 marks]*

[question 9d, Autumn 1987]

(b) Alan Walsh runs 'The Corner Stores'. He buys all his supplies from a 'cash and carry' warehouse. Six weeks before Christmas he tells you that he wants to stock up the shop with Christmas "goodies" - puddings, crackers, chocolates, wine, etc. Unfortunately he hasn't the cash to buy all the goods which he thinks he can sell. *[5 marks]*

(c) John and Jennie Williams set up in business last year manufacturing high quality kitchen units, which they sell to major retailers and kitchen installation companies. Business is going well and, this year, sales are expected to be £400,000. However, the businesses that they sell to are slow payers - but they pay in the end - and the Williams' always have debtors of £100,000 at any one time. This means that they are always short of cash, and this slows expansion of their business. *[5 marks]*

Chapter Fifteen
Banks and Competition

In recent years the banks have expanded their services in order to be able to offer a full range of services which meet the financial requirements of their personal (and business) customers. Examples of this expansion are:

- interest-bearing current accounts
- savings accounts offering a range of interest rates
- development of mortgage lending
- marketing of life assurance to customers
- selling unit trusts and other savings schemes

At the same time, a number of financial organisations have moved into services that, at one time, were traditionally provided by banks. Examples are:

- building societies offering current accounts
- major retailers offering charge and credit cards
- personal loans available from building societies

In this chapter we shall look at the major competitors of banks in the provision of financial services for personal customers. Remember, also, that banks compete aggressively amongst themselves for an increased share of the market.

15.1   Who are the Competitors?

The main competitors of banks for personal financial services are shown in fig. 15.1, and include:

- *building societies* - deposit-taking, money transmission, personal lending and credit cards, mortgage lending, investment, insurance services
- *Girobank* - (owned by the Alliance and Leicester Building Society) - deposit-taking, money transmission, personal lending, mortgage lending services
- *retail groups* - personal lending and credit cards, investment services
- *National Savings Bank* - deposit-taking
- *National Savings schemes* - a number of investment services
- *finance houses* - personal lending, and hire purchase

- *insurance companies* - investments and insurance services
- *moneyshops* - deposit-taking, money transmission, personal lending, mortgage lending, insurance
- *unit trusts* - investment services
- *investment trusts* - investment services
- *pension funds* - long-term savings and investment

Service	Main competitors
Deposit-taking	Building societies National Savings Bank Girobank Moneyshops
Money transmission	Building societies Girobank Moneyshops
Personal lending and credit cards	Building societies Girobank Moneyshops Finance houses Retail groups
Mortgage lending	Building societies Girobank Moneyshops
Other main services *Investment*	Building societies Unit trusts Investment trusts Retail groups Insurance companies National Savings Pension funds
Insurance	Building societies Insurance companies Moneyshops

Fig. 15.1   Main competitors of banks

Clearly, the major competitors of the banks in the provision of personal services are the building societies, with their large branch networks, long opening hours, and expanding services. However, the distinction between banks and building societies, which was at one time very clear, has become blurred. For example, in 1989 the members of Abbey National Building Society voted to convert the society into a public limited company (now called Abbey National plc), which has now been granted authorisation from the Bank of England to become a bank (Abbey National had already become a member of the general cheque clearing in 1988). Also, Girobank, which was for 20 years the Post Office's bank, was sold to Alliance and Leicester Building Society in 1989. It seems only a matter of time before other building societies move more closely to becoming banks.

Another area of considerable competition comes from the retail trade. Almost all large retailers offer their own credit card (although, in practice, many of these are operated on their behalf by credit card companies owned by banks). In 1988 Marks and Spencer launched its own unit trust, and in 1989 introduced personal loans and Personal Equity Plans. It cannot be long before a major retailer offers bank account services through its retail outlets (in a similar way to that operated by the Co-op bank).

15.2   Building Societies

Building societies have their origins in the late 18th and early 19th centuries from agreements between their members to save money in order to buy land and build houses for their members. During the middle of the 19th century they were permitted by law to accept the deposits of savers who did not wish to have a house built. From this time on, building societies developed the two main areas of their activities:

- deposit-taking
- granting mortgages

In 1986, the Building Societies Act was passed which allowed societies to expand their services to include:

- current accounts, with cheque books and cheque cards
- overdrafts and personal loans
- credit cards
- selling insurance
- giving investment advice
- dealing in stocks and shares, and unit trusts
- ownership of estate agents
- form public limited companies if the members so wish

Today, most societies are *mutual societies,* i.e. they are owned and operated for the benefit of their members, the savers and borrowers. However, in 1989, the members of the Abbey National Building Society voted to convert the society into a public limited company with its shares quoted on the stock exchange. The advantage of this is that, by issuing shares, the society has been able to raise money for expansion; the disadvantage is that it could be taken over by another company.

Building societies are supervised by the Building Societies Commission, which monitors the financial performance of each society. (Note, however, that when a building society is authorized to become a bank, e.g. Abbey National plc, supervision is then by the Bank of England).

Functions

- deposit-taking
- granting mortgages
- provision of personal financial services

Main services

Deposit-taking
Most building societies offer a range of accounts which include the following:
- share account
- regular savings account
- investment account

The terms under which these accounts operate vary from society to society with regard to maximum and maximum amounts, notice of withdrawal, and interest rates. You are advised to

BUILDING SOCIETIES: DEPOSIT-TAKING ACCOUNTS

Account	Features	Suitability	Advantages/disadvantages
Share account	• basic account • passbook issued • withdrawals on demand • no minimum balance to be maintained	• for those who require interest with immediate access to funds	*Advantages:* • an account that is easy to operate • immediate access to funds without penalty *Disadvantage:* • lower rate of interest than other accounts
Regular savings account	• regular monthly savings	• for those who wish to save on a regular basis, perhaps for a specific item	*Advantages:* • higher interest rates than a share account • monthly payments can be varied *Disadvantage:* • there may be loss of interest for early withdrawals
Investment account	• high interest rates paid on larger deposits	• for those who require high interest rates	*Advantages:* • high interest rates • 'tiered' interest rates paid, i.e. the higher the balance, the higher the interest rate *Disadvantage:* • there may be a period of notice, e.g. 90 days, or loss of interest for withdrawals on demand

Fig. 15.2   Building societies: types of deposit-taking accounts

obtain leaflets and make comparisons yourself. Fig. 15.2 gives details of the three main types of deposit-taking accounts, although each society will give its own 'brand name' to each account.

The following points apply to most building society deposit-taking accounts:

• Accounts can be in a sole name, or joint names, e.g. husband and wife.

• Interest is calculated on a daily basis and credited to the account either half-yearly or annually (variations include interest credited monthly, and interest paid by cheque to the account holder).

• Interest is paid net of basic rate income tax, i.e. there is no further tax to pay unless the account holder(s) pays higher-rate tax. However, non-taxpayers (e.g. some pensioners) cannot reclaim the tax paid and, for such people, building society accounts are a disadvantage.

- Rates of interest paid by building societies vary in accordance with the general level of interest rates.

- Withdrawals can be made in cash or by cheque, usually on demand, and often at any branch of the society.

- Certain of the accounts can be operated by ATM cards, the two main networks being MATRIX and LINK (the latter network is also used by Girobank and the Co-op Bank).

- Special savings accounts are offered to children and young people, with high interest rates and other 'goodies'.

Mortgages

Building societies were originally established in order to enable members to buy their own houses. This function, lending for property purchase by offering mortgages, still forms a major part of the societies' business. The main types of mortgages offered by building societies are the same as those offered by banks, i.e.

- repayment mortgage
- endowment mortgage
- pension mortgage

Fig. 15.3 shows the main features of each of these, together with their advantages and disadvantages. The following points apply to most building society mortgages:

- Mortgage accounts can be in a sole name, or joint names, e.g. husband and wife.

- Interest is charged annually to the mortgage account (and will be calculated either on a daily basis, or on the balance outstanding at a particular date).

- Rates of interest vary with the general level of interest rates.

- Some building societies offer slightly reduced interest rates for larger mortgages, e.g. above £60,000; 'low-start mortgages' are also available, which reduce the size of the monthly payments in the first few years.

- A building society will lend up to a certain amount, based on the income of the borrower, e.g. three times gross income, plus the annual gross income of a joint borrower, such as a wife, girlfriend, etc.

- The maximum amount lent will be up to 95% of the value of the property being purchased.

- The building society will require, as security, a first legal mortgage over the property, i.e. it has the right of sale under certain circumstances, and will hold the title documents of the property.

- The property must be insured against fire and other damage.

Provision of personal financial services

Since the passing of the Building Societies Act 1986, almost all societies have increased their range of personal financial services to include:

- current account
- automated teller machines
- credit cards
- personal loans
- home improvement loans
- insurance
- travel facilities
- financial advice

Fig. 15.4 shows the main features of each of these services in more detail. Some societies also have links with estate agents and, thus, are able to offer a complete service to the home buyer.

BUILDING SOCIETIES: MORTGAGES

Type of mortgage	Features	Suitability	Advantages/ disadvantages
Repayment mortgage	• finance for the purchase of residential property, i.e. house or flat • monthly payments include capital and mortgage interest	• home buyer seeking a straightforward method of purchase	*Advantages:* • long-term loan, up to 30 years • tax relief on interest on first £30,000 of mortgage • easy to extend/alter mortgage amount or term for subsequent house moves *Disadvantage:* • may not be as financially advantageous as endowment or pension-linked mortgages
Endowment mortgage	• finance for the purchase of residential property • monthly payments meet mortgage interest only • separate life assurance policy taken out (monthly premiums) • on maturity of the life policy, the capital amount of the mortgage is paid off	• home buyer seeking likelihood of capital sum after repayment of mortgage	*Advantages:* • long-term loan up to 30 years • tax relief on interest on first £30,000 of mortgage • full life assurance during term of mortgage • may produce a tax-free lump sum on maturity of life policy, after repayment of mortgage *Disadvantage:* • the term of the mortgage cannot be extended for subsequent house moves
Pension-linked mortgage	• similar to an endowment mortgage, except that regular payments are made by the borrower into a pension policy • mortgage is repaid from the lump sum received from the borrower's pension plan on retirement	• home buyer making contributions to a pension policy	*Advantages:* • long-term loan, up to 30 years • tax relief on interest on first £30,000 of mortgage • tax relief on payments into pension policy (within certain limits) *Disadvantages:* • the term of the mortgage cannot be extended for subsequent house moves • part of pension entitlement is used to repay mortgage

Fig. 15.3   Building societies: types of mortgages

BUILDING SOCIETIES: PERSONAL FINANCIAL SERVICES

Service	Features	Suitability	Advantages/disadvantages
Current accounts	• cheque book • cheque card • interest paid on credit balances • authorised overdrafts • standing orders/direct debits	• building society customer seeking 'banking' services	*Advantage:* • all basic banking services provided
Automated teller machines (ATM)	• cash withdrawals from ATM machines • balance enquiries • transfer money between accounts controlled by the card • payment of regular bills automatically (current account customers only)	• building society current account customers • also available for use with other types of accounts	*Advantage:* • can be used at any machine in either LINK or MATRIX networks
Credit cards	• credit facility	• customers seeking flexible borrowing	*Advantages:* • borrowing facility • flexible payments *Disadvantage:* • high interest rates charged
Personal loans	• loans for any purpose • loan period up to five years	• homeowners with or without a mortgage	*Advantage:* • lower interest rates because loan is secured on borrower's property
Home improvement loans	• loans for extensions or improvements to borrower's residential property • loan period can be full length of remaining mortgage term	• homeowners with or without a mortgage	*Advantages:* • lower interest rates because loan is secured on borrower's property • up to 95% of cost of improvement can be loaned
Insurance	• home insurance (buildings and contents) • life assurance	• homeowners with or without a mortgage • any other customer	*Advantages:* • premiums can be paid monthly • peace of mind
Travel facilities	• travellers' cheques • foreign currency	• customers travelling abroad	
Financial advice	• advice on investments, pensions, mortgages, tax management • purchase or sale of stocks and shares, and unit trusts	• customers requiring investment advice • customers requiring share and unit trust transactions	*Advantages:* • expert advice • low-cost share dealing service

Fig. 15.4   Building societies: provision of personal financial services

Differences from banks

Many people regard building societies as equals to banks and would be hard-pressed to point out differences between the two financial institutions. The distinction between the two has become more blurred by the move of one of the larger societies (Abbey National) to be authorised by the Bank of England to become a bank. The differences are:

- building societies provide services mainly for the personal customer; banks provide for personal and business customers.

- building societies are supervised by the Building Societies Commission, under the terms of the Building Societies Act 1986; banks are authorized by the Bank of England, under the terms of the Banking Act 1987.

- building society depositors are protected up to £20,000 to the extent of 90% of their funds, i.e. a maximum of £18,000; bank depositors are protected up to £20,000 and 75%, i.e. a maximum of £15,000.

- the majority of building society lending is for the purchase of residential property; most bank lending is for general personal and business purposes.

15.3 Girobank

Girobank (see also Chapter 4.5) operates through the Post Office and was originally established in 1968 in order to:

- provide a simple money transmission system
- offer current account banking to the personal sector, and particularly lower income groups who, at that time, tended to be reluctant to use the major banks

Nowadays, the bank has some 2½ million personal customers, and some 30,000 business account holders. However, many non-account holders use the Girobank 'Transcash' service for payment of bills such as gas, telephone, electricity, etc. at post offices. Major retailers use Girobank, with its longer post office opening hours, to deposit takings at the end of the day and on Saturday mornings. All accounting transfers are conducted at Girobank's computer centre at Bootle in Merseyside.

In 1989 the Government sold Girobank to the Alliance and Leicester Building Society, so the building society has access to current account banking services with which it can compete with the major retail banks both for personal and business customers.

Functions

The main functions of Girobank are:

- to provide a simple money transmission service
- provision of a current account banking to both personal and business customers

Main services

Girobank services are shown in fig. 15.5.

Differences from banks

- Girobank operates through 20,000 post office branches
- it operates a money transmission service outside the banking system
- it is owned by a building society

GIROBANK

Service	Features	Suitability	Advantages/disadvantages
Money transmission by 'Transcash'	• computerised transfer system • rapid funds transfer	• personal customers • business customers • non-account holders	*Advantages:* • simple and easy to use • 20,000 post office 'branches'
Current accounts	• cheque book • cheque encashment at certain post offices • cheque card • standing orders/direct debits • authorised overdrafts • high-interest current account available	• personal customers seeking basic current account services • business customers paying in takings	*Advantages:* • basic banking services • 20,000 post office 'branches' *Disadvantage:* • limited cheque encashment facilities without cheque card
Deposit accounts	• interest credited • higher rates of interest available for larger balances	• personal customers who wish to save	*Advantage:* • funds can be transferred easily between current and deposit accounts
Lending	• credit cards (VISA *'Girobank Classic'* card) • personal loans • mortgages • business loans	• personal customers • business customers	*Advantage:* • basic lending services to suit all types of customer
Travel facilities	• travellers' cheques • foreign money	• customers travelling abroad	
Automated teller machines (ATM)	• cash withdrawals • balance enquiries	• personal customers	*Advantages:* • member of LINK network • can also be used in MATRIX machines

Fig. 15.5   Services offered by Girobank

15.4   Retail groups

As mentioned earlier in this chapter, large retail businesses are increasingly competitors of the banks in the provision of personal financial services. The main areas of competition are:

• *store cards,* e.g. Marks and Spencer Chargecard, Argos Personal Account, Dixons Card, Currys Budget Card, etc.

• *personal loans and hire purchase,* e.g. for major purchases, such as furniture and carpets, electrical goods, etc.

- *unit trusts,* e.g. in 1988 Marks and Spencer launched two unit trusts
- *share dealing,* e.g. Debenhams has a number of 'share shops' situated in large stores
- *investment,* e.g. in 1989 Marks and Spencer commenced a Personal Equity Plan (PEP)

Retail groups are skilled at marketing and selling products, and often the sale of a financial service is made at the same time as the customer buys goods. For example, the sale of a hi-fi system can often lead to the use of a store card or a personal loan.

Some retailers will accept only their own store card (e.g. Marks and Spencer). The holder of a store card will be inclined to shop more often at the retail group and will spend more. Store card account-holders provide the retail group with a database of names and addresses who can be sent mail shots of new products - both retail and financial.

Unit trusts are a new venture for retailers, but Marks and Spencer's issue of two unit trusts in late 1988 was a great success. Far more money was invested in their unit trusts than was achieved by major financial services groups launching new unit trusts at the same time. Following on from this, in 1989, Marks and Spencer introduced a Personal Equity Plan.

Often there are links between retail groups and banks in the provision of financial services. For example, many store cards are operated on behalf of the retailer by credit card companies owned by banks; similarly personal lending and hire purchase is often provided by hire purchase companies owned by banks. Nevertheless, major retailers offer a considerable threat to banks in the provision of personal financial services.

15.5 National Savings Bank

The National Savings Bank (NSB) was established in 1861 as the Post Office Savings Bank. It was re-named in 1969 when it was separated from the Post Office and came under the control of the Government's Department for National Savings.

The NSB is operated through post offices and has the advantage of almost 20,000 post office 'branches' with longer opening hours than banks. However, its customers have to share post offices services with other users of the post office.

Functions
- deposit-taking from mainly personal customers
- investing depositors' funds in Government Stocks.

NSB accounts are suitable for small personal savers who want simple accounts without a full banking service, and the convenience of 20,000 post office 'branches'. NSB invests its customers' deposits, through the National Debt Commissioners, in Government Stocks, so helping to finance Government borrowing: in this way depositors' funds are guaranteed by the Government. NSB does not grant loans to its customers.

Main services
National Savings Bank offers two accounts, both of which use pass books:

- Ordinary Account
- Investment Account

Details of these accounts are shown in fig. 15.6.

NATIONAL SAVINGS BANK

Account	Features	Suitability	Advantages/ disadvantages
Ordinary Account	• simple savings account • passbook issued • minimum £5, maximum £10,000 • fixed interest rate for year • higher interest rate for balances above £500	• personal customers (including children) • clubs and societies • voluntary bodies	*Advantages:* • first £70 of annual interest is tax free (£140 for joint accounts) • withdrawal on demand of up to £100 at any post office (larger amounts arranged within a few days) *Disadvantages:* • low rate of interest paid • interest calculated on complete calendar months only
Investment Account	• longer-term savings account • passbook issued • minimum £5, maximum £100,000 • variable interest rate	• personal customers (including children) • clubs and societies • voluntary bodies • companies	*Advantages:* • interest paid gross of tax (particularly suitable for non-tax payers) • interest calculated on a daily basis *Disadvantage:* • one month's notice of withdrawal

Fig. 15.6   National Savings Bank accounts

Differences from banks
• National Savings Bank accounts are designed for those who require very simple accounts with deposit and withdrawal facilities but without full banking services

• operated through 20,000 post office branches

• tax concessions with Ordinary Account

• interest paid gross for the Investment Account

15.6   National Savings schemes

The Government's Department for National Savings offers a number of savings schemes in addition to the National Savings Bank. As with all National Savings, the saver's funds are used to finance part of Government spending:

NATIONAL SAVINGS

Service	Features	Suitability	Advantages/ disadvantages
National Savings Certificates	• investment certificates with a guaranteed return after five years. • the value of the certificates increases the longer it is held • each certificate costs £25 • maximum holding is 40 certificates (£1,000)	• personal savers wishing to hold certificates for five years	*Advantages:* • completely free of all taxes • protection against falling interest rates *Disadvantage:* • lower rate of growth if certificates cashed early
Index-linked National Savings Certificates	• investment certificate with growth rate linked to the Retail Prices Index (RPI) • each certificate costs £25 • maximum holding is 200 certificates (£5,000)	• personal savers wishing to hold certificates for five years • personal savers seeking inflation-proof savings	*Advantages:* • completely free of all taxes • inflation-proof savings • extra interest added to value of certificate above rate of inflation *Disadvantage:* • lower rate of growth if certificates cashed early
Yearly Plan Certificates	• regular savings scheme • between £20 and £200 monthly for 12 months • Yearly Plan Certificate issued at end of 12 months, which should be held for further four years to obtain maximum growth • interest rate fixed at start of scheme	• personal savers wishing to save regular amounts monthly • personal savers seeking long-term savings to be held for up to five years	*Advantages:* • completely free of all taxes • protection against falling interest rates *Disadvantage:* • lower rate of growth if certificates cashed early
Capital Bonds	• investment scheme for lump sums of money • bonds are bought in units of £100, with no upper limit • at the end of five years bonds are repaid in full with interest earned	• persons with a lump-sum to invest • non-tax payers	*Advantages:* • the interest rate is guaranteed for five years • interest is added to the value of the bond each year, gross of tax *Disadvantages:* • holder of the bond is liable for income tax on interest earned • lower rate of interest for repayment in less than five years • three months' notice of encashment required

(continued on page 192)

Fig. 15.7 National Savings schemes

NATIONAL SAVINGS (continued)

Service	Features	Suitability	Advantages/ disadvantages
Income Bonds	• lump sum deposits, minimum £2,000, maximum £100,000 • interest paid monthly, gross of tax	• persons with a lump sum to invest • investors who require regular monthly income • non-tax payers	*Advantages:* • monthly income • interest paid gross of tax (suits non-tax payers) *Disadvantages:* • variable interest rates • holder of the bond is liable for income tax on interest • three months' notice of encashment is required
Premium Bonds	• minimum £100; maximum £10,000 • each bond is entered into weekly and monthly draw • prizewinners picked by ERNIE (Electronic Random Number Indicator Equipment) • bonds can be encashed quickly	• savers who wish to speculate on possibility of winning a prize	*Advantages:* • prizes are tax-free • possibility of winning a large prize • easy to encash *Disadvantages:* • no interest earned • value of savings will fall if no prizes are won
Government Stocks (on National Savings Stock Register)	• purchase of Government Stocks (often called 'gilts') • interest paid gross of tax	• persons with a lump sum to invest • non-tax payers	*Advantages:* • no capital gains tax • easy to encash *Disadvantages:* • holder of the stock is liable for income tax on interest • limited range of Government Stocks on National Savings Stock Register

Fig. 15.7   National Savings schemes (continued from page 191)

Functions
National Savings schemes
• provide a range of savings facilities for the public
• generate a source of cash for the Government

As all National Savings schemes are guaranteed by the Government, there is no danger of loss for the saver.

Main services
The schemes currently on offer (see fig. 15.7) are:

• National Savings Certificates
• Index-linked National Savings Certificates
• Yearly Plan Certificates
• Capital Bonds
• Income Bonds

- Premium Bonds
- Government Stocks (on the National Savings Stock Register)

Each scheme is available from post offices; most banks sell National Savings Certificates and Premium Bonds.

15.7 Finance Houses

Finance houses have their origins in the second half of the nineteenth century when they helped to finance machinery for the industrial revolution by means of hire purchase. In the twentieth century they began to finance consumer goods, such as cars. Nowadays most major banks own a finance company, e.g. Midland Bank owns Forward Trust, and National Westminster Bank owns Lombard North Central.

Finance houses provide hire purchase and lending facilities to both the personal and the business buyer. The finance houses obtain their funds for these activities from money market deposits (i.e. the surplus funds of banks, building societies, and other financial institutions), and from deposit-taking from personal customers in the form of term deposits.

Main services for personal customers

- *Hire purchase.* Here the customer pays for goods by putting down a deposit, and then pays instalments over an agreed period of time. Goods on hire purchase remain the property of the finance company until the hire purchase customer (the *hirer*) has made all the payments, the last payment usually incorporating an 'option to purchase'. Hire purchase agreements generally run for between two and four years and are used to buy consumer goods such as cars, caravans, boats, furniture, home improvements, electrical applicances, etc.

- *Credit sale.* This operates in a similar way to hire purchase except that, in law, the goods belong to the customer from the start. A credit sale is often used for lower value items such as clothes, furniture, cameras, etc.

- *Personal loans.* Identical in operation to bank personal loans, except that the rate of interest charged will be slightly higher.

- *Term deposits.* In order to partly finance their lending activities, finance houses accept deposits from personal customers. Most of these are term deposits, with a minimum amount, such as £500 or £1,000 for three months, six months, etc. Rates of interest paid are generally slightly above those paid by the banks.

Main services for business customers

- *Industrial hire purchase.* This operates in the same way as hire purchase for personal customers. It is used by businesses seeking finance for the purchase of assets such as machinery, motor vehicles, etc. By using industrial hire purchase, the use of the asset is obtained for very little outlay.

- *Leasing.* Here the finance house buys a vehicle or a machine and leases or rents it to the business which makes regular leasing payments to the finance company. Unlike hire purchase, however, the asset never belongs to the business - legal ownership remains with the finance company. There are two types of lease: a *finance lease,* which is long-term (usually up to five years) and an *operating lease,* which is shorter term and often includes repair and maintenance of the asset. Generally, with a finance lease the asset is leased to one business customer only; with an operating lease the asset could be leased through its life to several different customers. Like industrial hire purchase, leasing enables a business to have the use of an asset for very little outlay, so putting less strain on a business' finances.

- *Money market deposits.* These are the major source of deposits through which a finance house funds its activities. The depositors are banks, building societies, other financial organizations, and commercial companies who deposit their spare cash, generally for fixed terms (e.g. one month, three months, etc.). Interest paid on these deposits will be at rates which vary with money market conditions, but will be competitive with other rates.

15.8   Insurance Companies

Insurance companies are major competitors of banks, particularly in the provision of life assurance and savings schemes. Insurance has a history which spans as long a period as banking. It has its origins in the sixteenth century and originally provided marine insurance to meet the needs of developing international trade, and fire insurance to meet the needs of people owning property. Life assurance started in the early seventeenth century. Today, insurance falls into the following categories:

- life assurance
- property insurance
  - buildings
  - contents
- transport insurance
  - motor vehicle
  - marine
  - aviation
- third party liability insurance
- personal accident and sickness

The term *assurance* is used with the first of the above categories, i.e. life. The word 'assurance' means that the event covered by the insurance policy is *certain,* or assured, to happen: e.g. a person with a life assurance policy will either reach a certain age or die before reaching that age. *Insurance,* by contrast, is taken out to cover events which *may* happen: e.g. the law requires us to take out insurance before we drive motor vehicles on public roads - we hope that we will not have an accident and make a claim on the policy, but we insure against the possibility.

As life assurance is the main area where insurance companies compete with banks, we shall study this aspect in more detail.

Contract of life assurance

The following key points will be present in any contract of life assurance:

- *name of proposer,* the person who fills in a proposal form to take out a life policy

- *name of life assured,* the person on whose life the policy is taken out

- *name of beneficiary,* the person to whom benefits under the policy are to be paid
  (Note: the proposer, life assured, and beneficiary are often the same person, but it is common for a husband to take out a policy on his life naming his wife as beneficiary.)

- *sum assured,* the amount payable

- *date of payment,* when the sum assured is to be paid, either on the death of the life assured or at a future determinable or stated date

- *premiums,* the amounts payable - usually monthly, quarterly, or annually - to the insurance company; premiums will vary dependent upon:
  - age of assured
  - sex of assured
  - health of assured
  - occupation, and any dangerous hobbies (e.g. hang gliding) of assured
  - sum assured
  - term of the policy

- *name of policyholder,* the person who holds the policy, usually the life assured

When completing a proposal form for life assurance, all questions must be answered truthfully, and all material facts (e.g. medical history) must be disclosed. If full and correct answers are not given, the insurance company could declare the contract to be void, i.e. it would refuse to make payment under the policy.

Functions of life assurance companies
- to provide life cover for the protection of dependants
- to provide savings facilities linked to life assurance
- to provide regular income through the use of annuities

Main services
- *life cover* is provided through
  - whole life policies
  - term assurance

- *savings facilities* are provided through
  - endowment policies
  - regular savings policies

- *regular income* is provided through the use of annuities

The main services are shown in fig. 15.8.

With and without profits policies
All whole-life and endowment policies can be taken out *with profits* or *without profits*.

- *With profits*
  The policyholder shares in the profits of the insurance company, which are made from investing the premiums paid by policyholders in stocks, shares and other investments. The premiums for a with profits policy will be slightly higher than for an equivalent without profits policy. The share of the profits is added (usually annually) to the original sum assured as a *reversionary bonus:* once the bonus is added, it cannot be taken away. Most insurance companies also pay a *terminal bonus* when the sum assured is paid out. Both types of bonus add to the amount paid out either on maturity of the policy, or upon the death of the life assured, depending on the type of policy. A with profits policy is to be recommended because, during times of inflation, it helps the sum assured to retain its purchasing power, but there is no guarantee that it will do so.

- *Without profits*
  With this type of policy, only the sum assured is paid out: the policy does not share in the profits of the insurance company. Premiums are lower than an equivalent with profits policy. The disadvantage is that the sum assured does not increase with inflation.

Surrender value
Whole-life and endowment life assurance policies usually have a *surrender value* if the policy is cashed in by policyholder. Surrender value is calculated as follows:

premiums paid, *add* bonuses, *less* cost of life cover, *equals* surrender value

Most policies do not acquire a surrender value until the policy has been in force for two years and, during the early years, surrender value may be less than the value of premiums paid.

LIFE ASSURANCE COMPANIES

Service/policy	Features	Suitability	Advantages/ disadvantages
LIFE COVER			
Whole life policy	• benefits payable on death of life assured • can be 'with profits'	• person wishing to provide for dependants	*Advantages:* • low cost • surrender value • 'with profits' policies available *Disadvantages:* • sum assured payable only on death • surrender value low in early years
Term Assurance	• life assurance policy for specified term, e.g. 10 years • benefits payable on death of life assured within the term	• person wishing to provide for dependants for limited term (often used as family protection by young couples)	*Advantage:* • low cost *Disadvantage:* • sum assured only payable on death
SAVINGS FACILITIES			
Endowment policies	• combination of life cover and savings facilities • lump sum payable at end of specified term, e.g. 20 years • usually 'with profits' • some policies can be 'unit-linked' • often linked to an endowment mortgage (see Chapter 13.9)	• person wishing to provide for dependants • regular savers, seeking capital growth • person requiring an endowment mortgage	*Advantages:* • 'with profits' policies should provide a good rate of growth • 'unit-linked' policies available • can be used as the means of repayment for an endowment mortgage • surrender value *Disadvantages:* • long-term policy • surrender value low in early years
Regular savings policies	• savings terms, often up to 10 years • savings can be linked to unit trusts • life cover included	• regular savers, seeking capital growth	*Advantages:* • life assurance cover • good rate of growth • surrender value *Disadvantage:* • surrender value low in early years
REGULAR INCOME			
Annuities	• regular income in return for a lump sum investment • different types of annuities available (see Chapter 12.7): - immediate - deferred - reversionary (or joint-life) - guaranteed - temporary	• suitable for older people seeking regular income (usually for the rest of their lives)	*Advantage:* • regular income (usually for rest of life) *Disadvantages:* • possible loss if annuitant dies early • lump sum withdrawals not available

Fig. 15.8 Main services of life assurance companies

Policyholders may consider surrendering a policy because they can no longer afford to pay the premiums, or because they need a lump sum of money. Surrendering a policy is very 'final' and should be avoided if at all possible. Alternatives are:

- The insurance company can be asked to make the policy *paid up*. This means that no further premiums are paid for the term of the policy, but bonuses that have already been added to the policy are maintained, and reduced bonuses may continue to be added. On maturity of the policy, an amount will be paid, but this will be less than if the premiums had continued to be made.

- If a lump sum of money is needed, the policyholder can ask the insurance company to make a loan against the surrender value of the policy. Interest will be payable on the loan, premiums continue to be paid, and the policy remains in force. The loan can be repaid either by agreed instalments, or from the proceeds of the policy on maturity. (Instead of seeking a loan from the insurance company, the policyholder could consider a loan from a bank: a life policy is acceptable security to a bank - see Chapter 13.2.)

15.9 Moneyshops

The idea of a moneyshop is to provide mainly personal customer banking services (including lending) in a relatively informal atmosphere. Moneyshops have been developed in the last 10-15 years, by some of the American banks, e.g. Citibank, HFC Bank and by finance houses, as a way of obtaining a 'High Street' presence. The features of moneyshops are:

- long opening hours (usually linked to local shopping hours)
- retail premises (rather than imposing bank premises)
- a friendly and comfortable atmosphere in relatively informal surroundings

To a large extent, the moneyshop idea has been taken up and developed by the major UK banks, as they 'revamp' branches to make them more attractive and, indeed, some branches have been designed mainly to attract the personal customer.

Functions
- provision of personal customer banking services

Main services
- current and deposit/savings accounts, mainly for the personal customer
- lending for the purchase of consumer goods by means of personal loans, hire purchase and loans secured against property
- mortgages
- insurance
- foreign travel services

15.10 Unit Trusts

A unit trust is a trust which collects savings from the public, pools the funds, and makes investments in stocks and shares, in accordance with the trust deed. It operates as follows:

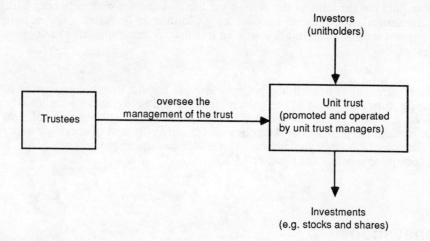

Unit trusts were first established in the 1930s, and nowadays there are over 1,000 different trusts for the investor to choose from. The main choices are:

- *capital growth*
- *income*
- *mixed* (some capital growth and some income)
- *general unit trust,* investing generally in shares with no particular emphasis on industries
- *specialist unit trust,* investing in particular shares, or overseas stock markets, or the shares of one particular sector

The three parties to a unit trust, as we have already seen in Chapter 12.5, are:

- unitholders
- unit trust managers
- trustees

Most banks operate their own unit trusts as managers, and are often trustees for trusts run by others.

Unit trusts are promoted and managed by:

- banks
- insurance companies
- professional savings companies

Investors in unit trusts hold a certain number of units, which they buy from the managers - either directly or through an intermediary such as a bank - at the managers' *offer price* and sell back at the *bid price*. The price of units varies with changes in the value of the stocks and shares bought by the managers. Unit trust prices are quoted daily in the 'quality' newspapers.

Dividends on stocks and shares held by the unit trust are collected together by the managers and, after deduction of management charges, are paid as distributions to the unitholders. Some of the income trusts pay distributions on a regular basis, e.g. quarterly, but the distributions on trusts whose aim is capital growth may be paid annually and, with some trusts, there is insufficient income to distribute.

Functions
- to enable 'smaller' investors to make an indirect investment in stocks and shares
- to reduce the risk of investment in shares

Services
- professional investment management for the 'smaller' investor
- lump sum investment and savings schemes
- can be linked to life assurance, mortgages, and pensions

The advantages and disadvantages of investing in unit trusts are shown in fig. 15.9.

UNIT TRUSTS

Advantages to investor	*Disadvantages to investor*
• an easy way to invest indirectly in stocks and shares	• the value of units may fall
• risk is spread	• a higher risk investment than placing the money on deposit with a bank or building society
• professional investment management	• should be regarded as a long-term investment
• investor can choose a unit trust which gives - capital growth - income - a mix of both	• a wide variety of unit trusts to choose from - the investor may be confused
• some unit trusts pay income quarterly	• past growth/income performance of a particular unit trust is no guarantee of future performance
• buying and selling is easy	
• a wide variety of unit trusts to choose from	
• opportunities to invest in overseas markets	
• an investment that can be sold quickly and the proceeds received within 7/10 days	
• lump sum investments and savings schemes available	
• unitholders' interests are protected by the trustees	
• managers' charges are relatively inexpensive	
• unit trusts can be linked to life assurance, mortgages, and pensions	

Fig. 15.9 Advantages and disadvantages of investing in unit trusts

15.11   Investment Trusts

Investment trusts operate in a similar way to unit trusts, i.e. they pool the money contributed by their investors and buy a range of stocks and shares. The first investment trusts were set up in the second-half of the nineteenth century - long before unit trusts.

The main difference between investment trusts and unit trusts is that an investment trust is itself a *public limited company,* whereas a unit trust is a *trust.* Investors in an investment trust buy shares in the company through a stockbroker. The investment trust company uses the cash at its disposal, plus any borrowing it makes, to invest in the shares of other companies. The price of shares in an investment trust company varies according to supply and demand, and the value of its *portfolio of investments* in other companies.

An investment trust is usually seen as suitable for larger sums of money than unit trusts, although some investment trusts operate savings schemes for regular monthly amounts. In a similar way to a unit trust, an investment trust collects dividends on its investments, which are then paid to its shareholders.

Like unit trusts, there are investment trusts which aim for capital growth, income, or a mixture of both. There are also investment trusts which specialize in the shares of companies in particular sectors, or certain overseas markets.

Functions
*   to enable investors to invest in the stocks and shares of a number of different companies
*   to reduce the risks of investment in shares

Services
*   professional investment management for small and medium-sized investors
*   lump sum investment by buying shares in the investment trust company; savings schemes sometimes available

15.12   Pension Funds

Most working people pay a part of their earnings towards a pension. On retirement they will receive an income which continues for the rest of their life. The awareness of the need for pensions has developed particularly since the end of the second world war.

Types of pension
There are three types of pension and, on retirement, a person could receive a pension from more than one category. The three are:

*   *State pension*
    This is paid to all men aged 65 and over, and to all women aged 60 and over, provided they are no longer in full-time employment and are earning less than a particular amount. The state pension is funded partly from National Insurance Contributions, which are deducted at varying levels from an employee's earnings (the employer also makes a contribution), and from taxation.

*   *Occupational pension schemes*
    Many employers also provide a pension scheme for their employees. In most schemes the employee and the employer contribute a certain amount each week or month (some employers do not require the employee to make any contributions). Up to a certain maximum amount, contributions made by an employee towards a pension are tax deductible, i.e. they are deducted from the employee's income before tax is calculated. On retirement the employee receives a

pension, the maximum amount of which is two-thirds of final salary; a lump sum may also be payable on retirement, although the pension amount is often reduced if this is taken.

Occupational pension schemes are operated by large employers themselves. A smaller employer will often use a specialist company - such as an insurance company, or a pension company - to operate its pension fund.

- *Personal pension schemes*
These are available to the self-employed, and to employees not in an occupational pension scheme. There are certain maximum amounts that can be contributed, generally a percentage of earnings. Contributions are tax deductible, i.e. they are deducted from gross pay before income tax is calculated and, in this way, the contributor pays less tax.

There is also the opportunity for those in an occupational pension scheme to make *additional voluntary contributions (AVCs)* either to their employer's scheme or to a personal pension scheme. The object of this is to increase the amount of the pension, and is used particularly by people who did not contribute to a pension scheme in their first years of employment. Within certain limits - related to earnings - contributions to AVCs are tax deductible.

Personal pension schemes are sold by insurance companies, and by specialist pensions companies.

Pension fund investments
Contributions to most pension schemes and all personal pension schemes are invested by the pension fund in order to increase the value of the fund. Pension funds are major investors, and they buy investments in stocks and shares, property, and even works of art.

With some types of personal pension schemes, the contributor can direct his or her payments towards particular investments. e.g. property or shares (including investments in overseas shares, or cash investments, such as a bank or building society deposit account). This type of pension scheme is *unit-linked,* and changes can be made between different investments. The value of the pension fund is directly linked to the value of the investments.

Functions of a pension fund
- provision of pensions in the form of
  - state pension
  - occupational pension schemes
  - personal pension schemes

Main services of a pension fund
- long-term savings contributed by the employee (and often the employer)
- professional investment management of the pension fund
- provision of a pension to the employee on retirement (a lump sum may also be payable)
- pension-linked mortgages also available (see Chapters 13.9 and 15.2) - repaid from lump sum payable on retirement

15.13 Revision Points

❑ *Major competitors to banks*
- These are:
- building societies
- Girobank
- retail groups

- National Savings Bank
- National Savings schemes
- finance houses
- insurance companies
- moneyshops
- unit trusts
- investment trusts
- pension funds

- The main areas of competition are:
- deposit-taking
- money transmission
- personal lending and credit cards
- mortgage lending
- other services: investment, insurance

❑ *Building societies*
- Building societies are major competitors of banks in the provision of personal financial services. Their main function is deposit-taking, and the provision of mortgages.

- Deposit-taking
- share account
- regular savings account
- lump sum investment account

- Mortgages
- repayment
- endowment
- pension-linked

- Other services
- current account
- automated teller machines
- credit cards
- personal loans
- home improvement loans
- insurance
- travel facilities
- financial advice

❑ *Girobank*
- Provides a simple money transmission service

- Offers current account banking, mainly to personal customers

- Services
- money transmission by 'Transcash'
- current accounts
- deposit accounts
- lending: credit cards, personal loans, mortgages, business loans
- travel facilities
- automated teller machines

❑ *Retail groups*
- Large retail groups provide a range of personal financial services
- store cards
- personal loans and hire purchase

- unit trusts
- share dealing
- investment, e.g. Personal Equity Plans

❑ *National Savings Bank*
- Operates through the post office

- Deposit-taking from mainly personal customers

- Depositors' funds invested in Government Stocks

- Accounts offered
- ordinary account
- investment account

❑ *National Savings schemes*
- Provides a range of savings facilities for the public

- All facilities are guaranteed by the Government

- Generates a source of cash for the Government

- Facilities offered
- National Savings Certificates
- Index-linked National Savings Certificates
- Yearly Plan Certificates
- Capital Bonds
- Income Bonds
- Premium Bonds
- Government Stocks (on the National Savings Stock Register)

❑ *Finance houses*
- Provide a range of hire purchase and other loan facilities to personal and business customers

- Acceptance of money market deposits from banks, building societies, and other financial institutions

- Deposit-taking from personal customers in the form of term deposits

- Services for personal customers
- hire purchase
- credit sale
- personal loans
- term deposits

- Services for business customers
- industrial hire purchase
- leasing, both finance leases and operating leases
- money market deposits

❑ *Insurance companies*
- Major competitors of banks in the provision of life assurance, and savings schemes

- Main functions are to provide
- life cover for the protection of dependants
- savings facilities linked to life assurance
- regular income through the use of annuities

- Life cover
- whole-life policies
- term assurance

- Savings facilities
- endowment policies (which can be linked to an endowment mortgage)
- regular savings policies

- Regular income through annuities
- immediate
- deferred
- reversionary (joint-life)
- guaranteed
- temporary

❏ *Moneyshops*
- First established by American banks, and finance houses

- Provision of personal customer banking services through
- use of retail premises
- long opening hours
- friendly and comfortable atmosphere

- Main services
- current and deposit/savings accounts
- loans secured against property
- mortgages
- insurance
- foreign travel services

❏ *Unit trusts*
- Competitors of banks for customers' investments

- Enable small investors to make an indirect investment in stocks and shares

- By pooling investors' money, and investing in different shares, risk is spread

- Promoted and operated by unit trust managers, overseen by trustees

- Types of unit trust
- capital growth
- income
- mixed
- specialist

- Lump sum investment and savings schemes

- Can be linked to life assurance, mortgages and pensions

❏ *Investment trusts*
- Similar idea to unit trusts - the pooling of investors' money and spreading of risk

- Investors buy shares in an investment trust company

❏ *Pension funds*
- Provision of pensions in the form of
- state pension
- occupational pension schemes
- personal pension schemes

- Long-term savings contributed by the employer (and often the employee), or self-employed person

- Provision of a pension on retirement (and often a lump sum payment also)

- Pension fund manages the investments - some pensions can be unit-linked

- Pension-linked mortgages also available

15.14 Know your *Banks and Competition*

Multiple-choice Questions

Choose the *one* answer you think is correct.

1. Which of the following services are *not* provided by building societies?

   A Unsecured loans
   B Business accounts
   C ATMs
   D Credit cards

2. Girobank was set up to

   A compete directly with the clearing banks by providing a full range of bank services
   B expand the functions of the Post Office and to introduce longer opening hours
   C provide a simple money transmission service and extend current accounts to the personal sector
   D give the Government a bank through which it could raise money

3. Which of the following is *not* a basic role of a unit trust?

   A To allow individuals to share in a larger and more diversified portfolio
   B To involve small savers in share investment
   C To ensure more rapid and secure growth than normal savings accounts
   D To collect funds from a large number of investors and to invest in securities

4. Which of the following statements applies to both investment trusts and unit trusts?

   A Both are companies
   B Investors buy shares in the 'trust'
   C Managers invest the funds and manage the portfolio
   D Both buy and sell their own shares

5. A customer wants to insure his life for the maximum amount to protect his young family whilst they are being educated. Which insurance policy would be best?

   A Whole life
   B Endowment with profits
   C Annuity
   D Term

6. An annuity provides

   A an income in return for a lump sum investment
   B a savings policy which covers a life over a period
   C an insurance policy which pays out a lump sum on an agreed date
   D a unit-linked savings scheme which pays a pension on retirement

Short Answer Questions

7.   Give *two* reasons why the building societies are the banks' greatest competitors.

8.   Give *two* reasons for the establishment of Girobank.

9.   Name *two* services of National Savings.

10.   Give *two* advantages of using the National Savings Bank/Girobank.

11.   What do HP and NSC stand for?

12.   Give *two* forms of instalment credit.

13.   State *two* of the benefits to the borrower of an endowment mortgage.

14.   Give *two* reasons why moneyshops can be attractive to customers.

15.   Name *two* types of units offered by a unit trust.

16.   What does PEP stand for?

17.   List the *three* main types of pension.

15.15   Essay questions *Banks and Competition*

1.   Compare and contrast the services provided to personal customers by banks and building societies.

[The Chartered Institute of Bankers' specimen paper]

2.   Outline the additional powers given to building societies under the Building Societies Act 1986, and since, which have increased their ability to be major forces in the financial services market.

[question 8, Spring 1989]

3.   The clearing banks all have similar functions; the three main ones being deposit-taking, money transfer, and advances. The banks face competition from many institutions in all areas.

For *each* of the functions give one example of a financial institution that competes with the banks. Briefly outline the role that the institution plays. Which factors make it a competitor and which are its competitive services?

[question 8, Spring 1988]

4.   Explain the main services offered by finance houses to:

(a) personal customers
(b) business customers

5.   What are the advantages to a 'small' investor of a unit trust? Are there any disadvantages? How does a unit trust differ from an investment trust?

6.   In what areas do retail groups offer

(a) opportunities to banks
(b) competition to banks

in the provision of personal financial services?

7.   *Case problem questions*

What particular financial service or services would you suggest for the following? State the benefits to the customer to help explain your choice.

(a)   Dave Smith is becoming a little worried about his financial future. He hasn't saved much in the past but he thinks he could at present afford to put aside £30 a month, although he expects to be able to save more next year. Dave has a steady job and his salary is paid into his account monthly. Although he is not too knowledgeable about financial matters he does worry about the effects of inflation. Dave pays tax at the basic rate.

[5 marks]
[question 28a, Spring 1987]

(b)   Anne Smythe has recently retired and receives a monthly pension cheque from her employer to add to her state pension. Anne lives in a small village some 10 miles from the nearest town and, as she does not own a car, she does most of her shopping in the village store which doubles as a post office. She does, however, go into town once a month to the large supermarket to buy any special items that she cannot get in the village.

Anne lives on her own and has to organise her finances to pay the usual household bills.

[5 marks]
[question 28d, Spring 1987]

(c)   Michael Watson is a 15 year old student who is saving hard for a speedboat. He has saved £500 to date and hopes to save a further £700 over the next nine months to allow him to buy a secondhand boat next summer.

He has a job walking greyhounds for a couple of hours each day which pays him £20 per week.

He will also save Christmas and birthday money.

[5 marks]
[question 9c, Autumn 1987]

(d)   John Elway wants to buy a car from his local dealer. He does not have a bank or building society account (and does not want one) but wants to borrow the balance over 3 years rather than pay cash. He has a regular income and can easily repay the loan instalments.

How can John borrow the money (possible through the car dealer)? List the advantages and any disadvantages of the scheme you suggest.

[5 marks]
[question 9c, Spring 1989]

(e)   Elaine Wilson is a 28 year old teacher who has two children aged 8 and 6. Unfortunately, her husband died when the children were very young and Elaine is now left to bring up her family on her salary alone. She is concerned about what will happen to the children should anything happen to her. The children would live with her parents but they might have financial difficulties in supporting them. Elaine is very keen on the children's education and would like to give them a sum of money to help them through university.

[5 marks]
[question 28b, Spring 1987]

(f)   Frank and Christine Morton have just won £25,000 on the football pools. Both Frank and Christine are aged 35 and have good jobs and are not too worried about their financial future. They feel that they would like to give their winnings a chance to grow faster than they would if they were merely put into a building society or a bank deposit account.

Although neither know anything about the 'city' and have read about the possibility of shares rising or falling, they would be happy to invest their money for 10 years, thereby avoiding the short-term ups and downs of the market.

How would you suggest that they invest their money?   What are the advantages and disadvantages?

[5 marks]
[question 9b, Spring 1988]

(g)   Arthur Daley is a self-employed antiques dealer aged 40. He has a very profitable business and is able to save several hundred pounds per month. Having reached 40 he has started to think about making provision for his retirement.

Describe the service you would suggest to Arthur and name any other groups of people who would benefit from this service.

[5 marks]
[question 9b, Spring 1989]

(h)   George and Ethel Wainwright are aged 55 and 52 respectively. They have recently been left £15,000 in the will of Ethel's sister.

The Wainwrights have no children and their main ambition when George retires aged 60 is to have sufficient income to allow them to maintain their present standard of living. Unfortunately George has changed jobs several times in his career and he will not receive a very large pension.

[5 marks]
[question 9a, Autumn 1987]

(i)   Arthur and Irene James are both aged 66. Arthur retired last year and received a lump sum of £7,000 on his retirement. They receive a state pension and do not have any other income. They are concerned that their pension will not be enough to let them maintain their living standard. They want to ensure that their £7,000 savings give them the best possible return.

Which financial organisation would be best for Arthur and Irene, and what service would you recommend? Give at least *three* benefits of this service.

[5 marks]
[question 9a, Spring 1989]

Chapter Sixteen
Future Developments in Banking

As we move into the 1990s, there are many changes taking place which affect banks as providers of financial services. This chapter looks at some of the developments that have already started and which will continue to have an impact over the next few years. These include:

- the approach of the single European market (commonly referred to by the date '1992')
- the introduction of the government's student loan scheme in 1990
- the rapid acceptance of EFTPOS as a method of payment, and the wider use of debit cards
- the increasing use of Eurocheques and cards
- changes in the banker-customer relationship, as recommended by the 'Jack' Committee Report
- developments of home banking services for personal customers
- possible changes in the terms of issue of credit cards as a result of the report of the Government's Monopolies and Mergers Commission
- development of in-store banking
- experiments in the use of 'smart' cards

There will be plenty of mention of these topics in the press during the period of your studies. You are urged to read a quality newspaper and 'Banking World' to keep up-to-date on these topics. The current state of these topics at the time of writing (Summer 1989) is now considered.

16.1 '1992'

The date 1992 has featured prominently in newspapers and on the television during the last year or so. It signifies that, from 1 January 1992, the European Community (of which the UK is a member) becomes a. single market. Broadly, barriers to trade within the community will be removed, and businesses based in the EC will have free access to a potential market of 320 million consumers.

As far as banking is concerned, the European Community governments agreed (in June 1989) outline proposals for giving EC banks a 'passport' or licence to operate throughout the community. This will take effect from 1 January 1993. A common framework will be established for regulating banks and other financial institutions.

The effect of the proposals mean that banks will be able to do business anywhere in the EC, provided that they conform with minimum rules of financial soundness. This should lead to a more open and competitive market in banking services throughout the community. Thus UK-based banks will have a potential customer base of all the citizens of the community, which offers great scope for a huge increase in business. However, other EC-based banks will be able to operate freely in the UK and will be competing on equal terms with UK banks.

The agreement needs to be passed by the European Parliament before it can be introduced.

16.2   The Government's Student Loan Scheme

The Government's policy is for students to finance part of the costs of their higher education by means of loans, which will supplement grants. The banks will be heavily involved in financing and administering the loans scheme. The scheme will be operated through a private company, whose members will comprise banks, building societies and other financial institutions. The costs of running the company will be met by the Government.

The Government hopes the scheme will be ready for the start of the academic year commencing in Autumn 1990. Students will be able to borrow up to £420 to supplement their grants. In later years, loans for larger amounts will be available as students take more of a stake in their education by bearing more of the cost.

Students will obtain a *certificate of entitlement* to a loan from their university, polytechnic or college. The certificate is presented either to the administration company, or to a branch of a bank or building society which participates in the scheme. The loan, which will be interest-free, will be repaid when the student has commenced work. Repayments will be on the basis of equal annual amounts, increased each year for inflation. Graduates earning less than a certain amount will be able to delay repayment. A major question which remains unanswered at present is whether the Government will meet the cost of bad debts.

Banks already compete for student accounts and the loan scheme will strengthen their position with this important sector of the personal banking market.

16.3   EFTPOS

1989 has seen dramatic developments in EFTPOS, in particular the agreement for nationwide standards of terminals installed in retail outlets.

EFTPOS systems (as at Summer 1989) in use are for:

* credit cards
  - *Access*
  - *Visa*
  - other credit cards

* debit cards
  - *Connect,* from Barclays
  - *Visa Payment Card,* from Lloyds
  - *Switch,* from Midland, National Westminster and The Royal Bank of Scotland

The terminals installed in retail premises are becoming more sophisticated as they automatically switch from being *off-line* when transactions are below the retailer's floor limit, and *on-line* when a transaction needs to be authorised by the card issuer. (Off-line terminals deal with transactions more quickly; they store the details of transactions which are then passed to the banks' and credit card companys' computer systems in one batch.)

16.4 Eurocheques

In 1989 the use of Eurocheques has increased dramatically as most banks in Italy and France begin to issue both Eurocheques and cards to their customers (previously each of these countries had used their own cheques and cards).

The use of Eurocheque cards in ATMs throughout Europe is also set to increase to 12,500 ATMs in 15 different countries by the end of 1989. There are also plans to introduce an EFTPOS retail payments service linked to the card.

16.5 The 'Jack' Committee Report

The Jack Committee was commissioned by the Treasury and the Bank of England to study the bank-customer relationship, ranging from traditional aspects through to new technology. The full title is *the Review Committee responsible for the Report on Banking Services, Law and Practice.* Not surprisingly, the surname of its chairman, Professor Robert Jack, is used as a shorter title. The Jack Report was published in 1989 and recommends a comprehensive overhaul of banking law and practice. The report has four key aims:

- to achieve fairness in the bank-customer relationship
- to maintain confidence in the banking system
- to promote the efficiency of the banking system
- to preserve and consolidate the bank's duty of confidentiality to the customer

The main recommendations are dealt with below.

Code of Banking Practice
- A code of practice is recommended setting out the rights of both banks and customers.

- The code would also require banks to explain details of charges to customers.

Cheques
- Cheques should continue to be transferable (by endorsement), but that only one crossing should be used with the meaning of 'not negotiable'. A new *Negotiable Instruments Act* is proposed to define negotiability and to set out the protections available from forgeries.

- A *Cheques and Payment Orders Act* is proposed to allow the introduction of a new method of payment. This is proposed to be called a bank payment order, which will
  - only be paid into a bank
  - only be paid into the payee's account

  As this is what happens with the majority of cheques anyway, few people would be inconvenienced and the scope for theft and fraud would be reduced considerably.

- Changes in the law are recommended to speed up the cheque clearing system by enabling the collecting bank to truncate cheques (see Chapter 10.5) and pass on the information to the paying bank in electronic form. The customer's existing legal rights in the event of forgery would be preserved.

Electronic funds transfer and 'new technology'
- Changes in the law are recommended to give a £50 limit on customers' liability for losses due to fraud for unauthorised ATM withdrawals.

- The banks are recommended to be made legally liable for customer losses due to the failure of Electronic Funds Transfer (EFT) equipment.

- Losses on disputed transactions are recommended to be shared equally between customer and bank.

- The banks are recommended to introduce a code of practice with certain minimum standards of security for the issue of EFT cards and PINs.

- Banks are urged to ensure that their technology is not susceptible to fraud, by introducing methods such as technology capable of recognising signatures.

Confidentiality

- The banks' duty of confidentiality is recommended to be defined in law by a proposed *Banking Services Act*. Broadly, the duty of confidentiality is proposed to be based on the judgement in the *Tournier case* (see Chapter 6.7), subject to removal of the 'public duty' defence, and also subject to stating the circumstances in which disclosure of information may be made 'in the interests of the bank'.

- Banks will be required to explain to customers the rules regarding confidentiality and the circumstances in which it can be breached.

- Disclosure by banks of financial information about their customers is recommended to be more closely controlled. In particular, banks are criticised for being too free with customer information, especially by supplying information for marketing purposes to subsidiary companies (such as insurance brokers, credit card companies, etc.), and for proposals allowing banks and credit reference agencies to swap information on customers (both the 'good' and 'bad' customers).

Banking Ombudsman

- The report recommends that the Banking Ombudsman (see Chapter 6.5) should become legally recognised, instead of voluntarily as at present.

- The powers of the Banking Ombudsman to be widened.

Conclusion

The recommendations of the Jack Report are wide ranging and will require changes in the law during the next year or so, with three new Acts of Parliament recommended:

- Negotiable Instruments Act
- Cheque and Bank Payment Orders Act
- Banking Services Act

Many of the proposals contained in the report will be left to a voluntary *Code of Banking Practice* to be written by the banks themselves. Consumer groups are concerned that the Government should monitor banks to ensure that they are following the standards of best practice: if not, then legal backing will need to be given to the standards.

16.6 Home Banking

The next few years will see major developments in the provision of home banking services, using the telephone as the link to the bank's computer. Reference has already been made to home banking in Chapters 10.6 and 11.12. Several major banks have introduced some form of home banking for personal customers, either on a trial basis or available to all customers.

Most systems use the tones of a modern push-button telephone for communicating with the bank's computer (separate tonepads are available for use with older telephones). Some systems use voice recognition technology by which the bank's computer is programmed to recognise numbers and a few words.

As at Summer 1989 two bank schemes are available on a nationwide basis:

- *TSB Bank* introduced its 'Speedlink' service in 1987 using either the tones of a telephone keyboard or a tone pad, to give instructions to the bank's computer. The service was extended in 1988 to link up with fax machines: Speedlink customers can now request, by telephone, that a bank statement be faxed to them automatically. The 'Speedlink' service is available to both business and personal customers.

- *National Westminster Bank* offers 'Actionline' to personal customers. The service uses voice recognition technology to respond to customer requests; tone pads are also available.

Other banks have been involved in running pilot schemes. Lloyds Bank's version, called 'Homebank', is worth especial mention because the customer has a small card reader machine installed next to the telephone at home. To 'sign on', the customer must 'swipe' his or her Cashpoint card through the reader. Lloyds considers that this method is more secure than keying in numbers through a telephone keyboard. Lloyds is currently evaluating its trials, and we shall see if the card reader is used in the final version, if the bank decides to go nationwide with the service.

Besides the banks, a number of major competitors also operate home banking services. In fact, it was a building society - the Nottingham Building Society - which pioneered home banking in 1983, with a system linked to British Telecom's Prestel viewdata service. The system is still in use, with users able to see their account on a television set, linked to the bank's computer by telephone. (The Bank of Scotland uses a similar system for its 'HOBS' - Home and Office Banking Service.) Another building society - the Nationwide Anglia - offers a telephone-linked service using telephone tones to communicate with the computer.

A professional savings company - Save and Prosper - offers a computer-linked telephone service to enable customers to obtain up-to-date valuations of their unit trust holdings, the balance on their Save and Prosper bank account, current prices of unit trusts, and an overview of the stockmarket. Again, telephone tones are used as the method of instructing the computer.

Girobank has just started a major pilot scheme of its 'DIALOG' service. This is solely a voice recognition service: no tone pads will be used.

Home banking is still very much in its infancy and only time will tell how much the service will be demanded by personal customers. Most banks already operate a similar service for business customers - usually called a *cash management service* (see Chapter 14.5) - which links by telephone direct to a customer's computer system.

16.7 Credit Cards

During the last two years, the Government's Monopolies and Mergers Commission has been carrying out an investigation into credit cards. Although the report has not yet been published, a number of points are likely to be proposed. These include:

- Scrapping the 'no discrimination' clause under which retailers must offer to charge the same price to credit card customers as to other customers. (If this is scrapped, retailers would charge a higher price to credit card customers to offset the discount they must allow to the credit card company.)

- Consideration as to whether cardholders who pay off their debts before interest is charged are being subsidised by those who do not. (It is likely that the card companies will, themselves, resolve this problem before too long by charging an annual fee and/or by reducing the interest-free period.)

16.8 In-Store Banking

Links between banking and retailing are growing closer all the time. On the one hand there is co-operation between banks and retailers in the handling of modern payment systems - the retailer is there to sell a product and wants the method of payment to be as speedy and efficient as possible. On the other hand, large retailers have developed their own personal financial services (see Chapter 15.4) in the form of charge cards, credit cards, personal loans, and now moving into unit trusts and Personal Equity Plans.

Areas of co-operation between banks and retailers

- 'stand-alone' ATMs installed by banks in shopping centres and in large stores
- opening times of bank shopping centre branches adjusted to fit in with local shopping hours
- development and installation of EFTPOS terminals (some large stores use machines to write the customer's cheque - this speeds up the time taken to pay for purchases)

Areas of competition between banks and retailers

- charge cards and credit cards marketed by retailers in direct competition with banks
- personal loans and hire purchase offered at the point of sale by retailers
- development of investment products by retailers, e.g. unit trusts and Personal Equity Plans
- banking services provided by in-store banks, e.g. Co-op Bank

It seems only a matter of time before a major retailer offers personal banking services, through its retail outlets, in direct competition with banks.

16.9 Smart Cards

These are cards which are the same size as credit and debit cards. They contain a microchip which is able both to store and process data.

Smart cards are widely used in France where they are used for EFTPOS transactions - the chip in the card provides the retailer's terminal with details of the account which is to be debited. In Britain limited trials are taking place at present.

Smart cards can be used:

- for EFTPOS transactions, where payments are debited to the customer's bank account
- as an 'electronic purse' for low value transactions, where the holder can charge up the chip with funds from his or her bank account, which can then be debited by retailers' terminals

16.10 Revision Points

❑ From 1 January 1993 banks, subject to financial soundness, will be given a licence to operate throughout the European Community. This presents
  - *opportunities,* a market of 320m consumers
  - *threats,* competition in the UK from other European Community banks

❑   The European Community will establish a common framework for regulating banks and other financial institutions

❑   From Autumn 1990, banks will participate in the Government's student loan scheme:
   • top-up loans of up to £420 per year
   • operated through a private company, in which banks and other financial institutions will become members
   • loans to be repaid when student has commenced work

❑   EFTPOS has developed a nationwide standard of terminals for use with credit and debit cards. Terminals can automatically switch between *off-line* and *on-line*

❑   Increasing use of Eurocheques throughout Europe, including ability to use Eurocheque cards at ATMs

❑   The Jack Committee Report recommends
   • a Code of Banking Practice to set out the rights of bank and customer
   • the use of one crossing on cheques, with the meaning 'not negotiable'
   • the introduction of a new bank payment order
   • an upper limit of £50 on the customers' liability for losses due to unauthorised ATM withdrawals
   • the development of truncation of cheques

❑   Homebanking
   • operated either by tones from a telephone keypad, or voice activated
   • major banks now working on systems for the personal customer

❑   The Monopolies and Mergers Commission report on credit cards is expected to propose
   • scrapping the 'no discrimination' clause whereby retailers charge the same price to both credit card and cash customers
   • changes in the way interest is charged, perhaps by reducing the interest-free period

❑   In-store banking
   • 'stand-alone' ATMs in stores and shopping centres
   • development of EFTPOS terminals
   • charge and credit cards marketed by retailers
   • personal loans and hire purchase offered by retailers
   • other services, e.g. unit trusts and PEPs offered by retailers

❑   Smart cards contain a microchip which is able both to store and process data. Can be used
   • for EFTPOS transactions
   • as an electronic purse

Index

'Account payee' crossing, 105-6
Administration, letters of, 135
Administrators, 78, 135
Adult customers, 72-6
Advisory services, 175
Agency broker, 39
Agent (bank as), 62
Articles of Association, 87
Association for Payment Clearing Services (APACS), 96
Assurance, *see* Insurance
ATM card, 128
Automated Teller Machines (ATMs), 119-20

BACS Ltd., 115-17
Bailee, 135
Bailment, 63, 135
Bailor, 135
Balance sheet (bank), 49-55
Bank deposits, 17
Bank capital, 53
Bank (collecting), 102-7
Bank and customer, 60-8
Bank drafts, 138
Bankers' Automated Clearing Services, *see* BACS Ltd.
Bank giro credits, 108
Banking Acts, 54
Banking ombudsman, 65
Banknotes, 10-11
Bank of England, 32, 54-6
Bank (paying), 99-102
Barter system, 7
'Big Bang', 38-9
Bills of Exchange, 18-19
Bills of Exchange Act 1882, 18-19, 101
Bridging loans, 165
Budget accounts, 160, 162
Building societies, 182-7
Business customers, 171-6
Business development loans, 173

Cash cards, *see* Automated Teller Machines
Cashflow accounts, 162-3
Cash management service, 121, 213
Certificate of deposit market, 43
Charge cards, 25
Charities, 92
Cheque cards, 23-4, 66, 128

Cheques
    bearer cheques, 22
    crossings, 103-6
    definition, 19
    endorsements, 21-2, 102-3
    history, 18
    open cheques, 22
    order cheques, 22
    parties, 18
    returned, 99-101
Cheques Act 1957, 102, 107
Clearing House Automated Payments System (CHAPS), 118
Clearing system, 96-109
    Association for Payment Clearing Services (APACS), 96
    Bankers Automated Clearing Services (BACS), 115-17
    Clearing House Automated Payments System (CHAPS), 118
    credit clearing, 108-9
    Electronic Funds Transfer at Point of Sale (EFTPOS), 118-19
    general cheque clearing, 97
    Girobank, 97
    settlement, 97
    special presentations, 107-8
    Town clearing, 107
    truncation, 120
Clubs and associations, 91
Coins, 9-10
Collecting bank, 102-7
Commercial paper market, 43
Computer services, 176
Consortium banks, 39
Consumer Credit Act 1974, 165
Contracts (bank/customer), 62, 66-8
Conversion, 102, 107
Co-operative Bank, 37
Country banks, 33
Credit cards, 24-5, 109, 130-1, 135, 163, 213
Credit clearing, 108-9
Credit creation, 17, 32
Credit scoring, 158
Crossings, 103-6
Current account, 126-8, 158-9

Debit cards, 24, 109, 128
Debtor/creditor (bank as), 62
Deflation, 11

Deposit account, 129, 147
Deposit protection fund, 54
Direct debits, 115, 116
Discount houses, 40, 43
Discount market, 43
Drafts (bank), 138

Electronic Funds Transfer at Point of Sale
    (EFTPOS), 118-19, 210
Endorsements, 21-2, 102-3
Estate agency, 138
Eurocheques, 133-4, 211
Eurocurrency market, 13
Exchange Equalisation Account, 56
Executor and trustee department, 135
Executors, 78, 135

Factoring, 174
Farmers' loans, 173
Fiduciary issue, 36
Finance house market, 43
Finance houses, 193-4
Financial intermediaries, 40
Financial Services Act 1986, 144-6
Foreign banks, 39
Foreign currency, 132
Foreign exchange market, 45
Foreign travel services, 132-5
    credit cards, 135
    Eurocheques, 133-4
    foreign currency, 132
    travel insurance, 134
    travellers' cheques, 132-3
Franchise loans, 173

GEMMS, 56
General cheque clearing, 97
General crossing, 103-4
Girobank, 37, 97, 187-8
Goldsmiths, 10-11, 31-3
Grant of probate, 135

Hire purchase, 174
Home banking, 121, 137, 212-3

Inflation, 12
In-store banking, 214
Insurance, 136-7, 194-7
    business, 176
    general, 136-7
    life, 136, 150-2, 194-7
    travel, 134, 137
Interbank market, 43
Inter-company market, 43
Interest rates, 146

International services, 175-6
Investment, 144
Investment banks, 38-9
Investment management services, 152
Investment trusts, 200

'Jack' Committee, 68, 211-2
Joint accounts, 76-7
Joint and several liability, 76, 85
Joint stock bank, 33

Leasing, 174
Legal tender, 16
Lending
    business customers, 171-3
    personal customers, 156-65
    principles of lending, 156-8
Letters of administration, 135
Lien, 65
Life assurance, 136, 150-2, 194-7
    annuities, 151-2, 196
    endowment, 136, 151, 196
    investment bonds, 151
    regular savings, 151, 196
    term, 136, 196
    whole life, 136, 196
LIFFE, 45
Limited companies, 85-91
Liquidity (bank), 49-53, 55
Local authority accounts, 92
Local authority market, 43
London International Financial Futures
    Exchange (LIFFE), 45

Market maker, 39
Market segmentation, 138
Married women (accounts for), 77-8
Memorandum of Association, 86
Merchant banks, 38
Minors, 77, 158
Minors' Contracts Act 1987, 158
Monetary policy, 55-6
Money,
    definition, 6
    functions, 8-9
    qualities, 7-8
Moneylenders, 31
Moneyshops, 197
Mortgagee (bank as), 63
Mortgages,
    bank, 164-5
    building society, 184
    commercial, 173

National Savings, 190-3
National Savings Bank, 189-90

Near money, 25-6
Night safes, 176
'Not negotiable' crossing, 104-5

Overdrafts, 158-9, 172-3

Parallel money markets, 41-3
Partnerships, 84-5
Paying bank, 99-102
Pensions, 137, 200-1
Personal customers, 125-38
Personal Equity Plans, 152
Personal Identification Number (PIN), 119, 128
Personal loans, 159-60
Polarisation, 145
Probate (grant of), 135

Quasi money, 25-6

Retail banks, 36-7
Retail groups, 188-9
Retail Price Index, 12
Returned cheques, 99-101
Revolving credit (cashflow) accounts, 162-3

Safe custody, 135
Savings, 144

Savings account, 129, 147
Secrecy (of accounts), 66
Share dealing service, 150
Small Firms Loan Guarantee Scheme, 173
Smart cards, 119, 214
Sole trader, 83-4
Special crossing, 104
Special presentations, 107-8
'Special relationship', 63-4
Standing orders, 115
Stock Exchange, 38
Student accounts, 126
Student Loan Scheme, 210

Tax and Price Index, 12
Term deposit, 130, 147
Token money, 27
Town clearing, 107
Travel insurance, 134
Travellers' cheques, 132-3
Truncation, 120
Trustees, 78-9
TSB Bank, 37

Ultra vires principle, 90
Undue influence, 63-4
Unit trusts, 147-9, 198-9

Wholesale Price Index, 12